CW00545587

AVATAR: TH
AIRBENDER
AND PHILOSOPHY

The Blackwell Philosophy and Pop Culture Series
Series editor: William Irwin

A spoonful of sugar helps the medicine go down, and a healthy helping of popular culture clears the cobwebs from Kant. Philosophy has had a public relations problem for a few centuries now. This series aims to change that, showing that philosophy is relevant to your life – and not just for answering the big questions like "To be or not to be?" but for answering the little questions: "To watch or not to watch *South Park*?" Thinking deeply about TV, movies, and music doesn't make you a "complete idiot." In fact it might make you a philosopher, someone who believes the unexamined life is not worth living and the unexamined cartoon is not worth watching.

Already published in the series:

AVATAR: THE LAST AIRBENDER AND PHILOSOPHY

WISDOM FROM AANG TO ZUKO

Edited by

Helen De Cruz and Johan De Smedt

WILEY Blackwell

This edition first published 2023
© 2023 John Wiley & Sons, Inc.

Registered Office
John Wiley & Sons, Inc., 111 River Street, Hoboken, NJ 07030, USA

Editorial Office
9600 Garsington Road, Oxford, OX4 2DQ, UK

For details of our global editorial offices, customer services, and more information about Wiley products visit us at www.wiley.com.

Wiley also publishes its books in a variety of electronic formats and by print-on-demand. Some content that appears in standard print versions of this book may not be available in other formats.

Library of Congress Cataloging-in-Publication Data applied for
Paperback ISBN: 9781119809807

Cover Design: Wiley
Cover Image: © YUNHEE SON/Getty Images, © Peratek/Shutterstock, © d1sk/Getty Images

Set in 10/12pt Sabon by Straive, Pondicherry, India
Printed and bound by CPI Group (UK) Ltd, Croydon, CR0 4YY

C004533_311022

Contents

Contributors
Drawing Wisdom from Many Different Places

Thomas Arnold is an assistant professor of philosophy at the University of Heidelberg, Germany, working on metaphysics, phenomenology, and phenomenological metaphysics (and, possibly, vice versa). He engages in bouts of public philosophy whenever the demands of life in Bang Sing Se, er, academia allow it. Wishes he knew as many jings as Momo.

Miranda Belarde-Lewis is a citizen of Zuni Pueblo in New Mexico and a member of the Takdeintáan Clan of the Tlingit Nation. She is an independent art curator, and an assistant professor in the University of Washington's Information School. As a professor Miranda researches and teaches about Indigenous Systems of Knowledge, exploring how knowledge is transferred and communicated through art. Miranda was introduced to ATLA by her then eight-year-old son, and scored the thrift of a lifetime when she found a hand-sized Aang and Appa in a bag at a Value Village. Little Aang is now a treasured family member.

Clementine Bordeaux is a doctoral candidate in the World Arts and Cultures/Dance department at the University of California, Los Angeles. Clementine is Sičáŋǧu Oglála Lakóta and grew up on the Pine Ridge Reservation. Their academic interests include Lakota ontology, Northern Plains creative practices, Indigenous feminisms, Indigenous representation, visual anthropology, digital and new media, and community-based participatory research.

Brad Cloud indizhinikaaz. Migizi indoodem. Mashki-Ziibing indoonjibaa. Ingoji go Gakaabikaang indaa noongom. Gekinoo'amaageyaan gabegikendaasoowigamigong, University of Minnesota ezhinikaadeg zhaaginaashimong. Ingikinoo'amawaag Anishinaabe-gikinoo'amaaganag igaye. Indian Education ezhinikaadeg. Niminwendam nanda-gikendamaan Anishinaabemazina'iganan. Gichi-apiitendaagwad nindibaajimowininaan. Booch indaagaagige-dibaajimomin. My name is **Brad Cloud**. I'm Eagle Clan. I'm from Bad River, and I live near Minneapolis these days. I'm an instructor at the University of Minnesota. I also teach Native students in a program called Indian Education. I enjoy studying Native American literature. Our stories are very important and we should always tell them.

Kody W. Cooper is UC Foundation Assistant Professor of Political Science at the University of Tennessee at Chattanooga. He is the author of numerous scrolls – er – articles considering various topics in political theory from a natural-law philosophical perspective, including jurisprudence, the family, religion, and bioethics. He is also the author of two books: *Thomas Hobbes and the Natural Law* (2018) *and The Classical and Christian Origins of American Politics: Political Theology, Natural Law, and the American Founding,* co-authored with Justin Dyer (2022). Is it real or a legend that he and his lover bent earth to be together and become the parents of nine children (and counting)? Oh, it's a real legend.

Helen De Cruz holds the Danforth Chair in the Humanities and is Professor of Philosophy at Saint Louis University, Missouri. In her philosophy, she aims to bend minds, not only of students and fellow philosophers, but also of the public at large. For this purpose, she has edited and co-edited several works of public philosophy, including *Philosophy Through Science Fiction Stories* (with Johan De Smedt and Eric Schwitzgebel, 2021) and *Philosophy Illustrated* (2022), as well as sole and co-authored essays in *Aeon/Psyche, The Conversation,* and *The Guardian.* The successful longtime collaboration with fellow philosopher and husband Johan De Smedt in many academic works indicates that philosophy need not be a lonely and solitary pursuit. In her spare time she bends words into speculative fiction, notes into soulful music, and pixels into digital art.

Johan De Smedt is a research professor (non-tenure track) at Saint Louis University, working as co-PI on a project on oneness and interconnectedness. He has written and edited several books such as *The Challenge of Evolution to Religion* (with Helen De Cruz, 2020) and *Empirically Engaged Evolutionary Ethics* (with Helen De Cruz, 2021). He hopes to bend the world toward the good, one article and book at a time. The designated firebender of his family, he cooks recreationally as well as of necessity as, if Helen cooked, they would all starve – or so his family claims.

Savriël Dillingh is a PhD candidate in political philosophy and business ethics at the Erasmus Institute for Philosophy and Economics. His research focuses on the political philosophy of the market and the place of the firm within it. Upon receiving his PhD, he plans to restyle himself as "the Phoenix Professor." To Savriël's great chagrin, however, all of the online tests claim that he is a waterbender.

Barrett Emerick is an associate professor of Philosophy at St. Mary's College of Maryland in the United States. He works mainly on social philosophy and moral psychology, focusing throughout on gender and racial justice. In collaboration with his friend, co-author, and favorite Waterbender, Audrey Yap, he is developing an anti-carceral, feminist, social ethic that starts from the fact that persons are fundamentally vulnerable, social, and fallible. He asks how, like Uncle Iroh, we can simultaneously hold others accountable for their actions without giving up on them.

Saba Fatima got her bachelor's in computer science but then decided to change her element from bending programming to bending philosophy, all in an effort to make life more meaningful for herself. Today, she loves teaching about feminism, racism, capitalism, and Islamic thought at Southern Illinois University Edwardsville. She also writes amazingly thought-provoking pieces about that kind of stuff and gives one-too-many public talks in her mission to make philosophy accessible. Her scholarship centers on Muslim social epistemology, Muslim critical thought, Islamic feminism, and the racialization of Muslims. A few years back, she started a podcast in which she interviews Muslim women academics, called *She Speaks: Academic Muslimahs*. You can learn more about this philosophy bender on her personal website: https://sites.google.com/view/sabafatimaphd.

Nicole Fice is a PhD candidate in philosophy at Western University in London, Ontario. Her research interests are in feminist philosophy, moral and political philosophy, and applied ethics. Outside of her studies, she tries to earthbend like Toph by throwing pottery on the wheel. So far, it's about as close as she can get. She grew up watching *ATLA* with her younger sister and brother, to whom her chapter is dedicated.

Johnathan Flowers is an Assistant Professor in the Department of Philosophy at California State University Northridge. Flowers's research areas include East Asian philosophy, American pragmatism, philosophy of disability, philosophy of race, and philosophy of technology. His current research focuses on the affective ground of experience, identity, and personhood. His first monograph, Mono no Aware as a Poetics of Gender is forthcoming in 2022. In addition to his academic studies, Flowers has been a student of the martial arts for over 20 years. Despite the results of several online quizzes, Flowers consistently argues that he is most like waterbenders, if not in temperament then in martial style.

Mike Gregory is a PhD student at the University of Groningen in the Netherlands researching political philosophy and ethics in the history of philosophy, especially Kant and Kantian philosophy. He also teaches a variety of courses about political philosophy and human rights. On the side, Mike has started a small business selling cactus juice because "It'll quench you! Nothing's quenchier! It's the quenchiest!" Coming soon to a desert near you.

Zachary Isrow holds a PhD in humanities (philosophy and anthropology) from Alma Mater Europaea. His research and teaching revolves around the ontological foundations of human nature, value theory, and the history of philosophy (East and West). He has studied Buddhism and Daoism, reflecting on their influence on Western thought, along with being a practitioner of Baguazhang for over 12 years. Like Uncle Iroh, he has an extensive tea collection.

Holly Jones is an emerita associate professor of English at The University of Alabama in Huntsville. She publishes on issues of race, identity, and citizenship as they relate to literature. She has two young sons, with whom she watches the show. Like Toph, she aspires to be Melon Lord in her free time.

Nicholaos Jones is a professor of philosophy and director for the Humanities Center at The University of Alabama in Huntsville. He enjoys philosophizing about a wide range of topics, from scientific explanation to Buddhist metaphysics. His wife and co-author, Holly Jones, gives him all his best ideas. He gets excited over nothing and, like Zuko, doesn't need any calming tea.

Nathan Kellen is an Instructor of Philosophy at Owensboro Community & Technical College. His primary interests are in the study of truth and logic, and he has published articles on the metaphysics of truth and logical pluralism. His other contributions to philosophy and popular culture can be found in *More Doctor Who and Philosophy*, and with Roy T. Cook in *The Ultimate Star Wars and Philosophy*, *Star Wars and Philosophy Strikes Back*, and *Wonder Woman and Philosophy*. He doesn't yet know 10,000 things, but he's trying.

Yao Lin holds a PhD in political science from Columbia University, a JD from Yale Law School, and a MA in philosophy from Peking University. He researches and teaches in moral and political philosophy, comparative law and politics, and comparative social and political thought. Yao writes extensively for the Chinese public, including philosophizing on various films and TV shows such as *Arrival*, *BoJack Horseman*, and *Coco*. This is the first popular philosophy he has written in English, and hopefully not the last. The draft was reviewed by his nine-year-old daughter, the most devoted *Avatar: The Last Airbender* fan in the family, and was revised accordingly. Like everyone else, Yao occasionally fancies having superpowers, which he wields to bring peace and justice to the world. Alas, he then reminds himself, a world where superpowers exist isn't quite worth wishing for.

James William Lincoln completed his PhD in philosophy (2020) from the University of Kentucky with graduate certificates in gender and women's studies, social theory, and college teaching and learning. Currently, he serves as a senior instructor in the Department of Philosophy at the University of Louisville where he teaches online classes in ethics, Asian philosophy, and social philosophy. He is also an instructor at Lasell University in their Junior Ethics Program. Notably, if he lived in the world of *ATLA*, he hopes he would be an airbender, but recognizes that he would probably be an earthbender.

Kerri J. Malloy is an assistant professor of global humanities in the Department of Humanities at San José State University. His research focuses on Indigenous genocide, healing, and reconciliation in North America and the necessity of systemic change within social structures to advance transitional justice. He is the author of several book chapters, including "Renewing the World: Disrupting Settler-colonial Destruction" in *The Routledge Handbook of Religion, Mass Atrocity, and Genocide* (2022) and "Remembrance and Renewal at Tuluwat: Restoring the Center of the World" in *Remembrance and Forgiveness: Global and Interdisciplinary Perspectives on Genocide and Mass Violence* (2020). He is co-authoring a monograph *The Politics of Defining Genocide: International Relations, Denialism, and Prevention*, which is in preparation. He currently serves on the Advisory Board of the International Association of Genocide Scholars.

Sofia Ortiz-Hinojosa is an assistant professor of philosophy at Vassar College, where she teaches courses on philosophy of mind, epistemology, Latin American philosophy, and ancient global philosophy. So far her tea-drinking has fueled her study of the nature and epistemology of imagination, which is key for Aang to imagine a peaceful future for the Four Nations. She also studies the seventeenth-century polymath Sor Juana Inés de la Cruz, who would probably have chosen to stay behind with Professor Zei and be buried with the books of Wan Shi Tong's Library. When not writing, Sofia likes to practice the water-whip and play with her two cat-owls, Zsa Zsa and Widget.

Brett Patterson teaches religion, ethics, and literature at Clemson University. He has written essays for various Pop Culture and Philosophy collections (including Batman, Iron Man, *Ender's Game*, and *Lost*) and has devoted much research to speculative fiction, most recently to the work of Gene Wolfe and Connie Willis. He also has been developing a taste for jasmine tea, based on Uncle Iroh's recommendation, of course.

David Schwitzgebel is studying cognitive science as a PhD student in Paris. He is affiliated with the École Normale Supérieure, PSL University, and the Institut Jean Nicod, where he researches cognition, linguistics, visual perception, knowledge, and collective intelligence. In his free time, he binges science fiction, hunts for delicious crêpes, and listens to experimental electronic music. Whatever you do, do not engage him in a philosophical debate about the distinction between tea and hot leaf juice.

Eric Schwitzgebel is a professor of philosophy at University of California, Riverside, and author of *A Theory of Jerks and Other Philosophical Misadventures*. He is the world's leading authority on the moral behavior of ethics professors. (Yes, really.) Few appear to be as wise as Iroh.

Justin Skirry is Professor and Chair of the Philosophy and Religion Department at Nebraska Wesleyan University in Lincoln, Nebraska. His philosophical interests are in Native American philosophy, ancient Egyptian philosophy, and in the philosophy of the seventeenth-century philosopher René Descartes. In watching *ATLA* with his sons Sam and Charlie, Dr. Skirry became fascinated with the philosophical depth of the series. He has Sam's noodle portrait of the Fire Lord proudly displayed in his office.

Samuel Skirry is an English Major at Nebraska Wesleyan University in Lincoln, Nebraska. He became interested in Native American philosophy because of Katara and Sokka in *ATLA*. Sam is also interested in film studies and criticism. He is currently searching for his noodle portrait of the Fire Lord; so far, no luck.

Joseph A. Stramondo is an associate professor of philosophy and director of the Institute for Ethics and Public Affairs at San Diego State University. His philosophical research makes the case that bioethics should focus on the lived experiences of disability as a crucial source of moral knowledge that should guide clinical practice, biomedical research, and health policy. Specifically, he has argued that we need to do a better job of taking disability experiences seriously when thinking about topics such as informed consent procedures, reproductive ethics, pandemic triage protocols, and assistive neurotechnology. When he isn't writing or teaching philosophy, he is hanging out with his spouse and their two young kids, who may themselves be aspiring earthbenders, considering that they are often covered in a "protective layer of earth."

Natalia Strok has a PHD from the University of Buenos Aires (UBA). She is an associate researcher on the history of philosophy at the National Research Council of Argentina and teaches at UBA and the National University of La Plata. She has been studying the Platonic tradition since forever, but currently she concentrates on Ralph Cudworth and Anne Conway, while developing a project on necessity and contingency topics in different authors. She has presented papers on *Star Wars* and Harry Potter at philosophical conferences. She wishes, someday, to only write and talk about pop culture.

Hello, **Robert H. Wallace** here. He is an assistant professor of philosophy at California Polytechnic State University, San Luis Obispo. He works on issues at the intersection of metaphysics, ethics, and the philosophy of action, with a special focus on free will and moral responsibility. When asked if he ever gets sick of his job, he'll say: "sick of philosophy, that's like being sick of breathing!"

Daniel Wawrzyniak studied philosophy and English language and literature at the University of Göttingen, Germany, where he also received his PhD in philosophy. He writes and gives talks about human–animal relations, in particular concerning animal well-being in livestock husbandry systems, genetic engineering, and other uses of animals for human purposes. In fact, this agenda is so important to him, he heavy-heartedly dropped his initial idea of writing a contribution on his role model Uncle Iroh and the philosophy of tea drinking – please, note: in tea as in food "the secret ingredient is love" not lemur.

Justin F. White is an assistant professor of philosophy at Brigham Young University. His research focuses on nineteenth- and twentieth-century European philosophy (especially Kierkegaard, Nietzsche, Heidegger, and Merleau-Ponty) and on contemporary philosophy of agency and moral psychology. He is interested in regret, skill, self-deception, self-ignorance, and aspiration. He has published in *The Monist*, *The Southern Journal of Philosophy*, *The Kierkegaardian Mind*, *The Routledge Handbook of Phenomenology of Agency*, *European Journal of Philosophy*, and *The Cambridge Heidegger Lexicon*. An avid distance runner, Justin has explored the possibility of a cactus-juice-based sports drink. Although a brand slogan was ready to go – "Nothing's quenchier. It's the quenchiest!" – investors became hesitant after preliminary trials in desert conditions had mixed results.

Nicholas Whittaker is a doctoral candidate in the philosophy department of the City University of New York, Graduate Center. Their work centers on a cluster of interrelated questions spinning out of philosophy of art, philosophy of race, and phenomenology; abolitionist theory and politics guides much of that work. Their writings can be found in *Journal of Aesthetics and Art Criticism*, *British Journal of Aesthetics*, *Film and Philosophy*, *The Point*, *The Drift*, *LA Review of Books*, and more. They are a lifelong *Avatar* fan; in fact, as far as they are concerned, being a part of this collection is the adult equivalent of pretending to be a waterbender at the beach as a child. (You should've seen them when the moon rose . . .)

Isaac Wilhelm is an assistant professor of philosophy at the National University of Singapore, whose research focuses on metaphysics and the philosophy of science, and who is developing a logic textbook – called

"Logic and Justice" – which motivates the study of formal logic by connecting it to various social and political issues.

Audrey Yap is an associate professor of philosophy at the University of Victoria in Canada that stands on unceded ləkʷəŋən (Lekwungen) territory. She works mainly on social philosophy, and is working on a larger project on anti-carceral feminism together with her friend, co-author, and favorite Earthbender, Barrett Emerick. However, credit for her contribution to this volume goes in large part to her real-life Appa, fierce protector, and deeply missed dog Beezie, who presided over much of the episode viewing and taught her all of the most important things she knows about not giving up on people.

Preface

Aaron Ehasz

What is the meaning and value of philosophy in *Avatar: The Last Airbender*? Why is it there?

A decade before I became head writer of *ATLA*, I was an undergraduate studying philosophy at Harvard University. At the time, one of the most feared courses was an introduction to Hegel, taught by Professor Fred Neuhouser. To be clear, it was the material that was intimidating; the professor himself was beloved. At any given moment, he seemed to be genuinely wrestling with the mind-bending puzzles of Hegel's philosophy. Walking about campus he always had a faraway look, lost in thought, as if perhaps he was just a single firing synapse away from fully synthesizing the material and reaching enlightenment.

However, one day something happened that shook Professor Neuhouser from his seemingly unbreakable intellectual reverie. I was sitting with several other students in the Adams House Dining Hall when we saw our brilliant professor dispose of the remains of his meal and walk over to select a dessert. His expression revealed his mind was still firmly anchored in some nuance of dialectical phenomenology. What he could not have expected was that when he got to the ice cream station the depleted tub of mint chocolate chip had just been replaced with a five-gallon cylinder of chocolate malted crunch, brand new and right out of deep freeze. Professor Neuhouser approached with his bowl, and we watched as he attempted to scoop the ice cream. Impossible! It was completely solid. Professor Neuhouser was not ready to concede, and after dipping the ice cream spade in the rinsing water, he attacked his frozen reward with all his might. For one instant, his face changed, and we knew: in that moment, there was no Hegel on his mind, nor Fichte or Rousseau for that matter, he was all about the ice cream! Man vs. Dessert.

When I think about *ATLA*, I think about how our characters' ideas, belief systems, and frameworks were tested against their humanity. We loved exploring ideas from both Eastern and Western philosophy, and I always hoped that on a "simplified-for-cartoons" level we still did those ideas some authentic justice. But maybe, in the end, the characters were just human beings – they were just kids – and no philosophy was ever really going to stand up in the face of their very real human needs. I think about Aang, trying to comfort himself with Buddhist philosophy when he loses Appa, but how ultimately his intellectualization of the loss fails. I think about Aang, trying to let go of Katara so he can unblock his last chakra and unlock the Avatar state . . . how can he possibly let go of his love?

Reflecting on *ATLA*, I wonder if perhaps this was the unconscious conclusion we had drawn in our writing – that cold intellectual philosophy ultimately cannot stand up to core drives of character and human needs. In the end philosophy was nothing, just weightless musings. It shrinks and vanishes in the face of loss, love, or especially hard ice cream.

But then I think about Uncle Iroh.

Uncle Iroh not only loves wisdom, he loves and studies wisdom and ideas from many cultures. In "Bitter Work," Iroh reveals that through his study of Water Tribe culture, he applied some of their ideas and techniques to things he already knew as a firebender – and he created a new technique that redirects lightning. He teaches this technique to Zuko, and these teachings end up being the key to the whole saga. This technique allows Zuko to stand up to his father, survive, and move forward on a new path that helps Aang, Katara, Toph, and Sokka save the world.

So, one unconsciously written lesson that I would like to take from *ATLA* is that our humanity is not just a measure and limit to the power of philosophy. Philosophy and our openness to new ideas are the key to unlocking the ultimate potential in our humanity. The other tacit lesson, as great thinkers from ancient to modern times, Eastern and Western cultures can agree on, is that if you just let the ice cream sit out for about ten minutes, it's a lot easier to scoop.

Introduction
"We are all one people, but we live as if divided"

Helen De Cruz and Johan De Smedt

"Water. Earth. Fire. Air. Long ago, the four nations lived together in harmony. Then everything changed when the Fire Nation attacked." The opening sequence of *Avatar: The Last Airbender* introduces us to the four elements of the show's universe and the historical events that precede the story. The narrator (Katara) goes on, "Only the Avatar, master of all four elements, could stop them. But when the world needed him most, he vanished."

On the face of it, *ATLA* seems like just another story that uses the "Chosen One" trope, which is familiar in science fiction and fantasy – think of Harry Potter, Luke Skywalker, or Neo. This trope usually unfolds in the following way: the world is in peril, but fortunately there is a Chosen One who will save it. The Chosen One is prophesied as the only one who can save humanity, or the world, or the universe, by virtue of his – or rarely her – special innate abilities. As speculative fiction writer Irette Patterson explains, "The Chosen One succeeds because they are, well, chosen, not because they have worked years to perfect their skill set. Their ability is innate."[1] She objects to the trope precisely because it underemphasizes collective struggle and learning. In reality, we cannot fix problems so easily by passively waiting around for a savior.

Indeed, the Avatar is exceptional. In a world where some people possess the ability to bend a specific element to their will, he is the only one who can bend all four elements. He is the one who brings balance to the world, the only one who can stop the militaristic Fire Nation in their relentless conquest.

However, *ATLA* subverts the Chosen One trope, in ways that make the show philosophically distinct from many other shows that feature superheroes and other larger-than-life characters. Though Aang as the Avatar is

Avatar: The Last Airbender and Philosophy: Wisdom from Aang to Zuko, First Edition. Edited by Helen De Cruz and Johan De Smedt.

indeed the only one who can master the four elements, his learning is slow and non-linear. He requires a dedicated teacher for each element, and finding teachers is not always a straightforward process. Moreover, he struggles and faces mental obstacles in his ability to earthbend and especially firebend. Even after he completes his training, he remains inferior in bending skill to some of his masters. Unlike Katara, he cannot bloodbend; unlike Toph, he cannot metalbend.

Saving the world is a team effort, embodied in Team Avatar, aka the Gaang. Aang is not the leader of Team Avatar (that is Katara). He's not the brains (that is Sokka). He's not the voice of reason (often Toph). As Aang points out, the sky bison Appa literally carries the members of Team Avatar ("The Chase"). Also, Aang needs spiritual as well as practical guidance, which he receives from his past incarnations and many wise individuals, including the Lion Turtle and King Bumi.

A major theme in *ATLA* is oneness, the philosophical idea that the world is one and that we can only flourish in relationship to others.[2] As Guru Pathik says, "The greatest illusion of this world is the illusion of separation. Things you think are separate and different are actually one and the same." When Aang asks if this applies to the four nations, Guru Pathik replies, "Yes. We are all one people. But we live as if divided" ("The Guru"). Huu, a waterbender from the Foggy Swamp Tribe, expresses a similar sentiment: "You think you're any different from me? Or your friends? Or this tree? If you listen hard enough, you can hear every living thing breathing together. You can feel everything growing. We're all living together, even if most folks don't act like it. We all have the same roots and we are all branches of the same tree" ("The Swamp").

We can find real-world analogues of Huu and Pathik in many philosophical traditions, notably in East and South Asian schools of thought, including Daoism, neo-Confucianism, and Huayan and Chan/Zen Buddhism. These philosophical traditions hold that the world and its inhabitants actually form a whole, and that our sense that we are separated (in nations, species, living and non-living things, etc.) is a harmful illusion. For example, the Chinese Buddhist philosopher Fazang (643–712) explained the idea of oneness to Wu Zetian, China's only empress. He taught her that reality is one, using a nearby golden lion statue as a metaphor for the oneness of reality. Like the different parts of the statue, "All is one, because all are the same in lacking an individual nature; one is all, because cause and effect follow one another endlessly."[3] Views that humanity is one whole and that we are one with the natural world also feature in many Indigenous philosophical traditions, as well as in feminist care ethics, environmental and animal ethics, and anarchism. The contributions to this volume engage with several of these traditions.

This book benefits from its authors' breadth of experiences and philosophical insights. Their experiences directly bear on their work; for example, two chapters that explore the bending arts of *ATLA* in detail are written by martial artists experienced in Chinese and Japanese martial arts. Other authors advocate for disability rights and Black abolitionism. Three of the chapters in this volume are written by Indigenous authors. This eclecticism and the importance of experience remind us of what Iroh teaches his nephew Zuko in "Bitter Work": "It is important to draw wisdom from many different places. If you take it from only one place, it becomes rigid and stale. Understanding others, the other elements, and the other nations will help you become whole."

This intertwining of experience, identity, and reflection illustrates how philosophy helps us deal with enduring problems that have no easy solutions. The imagined world of *ATLA* needs to deal with the imperialism of the Fire Nation and its destructive effects on ecology, culture, and people. We are regularly reminded that the Air Nomads became victims of a genocide (already in the show's title "the last airbender"), which is an unusual and serious topic for a children's show, especially given how genocide and ecological devastation continue to be swept under the carpet in the real world. Without serious reflection on these problems, that is, without *philosophy*, we cannot come to solutions. Far from an idle pastime, philosophy is central to human life and flourishing; it helps us to address societal ills in a creative way.[4]

For example, we can see how Ba Sing Se deals with challenges in a suboptimal way. Its government has installed an authoritarian and secret police force. Moreover, it cordons off the steady stream of refugees from its wealthiest citizens, and promotes lies ("There is no war in Ba Sing Se") over an honest confrontation with the imminent danger its citizens face. Like the characters in *ATLA*, we also have to grapple with ecological destruction, the enduring effects of genocide, imperialism, wealth inequality, and many other challenges. In *ATLA*, sage individuals in conversation with Team Avatar can come to reasonable solutions to these problems. Their philosophies can help us imagine alternative futures and better ways of life in our world too.

Much like Team Avatar is a collective effort, this book could not have come about without the collaboration and help of many people. Foremost are the 32 contributing authors, whose insights prompted us to rewatch numerous episodes and to discover new layers of meaning within them. We are also thankful to the people at Wiley Blackwell, including Will Croft, Marissa Koors, and Charlie Hamlyn, for their assistance throughout the project, and Louise Spencely for her careful copyediting. We are grateful to Katie Rackers, Helen's research assistant, for help with the preparation and formatting of the manuscript. We are indebted to our children, Gabriel and Aliénor, who watched the series with us and discussed the contributions as we were reviewing and editing them. Many thanks to Bill Irwin, the series editor and wordbender par excellence, for help and advice throughout the project. A final word of thanks goes out to our students, with whom we have discussed several of the topics of the show, and especially to John Nash, who drew our attention to the series.

Notes

1. Irette Patterson, "On Resistance: The Chosen One," *Strange Horizons*, January 28, 2019, at http://strangehorizons.com/non-fiction/on-resistance-the-chosen-one.
2. For an exploration of oneness in eastern philosophy, see Philip Ivanhoe, *Oneness* (Oxford: Oxford University Press, 2017).
3. Fazang, "Essay on the Golden Lion," in Justin Tiwald and Bryan Van Norden eds., *Readings in Later Chinese Philosophy: Han Dynasty to the 20th Century* (Indianapolis: Hackett, 2014), 88.
4. For a carefully outlined argument along these lines, see Mary Midgley, *What Is Philosophy For?* (London and New York: Bloomsbury, 2018).

PART I

THE UNIVERSE OF *AVATAR: THE LAST AIRBENDER*

1

Native Philosophies and Relationality in *Avatar: The Last Airbender*
It's (Lion) Turtles All the Way Down

Miranda Belarde-Lewis (Zuni/Tlingit) and Clementine Bordeaux (Sicangu Oglala Lakota)

> The true mind can wither all the lies and illusions without being lost.
> The true heart can touch the poison of hatred without being harmed.
> Since beginningless time, darkness thrives in the void, but always yields
> to purifying Light.
> (Lion Turtle, "Sozin's Comet, Part 2: The Old Masters")

Is *Avatar: The Last Airbender* (*ATLA*) a Native story? Possibly. Can Native peoples see themselves and their philosophies reflected in *ATLA*? Absolutely. At least we can. We are Native people from vastly different Native communities (Zuni Pueblo/Tlingit and Sicangu Oglala Lakota), and yet there are many events, themes, and underlying philosophical messages within *ATLA* that resonate with us both. These include having deep relationships with a specific territory and landscape, a consciousness of the sheer strength of the natural elements within that landscape, being aware of and at ease with the spirit realm, and the easygoing acceptance of supernatural and extra-human abilities as part of everyday life for those in the *ATLA* universe.

The everydayness of benders reflecting the physical properties of their elements reminds us of the work of the late Jicarilla Apache philosopher V.F. Cordova (1937–2002). Cordova describes "bounded space" as a land base defined by geographic features such as mountains, rivers, deserts, lakes, oceans, and canyons. Being from a specific bounded space provides a chance to develop a heightened awareness of one's physical location, as well as the plants, animals, weather, and seasons of that environment. Being from a bounded space obligates a person to be knowledgeable of, and responsible for, that space. Part of the obligation and responsibility of bounded space is

Avatar: The Last Airbender and Philosophy: Wisdom from Aang to Zuko, First Edition.
Edited by Helen De Cruz and Johan De Smedt.

knowing that on the other side of that mountain, river, desert, lake, ocean, or canyon live different sets of people in *their* rightful and bounded space.[1]

The *ATLA* universe contains multiple examples of bounded space. As the series progresses, we're taken on a tour through the different nations and learn to recognize the ways each nation's bounded space is reflected in the landscapes, animals, and plants, and how the landscapes have shaped the humans in those spaces – in everything from their personalities, clothing, and food, to their relation to the spirit realm, and, of course, their benders.

There is a Lakota saying: "the same as above, as below," which means that the events taking place here, in the physical world, affect what happens in the spiritual world and vice versa.[2] While we're given hints that there are amazingly big metaphysical and spiritual events going on when Aang's iceberg bubble first surfaces and when the statues' eyes light up with Avatar energy at the Southern Air Temple, our first explicit introduction to the spirit realm is "Winter Solstice, Part 1," where the Gaang witness the effects of a scorched earth terror campaign typical of a Fire Nation raid and discover a nearby village being terrorized by an angry spirit – Hei Bai. After Sokka and Aang are transported to the Spirit Realm and back, the experience helps Aang (and us) see that living humans and the spirit world coexist and are inextricably linked. The spirit realm might appear scary. But as we dive further into the series, we realize that it's all around us and that it deserves respect and is not to be feared. Aang learns it's impossible to separate the physical world from the spirit world, a sentiment shared by many Native peoples from different tribal nations.

As Indigenous peoples watching *ATLA*, we bring our specific tribal understandings of the physical world, spiritual world, and more-than-human kin defined by the bounded spaces we grew up in. For example, in Lakota, understanding spiritual journeys after death involves traveling along the Milky Way to the Spirit world, which reminds us of Aang's path along a starry ribbon toward the universe as he learns how to master the Avatar state ("The Crossroads of Destiny"). In both Zuni Pueblo and Tlingit understandings of reincarnation and rebirth, the genealogical connections of family and heritage live on through successive generations and are acknowledged as an identifiable strength of individuals, families, and clans (extended family groups). Past lives play a vital role in passing on knowledge and wisdom through the Avatar line. We can see Aang's journey as he tries to restore the balance between good and evil, dark and light, and master all the elements as his understanding of air, water, earth, and fire deepens his connection to the world he's tasked with protecting.

The Benders: Defined by Their Bounded Space

At the beginning of each *ATLA* episode, the audience is reminded: "Long ago, the four nations lived together in harmony." The sequence shows four individuals bending the water, earth, fire, and air elements. The four elements within the *ATLA* universe reflect the specific bounded space that obligates a person to be knowledgeable of and responsible for that space. *ATLA* characters within the Water Tribes, Earth Kingdom, the Fire Nation, and the Air Nomads are bound to and shaped by their relationships with their respective nations.

Two episodes specifically highlight the impact of relationships between other-than-human persons, including animals and spirits of the bending world. In "The Siege of the North, Part 1," the moon and ocean stories are revealed to explain waterbending. In "The Firebending Masters," stories are shared regarding earthbending, airbending, and firebending. These two episodes are excellent examples of bounded space and relationality. Relationality, as explored by contemporary Cree scholar Shawn Wilson, is a deep-seated responsibility to the territory one comes from, as well as all aspects of that territory – land, waters, people, animals, plants.[3]

In "The Siege of the North, Part 1," we are introduced to the Northern Spirit Oasis and the spirits Tui (push) and La (pull), who took the form of koi fish in the human plane of existence. Princess Yue tells Aang, Katara, and Momo that the moon taught waterbending to the people of the Water Tribes as they observed the push and pull on the ocean. Yue further explains that "our strength comes from the spirit of the moon; our life comes from the spirit of the ocean." She takes them to a spirit oasis, the most spiritual area in the North Pole. Later, Yue reciprocates the life that was gifted to her as a newborn, in order to reanimate Tui's slain fish body, and thus takes her new place in the sky as an ancestor, the Moon Spirit. This act of selfless love for family and community reminds us of Tlingit clan insignia in the Pacific Northwest. The symbols used to represent various Tlingit clans were earned by ancient ancestors who gave their lives to animals, supernatural beings, or landforms, like mountains. In exchange, their surviving family group is now able to use and draw strength from the image of that animal or mountain. Likewise, the waterbenders (and Sokka) know that Yue is in the sky, guiding and watching over everyone.

In "The Firebending Masters," Toph shares her story of learning earthbending from the badgermoles: "I was able to learn earthbending not just as a martial art, but as an extension of my senses." She explains that the badgermoles utilize earthbending as a way of "interacting with the world." Aang tells us he learned from the Air Nomad monks, but they learned from the flying bison, the original airbenders. He even remarks to Appa that "maybe you'll give me a lesson one day, buddy," thus reducing the hierarchy between humans and animals, introducing the possibility that Appa could be the leader of a situation, and not just a ride and a pet. The connection to koi fish, badgermoles and air bison demonstrates the deep relationship to other-than-human persons integral to bending.

Later, in "The Firebending Masters" episode, the last dragons are revealed to understand fire, furthering Aang and Zuko's firebending knowledge. The ancient protectors of this knowledge, the Sun Warriors, literally bring to light the way dragons continue to privilege and utilize firebending cultural knowledge. The Sun Warriors reveal an ontological formation that contemporary Quandamooka scholar and philosopher Aileen Moreton-Robinson describes as a matter of identity and state of being. She explains "we come to know who we are and who we claim to be, as well as who claims us and how we are connected to our lands."[4] Zuko and Aang's firebending suffers without a defined connection to the dragons and the land. Ultimately, Aang's apprehension toward firebending and Zuko's diminished firebending abilities are grounded in fear. As they witness firebending from the true masters, they see this ability as a responsibility rather than a right. Their commitment to firebending is present in their drive to bring balance to the universe. For each nation's benders, it's the connection to and awareness of the physical properties of their respective bounded spaces that results in their extra-human abilities and ultimately, the mastery of their bending.

The People

The specific bounded spaces of the respective nations are reflected in their people and their benders. In "Bitter Work," Uncle Iroh breaks down the main characteristics of the people and the four nations: the Fire Nation embody power and desire; the Earth Kingdom show endurance and diversity; the Air Nomads achieved freedom from worldly concerns (and also had a pretty good sense of humor); and the Water Tribes exude love and community, especially in the face of change. Contemporary Hawaiian philosopher and scholar Manulani Aluli Meyer states, "specificity leads to universality." [5] This idea about celebrating one's origins while still respecting differences is later expanded by Iroh and the others in the Order of the White Lotus, a point we'll return to later. The specificity of physically bounded places creates the unique traits of the people who live within those boundaries, which results in the incredible abilities drawn upon by each nation's benders.

Meyer writes that for Indigenous peoples, "one does not simply learn about the land, we learn best *from* land." She goes on to explain that we need to recognize and identify how "space has influenced our thinking. Because it has."[6] Prince Zuko's quest to reclaim his honor through his search for the Avatar leads him to experience every corner of the world with Uncle Iroh and his small crew. Later, when he achieves his long-standing goal of being at his father's side during a war meeting (shown as a flashback in "Sozin's Comet Part 1: The Phoenix King"), Zuko is looked to as the expert; he possesses nuanced insights that none of his father's advisors have. Zuko and Fire Lord Ozai realize that Zuko's interactions beyond the inner confines of the palace, where he is surrounded by servants and neighbors of other wealthy and noble Fire Nation folk, have shaped his understanding of the other nations. In other words, Zuko's world travels have provided him with valuable insights into the Earth Kingdom citizens, which Princess Azula then twists into a genocidal plan immediately endorsed by Ozai. The difference between Ozai and Zuko boils down to a fundamentally different ethical understanding of their responsibility to the world and their rights as the leaders of the Fire Nation. Ozai feels he has a right to power over the world, while Zuko recognizes a profound responsibility to leading the Fire Nation as a contributor, and not the ruler of the other nations. We see this again later (in "Sozin's Comet Part 1: The Phoenix King") when the Gaang looks to Zuko to find Aang because, as Katara points out, he "is the expert at tracking Aang." His senses and knowledge of the world have been shaped by his interactions with many different types of land and the people within the Earth Kingdom.

Toph Beifong first appears in Aang's vision in "The Swamp." In some Indigenous communities, such as with many Lakota families, experiencing a premonition, or vision, leads to responsibilities to the community. King Bumi advises Aang to seek an earthbending teacher who "listens to the earth." We finally meet Toph in "The Blind Bandit," when Aang recognizes that she is literally listening to the earth. The vision in the swamp that helps Aang identify Toph as his earthbending master reinforces Native values of relatedness and interconnection.

In "Bitter Work," we see Aang struggle with earthbending. Toph's personality and teaching style is another example of the stereotypes for different nations' citizens. Toph barks orders and mocks Aang. Her taunting is an attempt to shame Aang into earthbending, resulting in frustration for them both. It's not until Katara reminds the easy-going and playful Aang that the natural opposite of Air is Earth, that he realizes that he needs to be patient with himself as he adapts to the internal qualities required to be an effective earthbender. Many Native stories about the origins of the world include obstacles put in the path of a trickster/hero/protagonist, meant to challenge them and make them stronger. Aang and Toph both display personalities shaped by their physical environments and remind us that the eternal struggle for balance and reciprocity sought by the Avatar requires adaptation, understanding, *and* balance. The search for connection, relatedness, and harmony is in line with the goals of many Native stories, cosmologies, and religious practices.

ATLA Universe

The *ATLA* universe provides narratives that point to Indigenous intergenerational ways of knowing. The concept of the North American continent existing on a turtle's back comes from a wide variety of tribal nations. Cherokee novelist Thomas King playfully uses the line "It's turtles all the way down" throughout his book *The Truth About Stories*.[7] Turtles on top of turtles demonstrate relationality passed along intergenerationally and establish a spiritual foundation for those on the turtle's back. Within the *ATLA* universe, the experience of being on a turtle's back, or rather a Lion Turtle's back, signals a deep connection to the spirit realm. Additionally, the advice of the Lion Turtle mirrors the knowledge of elders that continues to present itself throughout the series. The *ATLA* universe transforms Aang's experiences into examples of long-standing intergenerational learning needed to solve problems within the human world.

In "Sozin's Comet Part 2: The Old Masters," two significant *ATLA* universe revelations illustrate the importance of relationality. The episode sets up Aang's first meeting with a Lion Turtle and introduces the Order of the White Lotus. Both revelations provide a way for the audience to understand the importance of intercultural collaboration for the safety and well-being of all nations. Furthermore, the introduction of a Lion Turtle reveals a more significant connection between bending and the spirit world. These plot developments ultimately shift our understanding to see that bending is not about power but rather a continuum of responsibility toward balance.

In "Sozin's Comet Part 1: The Phoenix King," Aang expresses inner turmoil as he contemplates whether he must kill Fire Lord Ozai. Throughout the series, Aang often takes a spiritual journey to visit his past Avatar lives or find advice from the spirit realm. However, when Aang goes missing in this episode, he is given the ability to ask his past Avatar selves what he should do, and he comes face to face with a Lion Turtle. By the end of his journey on the Lion Turtle's back, the Lion Turtle's advice leads him to realize an alternative to taking a human's life. Aang defeats Fire Lord Ozai (AKA the Phoenix King) by taking away his bending abilities rather than killing him. In a flashback, the Lion Turtle states, "In the era before the Avatar, we bent not the elements, but the energy within ourselves." Aang, reflecting on the Lion Turtle's advice, struggles to keep his spirit balanced. He accomplishes his task in taking Ozai's firebending away so that it can no longer be used to "hurt or threaten anyone else again." Aang's actions demonstrate that balance *across* the universe is more important than power *over* the universe.

Throughout his journey in the series, Aang realizes that an intergenerational connection to his past selves can ensure a future relationality grounded in the balance of the elements, nations, and spirit realm. His 100-year absence has caused the physical world to descend into chaos and selfishness. The power grab of the Fire Nation has disrupted the relationships to bounded space. Near the end of the final episode ("Sozin's Comet Part 4: Avatar Aang") Zuko states, "a hundred years of fighting has left the world scarred and divided." We are then reminded of the Lion Turtle's lesson to have an incorruptible spirit that relies on the ability to seek balance across generations.

Within the *ATLA* universe, intergenerational engagement is an essential aspect of relationality. In "Sozin's Comet Part 2: The Old Masters" we see the longevity of intergenerational wisdom and knowledge across the different kingdoms, tribes, and nations. The Order of the White Lotus exemplifies a connection to and continuum between land and place shaped and protected by knowledge of the elders. While the Gaang tries to find a solution to defeating Fire Lord Ozai, they seek out Uncle Iroh for advice. They discover him with other "great masters," including Sifu Pakku, Jeong Jeong, King Bumi, and Master Piandao – a non-bender from the Fire Nation. These "old guys," as Toph calls them, explain that they are a part of "an ancient secret society," a group that transcends the divisions of the four nations." The Order of the White Lotus illustrates that bringing balance to the world is not just a task for the Avatar, but for everyone from all nations, both benders and non-benders. As a young honorable leader, Zuko seeks to restore balance to the Fire Nation. At the same time, the members of the Order of the White Lotus return Ba Sing Se to the people of the Earth Kingdom.

The concluding episode of the series transcends bending, nation, element, and bounded space to prove that *ATLA* is a story about relationality. To counteract the failings of individual people, the intergenerational tasks set before the Order of the White Lotus, the Aang gang, and the Avatar rely heavily on stories and experiences of those who have gone before. Lakota communities, as well as many Indigenous Nations, often turn to spirit helpers or familial ancestors to guide decision making. The Avatar continues to call on his past selves for guidance while the Aang gang and the Order of the White Lotus rely on aspects of their respective nation to bring balance to the *ATLA* universe. From an Indigenous perspective, elder knowledge or spirit knowledge is shared through stories or the storying of a place.

The Order of the White Lotus represents the stories of bounded space coming together to re-establish a relationship with the Earth Kingdom, with representatives from each nation and both benders and non-benders doing their part to restore Ba Sing Se's sovereignty. For example, Uncle Iroh recognizes that his vision of conquering Ba Sing Se was a misguided understanding of his youth. He states "only now do I see that my destiny is to take it [Ba Sing Se] back from the Fire Nation" ("Sozin's Comet, Part 2: The Old Masters"), which is why Iroh gathered the Order of the White Lotus. Uncle Iroh recognizes that the stories and understandings from each nation are what should bring balance to the world. The stories of the relationships between other-than-human kin, spirits, landscapes, and generations are essential to the function of relationality within the *ATLA* universe.

Opening (Spirit) Portals

Within the *ATLA* universe, we witness regular connections with the spirit realm or spirit world. Vine Deloria Jr. demonstrates that communities in North America often call themselves "the people" to reflect their deep connection to the demands of the spirits of the land.[8] Deloria argues that the natural world dictates how Indigenous peoples engage with their land and cosmology. This engagement often takes the form of speaking to plants or animals, or connecting with spirits.[9] Many Indigenous scholars have explored these connections to the "spirit world" as understood in *ATLA*.

Our use of "spirit" in this chapter reflects the use of the word "spirit" in the series. David Delgado Shorter advises that the use of "spirit," "spiritual," or "spirituality," in regard to Indigenous peoples is a complex issue that often results in a dismissal of Indigenous ideas, concepts, and practices. Shorter supports the use of "related" instead, which is another reason why we focus on relationality to explain the spirit realm as it's depicted in the concepts of bounded space and bending in the universe of both *ATLA* and in *The Legend of Korra (LoK)*.[10] To transform a spiritual relationship with others requires a proactive stance as opposed to a passive engagement with the world. We witness the transformation from the passive individualism of Aang hiding from his responsibilities or Zuko's narrowed goal of restoring "honor" to an active relational interaction between the Nations and their inhabitants. Throughout the series, we get different perspectives and moments of spiritual connections that demonstrate how Indigenous spirituality involves a deep respect, which requires actionable accountability to self, family, friends, nations, and the universe.

Although it's not the focus of this chapter, the importance of the spirit realm lays the foundation for the ability to access the spirit realm and the Avatar origin stories shared in *LoK*. At the end of *LoK* Book One ("Endgame"), Korra's bending has been taken away by Amon, and it's Aang who restores her bending, even though he is already dead. He blurs the lines between the spirit realm and the physical realm and shows Korra that she can access her connections with her past selves by simply asking for their help. As demonstrated earlier, the otherworldly presence of the Lion Turtle sets up a narrative of the origins of bending that existed before the timeline we see in *ATLA*. *LoK*, Book Two ("Beginnings: Part I") reveals the importance of the Lion Turtles to the formation of benders in the *ATLA* and *LoK* universe. In *LoK*, the Lion Turtles were the original beings that granted bending to humans in order to navigate the spirit realms. By the end of the series, Avatar Korra has permanently opened the spirit realm and provides the balance that the avatars have continuously sought for 10,000 years. She displays her responsibility to the physical world and the spirit realms through her right to open the portals. The spirit portals are open across space and time and are no longer limited to just the Avatars.

Native understandings of the world are as complex and varied as the tribes themselves (there are over 570 Native nations in the US alone!), yet, our stories, histories, ceremonies, and philosophies have always emphasized a deep, respectful relationship with one's surroundings and a quest to achieve balance within ourselves and with our relatives – human and otherwise. The balance between rights and responsibilities to a specific landscape are reflected across both the *ATLA* and *LoK* universe and make for easy connections to Native and Indigenous philosophies that center relationality and accountability to community.[11] We can see ourselves reflected back in the gratitude of spirits such as Hei Bai and the Painted Lady, in the elders' knowledge shared through the Order of the White Lotus, and in the wisdom gained while on the back of a Lion Turtle. For us, the *ATLA* universe is turtles all the way down.

Notes

1. Kathleen Dean Moore, Kurt Peters, Ted Jojola, and Amber Lacy, eds., *How It Is: The Native American Philosophy of V.F. Cordova* (Tucson: University of Arizona Press, 2007).
2. Ronald Goodman and Alan Seeger, *Lakota Star Knowledge: Studies in Lakota Stellar Theology* (Mission, SD: Sinte Gleska University, 2017).
3. Shawn Wilson, *Research as Ceremony: Articulating an Indigenous Research Paradigm* (Melbourne: Monash University, 2004).
4. Aileen Moreton-Robinson, "Relationality: A Key Presupposition of an Indigenous Social Research Paradigm," in Jean M. O'Brien and Chris Anderson eds., *Sources and Methods in Indigenous Studies* (London and New York: Routledge, 2017), 71.
5. Manulani Aluli Meyer, "Indigenous and Authentic: Hawaiian Epistemology and the Triangulation of Meaning," in Norman K. Denzin, Yvonna S. Lincoln, and Linda Tuhiwai Smith eds., *Handbook of Critical and Indigenous Methodologies* (Thousand Oaks, CA: Sage, 2008), 217–232.
6. Aluli Meyer, 219.
7. Thomas King, *The Truth About Stories: A Native Narrative* (Minneapolis: University of Minnesota Press, 2008).
8. Vine Deloria Jr., *The World We Used to Live In: Remembering the Powers of the Medicine Men* (Golden, CO: Fulcrum Publishing, 2006).
9. Deloria, 125.
10. David Delgado Shorter, "Spirituality," in Frederick E. Hoxie ed., *The Oxford Handbook of American Indian History* (Oxford: Oxford University Press, 2016), 433–452.
11. Shawn Wilson, *Research as Ceremony: Articulating an Indigenous Research Paradigm* (Melbourne: Monash University, 2004).

2

Getting Elemental
How Many Elements Are There in *Avatar: The Last Airbender*?

Sofia Ortiz-Hinojosa

Avatar: The Last Airbender (*ATLA*) opens with the words: Water. Earth. Fire. Air. As all fans know, the "Four Elements" mythos pervades the series, depicting talented people called "benders" who are able to wield and manipulate these special substances. A spiritually blessed individual called the Avatar can learn to wield all four Elements, but most individuals can wield one at most.

Exactly how fundamental are these Elements in *ATLA*? Earthbender Toph Beifong discovers that she can bend metal, formerly thought unbendable, because there are trace amounts of Earth in it ("The Guru"). This suggests that metal is made of both Earth and other things that are not Earth. If that were true, then there would be Elements in the world of *ATLA* that are not mentioned in the opening sequence. In the *Wu Xing* or Five Agents system of ancient Chinese Daoist philosophy, for instance, there are actually five elements: water, fire, wood, metal, and earth.[1]

However, Guru Pathik tells Avatar Aang that, "Even metal is just a part of Earth that has been purified and refined" ("The Guru"). This suggests that metal and Earth are continuous. Nonetheless, it is the *impure* part of metal that Toph can manipulate, rather than the purified part of metal, because of its familiar Earthly resonance. Has this purified Earth become something else? If it has, then either there are more Elements than the four we learn about in the opening sequence, or there are materials made from one or more of the four Elements which most benders cannot manipulate.

By the word "Element," the inhabitants of *ATLA* are not referring to our atomic elements. In the world of *ATLA*, the special materials called Elements seem to be major and basic components of the universe. In our world, by contrast, air is a mixture of oxygen and other gases, fire is the visible portion of chemical combustion, water is dihydrogen monoxide, and earth is a mixture of various sorts of molecules. Where we live, there are many objects that are not composed of these materials, such as silicone,

Avatar: The Last Airbender and Philosophy: Wisdom from Aang to Zuko, First Edition. Edited by Helen De Cruz and Johan De Smedt.

wood, plastic, enamel, helium, and many others. In order to distinguish the four special materials called Elements in *ATLA* from how we use the word "element" in our world I will use an initial capital letter for each word that denotes them: so the Elements in *ATLA* are Water, Earth, Fire, and Air, and they compose most of the objects in the world of *ATLA*.

Fifth Element?

The division between Elements is not perfectly distinct, and there are some oddities. Some individuals can wield subsets of the Elements that other benders of that Element cannot: the inhabitants of the Si Wong desert can use earthbending to manipulate the desert sands, although most earth-benders cannot do so ("The Library"). It would be tempting to think that bending requires admirable traits. But it doesn't seem as if spiritual skill or moral fortitude are necessarily required for bending abilities to manifest: there are misguided characters in the world of *ATLA* who are very skilled at bending as well as very spiritually wise individuals who cannot use bending. Most individuals in the universe of *ATLA* cannot bend at all.

Some fans might have noticed that no characters seem to be able to bend dry wood, bone, leather, or natural fibers like wool, hair, or plant fiber. This adds more complexity to the metal problem. Perhaps it is the human fabrication process or the process of mixing with living creatures that con-verts the natural Elements into other materials, or that makes them unbendable given what benders currently know. Perhaps there is some other explanation. Maybe the Elements are fundamental but some objects are made of multiple Elements. For example, hydrogen and oxygen are basic chemical elements in our world, and each can be used to make up one molecule of H_2O or regular water, which has new and different properties from hydrogen and oxygen alone. A final possibility: perhaps the Elements in *ATLA* are each themselves derived from one still more basic substance.

This last idea finds some support in the series when a gargantuan Lion Turtle reveals the secret of energybending to Aang ("Sozin's Comet, Part 2: The Old Masters"). Energybending involves the ability to manip-ulate the energy inside other individuals and within oneself, including the energy or *qi* that allows them to use bending in the first place. Is energy itself a fifth Element? What if the four Elements are all themselves derived from energy?

This question of fundamental substances is central to the branch of phi-losophy called *metaphysics*. Metaphysics deals with the ways things exist or could exist, how they come to be or change, and how these things are related to each other logically and physically. For example, metaphysics (with the help of other areas of knowledge) might ask whether minds and brains are the same or different things, whether Pluto is a planet, or whether the number 2 depends for its existence on the number 1.

Metaphysics is not limited to our own physical reality, either. It is also appropriate for asking questions about merely possible or entirely fictional worlds, like the *ATLA* universe, as long as the rules of that universe follow some identifiable logic or pattern.

To enquire into the fundamentality of the Elements in *ATLA* is to just ask about what things are made out of, and whether everything is made out of the same things or out of different things. If all of the other Elements are made out of energy, then energy would be the most fundamental substance in the world of *ATLA*. Other materials like the four Elements would then be parts or differentiations of this fundamental substance.

This idea brings us to again ask what the *unbendable* materials are made of in *ATLA*. Are they complexes of the Elements? We do meet waterbenders who can bend Water inside plants, such as the Foggy Swamp Tribe ("The Swamp"). Some waterbenders, including Katara, can become healers by manipulating fluids inside the human body ("The Deserter"). We also meet waterbenders who can control humans by bloodbending, a chilling art developed by the waterbender Hama ("The Puppetmaster"). Presumably these bending skills are based on fluids in plants and animals that are mostly the Elemental Water. There's no indication that waterbenders could also bend organic parts of these organisms. For example, we would imagine benders could not bend a dried flower, dried herb, or dried seaweed. It is possible that living plants and animals are part Water and part other Elements, such as Earth. Perhaps some benders might be able to bend cloth, wood, or other materials if they had some further insight into their nature.

It could help to ask: what are the essential features of each Element? One hypothesis we might entertain is that the four Elements pick out one of the four states of matter we are familiar with in our world, such as solid, liquid, gas, and plasma. Some support for this line of thinking comes from the abilities of the firebenders Iroh, Zuko, and Azula to bend lightning ("Bitter Work"), which is matter in a plasma state, as well as from the ability of Toph to bend Metal as well as Earth ("The Guru"), both of which are matter in a solid state. However, the series disproves this otherwise attractive hypothesis a few times. For example, waterbenders including Katara are shown to be able to bend ice and snow, the solid state of Water, and even change the phase of water ("Jet"). Moreover, when at one point Katara disguises herself as the Painted Lady, she is able to bend both the liquid Water below her and the more gaseous fine mist she uses to cloak her comings and goings ("The Painted Lady"). Certain earthbenders, such as former Avatars Roku, Kyoshi, and Szeto, are shown in flashbacks with the ability to bend lava, which is probably molten Earth ("The Avatar State," "Avatar Day," "The Avatar and the Fire Lord"). There is also the fact that while metal, bone, and wood are all solid materials, Toph only ever applies her earthbending to the first of these. We therefore need another hypothesis.

Ancient philosophy might provide some inspiration. First, we'll extract some insights from the ancient Greeks, and then we'll look into Mesoamerican philosophy. Finally, we'll examine South and East Asian philosophy for clues.

One or Many

The ancient Greek philosopher Empedocles (c. 494–434 BCE) thought there were four ungenerated *rhizōmata* or "roots" making up the world, along with two forces. He identified the four roots as Earth, Fire, Water, and Air, and the two forces as Love and Strife, which help explain movement and change through attraction and repulsion. Pure Love makes for harmony, while pure Strife makes for chaos, but both forces, according to Empedocles, were required for life to exist.[2] This metaphysical structure resembles that of the world of *ATLA*.

If an Empedoclean theory turns out to be true about *ATLA*'s universe, then bending abilities are necessarily distinct and possibly discontinuous, just as the Elements are fundamentally distinct. That would mean that an earthbender would never be able to firebend without an extraordinary gift like that of the Avatar. Take the ability to bend lava. Although Avatar Kyoshi could bend lava, her dual firebending and earthbending could explain this skill ("Avatar Day"). While we see the firebender Sozin redirecting the heat from lava, we do not see him directly bending lava himself, which we do see his opponent Avatar Roku do ("The Avatar State"). There is some evidence from the life of a future Avatar named Korra, who meets two different earthbenders able to manipulate lava, that lava is a subset of Earth after all, or more easily accessible to earthbenders (*The Legend of Korra*, "Enter the Void").

But what if the Elements were continuous with each other? For example, suppose that we had evidence that either a firebender *or* an earthbender could learn to bend lava, because it shares characteristics with both Elements. We do watch both waterbender Katara and earthbender Toph have a mud fight using bending ("The Runaway"), which suggests mud is both water and earth, or that water and earth become continuous in mud. We may need a different hypothesis that allows the Elements some more continuity.

The earlier philosopher Anaximander (610–c. 546 BCE) believed that the substance that originated the universe was *apeirōn*, an undifferentiated, unlimited totality. The four distinct Elements were generated from this undifferentiated totality by the primary opposites, cold/hot and wet/dry, pulling or pushing it in different directions. According to Anaximander, the Elements could eventually return to being *apeirōn*.[3] He preferred this theory to other elemental theories, because it would explain why the world continued to exist in spite of things changing. For example, if it were possible for Water to become Fire, he reasoned that eventually there would either be no Water or no Fire left, because Water's wetness can douse Fire and because Fire's heat can boil or evaporate Water into nonexistence. If the fundamental substance were *apeirōn*, however, then any random imbalances would eventually be resolved, because any substance can be generated from or return to *apeirōn*.

Suppose the Elements were continuous like this. In the world of *ATLA*, energy could be similar to Anaximander's *apeirōn*. If so, then all of the Elements would be generated out of energy. However, the concept of energy in *ATLA* is in a few ways more complicated than the concept of *apeirōn*. For one thing, Anaximander did not think mortal individuals could wield *apeirōn*. But more crucially, when Zuko recovers his firebending abilities, he learns from the Sun Warriors that the Fire he produces comes from his "inner energy," implying a continuity between Fire and energy specifically ("The Firebending Masters"). While other benders require pre-existing Elements in their environment, firebenders can generate their own. This suggests either that Fire is an intermediate state between energy and another Element, or that not all of the Elements are easily generatable from energy by humans.

Heraclitus (535–c. 475 BCE) hypothesized that Fire was the fundamental substance out of which everything is generated, and that Strife was the main force in the universe, such that every object was made up of opposites and required Strife between these opposites for its existence.[4] One way this has been interpreted is as the idea that everything is constantly changing. Constant motion for *ATLA*'s universe seems supported by Guru Pathik ("The Guru"). However, it is not clear whether strife between opposites is essential to the makeup of the *ATLA* universe.

The ancient Nahua of Mesoamerica, sometimes called the Aztecs, shared a similar view of the universe with Heraclitus, a millennium and an ocean away. James Maffie suggests that the ancient Nahua believed that fundamentally everything is *teotl*, a constant and divine motion or energy, a constant *becoming*.[5] Zuko's experience with the Sun Warriors resonates with this idea. If the source of life is the sun, as the Sun Warriors and the Nahua believed, and people have such life inside of them, then there would be an intimate connection between the sun, fire, and life energy. In fact, the Nahua called themselves the People of the Sun. They understood themselves to be warriors living in the era of the Fifth Sun, fighting to maintain balance in the world so as to delay the sun's eventual death, for the sun was a god who had to sacrifice himself for the job, and would eventually end his tenure. The prior four suns were each gods of earth, air, fire, and water who, depending on the version of the myth examined, ended their time as sun by cataclysmically ridding the world of people due to fights between gods, impiety among their created subjects, or other calamities. The People of the Sun therefore felt great pressure to repay the sun-god for its life force by using their own life force (sometimes in the form of bloodletting, animal or human sacrifices, and other rituals and ceremonies). According to the Nahua, this would balance the universe and keep the cycle of life going. In this way, the sun fuels life and is itself fueled by life.

While theoretically we're getting warmer (excuse the pun), the *ATLA* universe is not quite like the Nahua cosmos. For one thing, we don't have evidence that Air or Water or Earth originate in Fire or energy. Although some waterbenders can manipulate and heal living beings, we're unclear whether this is a direct conversion of energy into something waterbenders use. For another thing, if the *ATLA* universe was like Heraclitus' or like the Nahua's, we might expect a lot more people to be firebenders than other kinds of benders because it would come more naturally to them to begin bending from the source. Moreover, Aang is able to waterbend, airbend, and earthbend even when he cannot or will not use firebending. Let us investigate energy a bit further now, using South and East Asian philosophy.

Energy and Spirit

The concept of energy or *qi* in *ATLA* definitely resembles the ancient Chinese concept of *qi*[6] or the Hindu concept of *prāṇa*.[7] Guru Pathik directly discusses chakras, the spiraling pools of energy through which this energy or *qi* flows, with Aang ("The Guru"). Chakras are mentioned by ancient Indian sources in both Hindu and Buddhist traditions of *tantra* meditation practices. It is clear then that in the *ATLA* universe energy can flow through people and through their chakras. Aang's conversation with Guru Pathik suggests that energy is present in the universe as well. Perhaps this system of energy flow is the overall mechanism by which benders are able to connect to the Elements: indeed, Aang unblocks his firebending abilities by unblocking one of his chakra. This suggests that the Elements have a very close relationship to energy.

Is energy a kind of life-force? Recall that Aang's world also harbors spirits, who live in a parallel space the characters call the Spirit World, and seem to be living creatures of a sort ("Winter Solstice, Part 1: The Spirit World"). This brings us to the complicating question: what is the relationship between energy and spirit?

Aang's connection to the Spirit World suggests that the Spirit World is a distinguishable space or reality from the human world, or that it is composed of different sorts of *substances*. Only the Avatar as the bridge between worlds can travel there. Aang leaves his body behind when he goes to the Spirit World, rendering him vulnerable to injury and even death. Only a handful of spirits are capable of assuming physical forms in the mortal world, and doing so requires them to give up their immortality ("The Siege of the North, Part 2"). This suggests that the physical Elements are only one part of the world, connected either exclusively or more strongly to physical bodies than to spirits.

If spirits and the Elements are separate kinds of substances, then it is possible that the *ATLA* universe is *dualistic*: that there are two types of fundamental things in that universe. During Aang's life, the Spirit World and the human world exist separately and rarely interact.

However, if energy were connected to spirit as well as to the Elements, it could point to another kind of metaphysical basis for the universe, a *monistic* one, where there is only one kind of fundamental thing that somehow differentiates itself to become all the other kinds of things or where, at minimum, all of the things that exist are ultimately interdependent. In different South Asian traditions, we find both *monistic* worldviews, such as the Vaiśeṣika or Mīmāṃsā school of Hinduism where mind-independent reality is primary, and *dualistic* worldviews, such as the Sāṃkya-Yoga schools of Hinduism where conscious material and unconscious material are separate parallel parts of the universe.[8] Which of these better describes *ATLA*'s universe is unclear until we solve the problem of what relationship energy has to spirit, on the one hand, and the Elements, on the other.

Unity of the Elements

So, our key problem remains: what is energy? Energy could correspond to a kind of entity or force altogether different from the four Elements, such as Anaximander's *apeirōn* or the Nahua *teotl*. Energy could also be a complement or subset of spirit, somehow connecting incorporeal life and corporeal life in the *ATLA* universe.

The conversation between Aang and Guru Pathik extends and complicates this thought. Aang, following Huu, the waterbending master from the Swamp, remarks, "We're all connected. Everything is connected," and Guru Pathik replies, "Even the separation of the four elements is an illusion. If you open your mind, you will see that all the elements are one. Four parts of the same whole" ("The Guru," "The Swamp"). Guru Pathik does not mention energy as a fifth element, nor does he reference spirits or the Spirit World. This suggests that energy is a distinct thing, either the whole that makes up the Elements or something that is itself not an Element.

Let's entertain the following theory. Suppose energy is the life energy in all living beings, distinct in kind from the physical Elements but able to influence them or generate them. If the bodies of *ATLA*'s inhabitants are, in fact, made of a mixture of multiple Elements, then perhaps a connection with a specific Element, like those developed by animal and human benders, is an extension of some part of their basic sensorimotor skills. Toph says, for example, that badgermoles earthbend as an extension of their own senses ("The Firebending Masters"). If so, then perhaps *all* living beings are actually benders – of their own bodies! It would then make sense that bending is intimately connected with the ways of life and natural environments of organisms, like those of the badgermoles, the Foggy Swamp Tribe, and the Sand People.

On this theory, most people cannot manipulate organic materials because doing so requires bending skills beyond those of a normal person. Now, suppose spirits are pure energy, and that the Avatar Spirit is an especially energetic, or especially well-connected spirit. This would explain the Avatar's ability to transcend their own individual way of life and experience, as well as their ability to manage bending other people's energy ("Sozin's Comet, Part 4: Avatar Aang").

This little theory is quite satisfying. It would suggest that energy, a semi-incorporeal life force, is the fundamental basis for change and stability in the *ATLA* universe. If all living and non-living beings depend on energy, it suggests the deepest reality of *ATLA* is a non-physical interdependence between beings. Like the Banyan tree, the four nations and their environments may all be one being that has forgotten its own nature ("The Swamp"). Were Aang, or another one of our heroes, to have a realization to this effect, would it help them to "restore balance" to their world?

This question troubles Aang throughout the series. As Avatar, he knows he has had past lives, and that he is spiritually connected to them. Ultimately, none of these former Avatars are certain about what it means to "restore balance" to the world. Each has had a different way of proceeding ("Sozin's Comet, Part 2: The Old Masters"). Aang, for his own part, disagrees with his predecessors, his own past lives.

Perhaps this returns us to the idea of constant change. Maybe the Elements are not separate, in the sense that the Elements themselves are impermanent, constantly able to become something else. Perhaps energy is not a fundamental substance like *teotl*, but instead the principle of this constant activity, a force like Empedocles' Love and Strife.

This reminds us that, just as in our own case, the inhabitants of *ATLA* do not have perfect information about their universe. Even Guru Pathik and the past Avatars may just be transmitting their best idea of how everything works without complete certainty. The protagonists' continuing but frustrated efforts to understand the organizing principles of their universe mirror our own. We, too, are not quite sure what the most fundamental things are in our own universe, even as we try very hard to investigate them.

While we may never know for sure whether energy generates or only controls all the Elements, and whether it is the basis for all of reality in *ATLA*, we have managed to rule out some possibilities for *ATLA*'s metaphysics. For one thing, there may not be only four Elements at all: there may be one, six, or even more fundamental substances, or four physical Elements plus a principle of change and an immaterial substance. For another thing, it is clear that the protagonists still have a lot to learn about their world. With increased understanding of the relationships between the Elements, energy, and spirit, our heroes may be able to invent new forms of bending that have never existed before.

Notes

1. Zhang Dainian, *Key Concepts in Chinese Philosophy*, trans. Edmund Ryden (New Haven, CT: Yale University Press, 2002), Part I §b.i.12, "Five Agents, *Wu Xing*," 95–103.
2. Richard D. McKirahan, *Philosophy Before Socrates: An Introduction with Texts and Commentary*, 2nd ed. (Indianapolis: Hackett Publishing Company, 2010), "Chapter 14: Empedocles," 230–292.
3. McKirahan, "Chapter 5: Anaximander," 32–47.
4. McKirahan, "Chapter 10: Heraclitus," 112–144.
5. James Maffie, *Aztec Philosophy: Understanding a World in Motion* (Boulder: University Press of Colorado, 2014), Chapter 1, "Teotl," 21–78.
6. Dainian, *Key Concepts in Chinese Philosophy*, Part I §a.i.5, "Qi," 45–62.
7. Sarvepalli Radhakrishnan and Charles A. Moore eds., *A Sourcebook in Indian Philosophy* (Princeton, NJ: Princeton University Press, 1957), "The Upanishads: 4. Praśna Upaniṣad," 50.
8. Roy W. Perrett, *An Introduction to Indian Philosophy* (Cambridge: Cambridge University Press, 2016), "Chapter 5: World," 140–167.

3

The Personalities of Martial Arts in *Avatar: The Last Airbender*

Zachary Isrow

Throughout the world there are practitioners of various forms of movement aimed at cultivating the natural energy around us in the environment as well as within our own bodies. These movement styles are commonly known as martial arts. As a practitioner myself for over 11 years, my studies have centered on the internal Chinese martial arts (Taiji, Xingyi, Baguazhang, and Liuhebafa), along with the more external Northern Shaolin and Bajiquan styles of Kung Fu. Each martial arts system has both a physical and a mental aspect to it, both of which must be developed before one can truly master any of them.[1] Each system of martial arts varies in terms of the physical movements and mental aspects involved; they also have their own unique focal points rooted in the philosophical system from which they arise.

In *ATLA*, each nation utilizes a different system of martial arts, which grants some members of a given nation the ability to manipulate that nation's defining element. Different bending styles showcase real Chinese martial arts – Taiji, Baguazhang, Northern Shaolin, and Hong Jia Kung Fu. The former two are rooted in the philosophy of Daoism and the latter two have Buddhist roots. Likewise, the former two are internal martial arts, which emphasize *qi* energy cultivation and mental control, whereas the latter two are external martial arts, which predominantly focus on strength and physical manifestation of *qi*. Each system focuses on a particular aspect of the philosophy from which it is derived.

The main characters in *ATLA* who practice the different styles of bending (Katara, Toph, Zuko, and Aang), each draw from the martial arts style that influenced the creation of the bending style, and they also take on personality traits that are representative of the philosophical principles that the martial art is based on. This chapter will explore these four main

Avatar: The Last Airbender and Philosophy: Wisdom from Aang to Zuko, First Edition.
Edited by Helen De Cruz and Johan De Smedt.

characters, the elemental categories to which they belong, the martial arts that influence their bending, and how their personalities are influenced by the philosophies from which those martial arts are derived.

Water, Waterbending, and Taiji

The Water Tribe learn the essential skill of adaptability. When water rushes downstream, it does not always go in a straight path. It curves and bends, flowing around corners. Water goes no slower or faster than it needs to, to end up where it is going. In short, water adapts to its path, taking the road of least resistance to conserve the energy with which it flows. The people of the Water Tribe are like water. As Uncle Iroh tells Zuko in his lesson about lightning bending in "Bitter Work": "The people of the Water Tribes are capable of adapting to many things. They have a sense of community and love that holds them together through anything." This adaptability is characteristic of not only the people of the Water Tribe, but of waterbending as well. The trait of adaptability characterizes the people of the Water Tribe and can be found within the martial arts style used in the art of waterbending.

Waterbending relies on movements aimed at shifting positions, and redirecting force. It utilizes a waterbender's adaptability by changing the pacing. A hard attack is met with a soft response, a redirection; waterbending becomes a passive force, but one which can be quite powerful. Waterbending is based on the martial art Tajiquan, more commonly known as Taiji. In Taiji, as with many of the internal Chinese martial arts systems, emphasis is not placed on force and attacking, but rather upon balance and redirection of energy. The movements are aimed at cultivating energy and in gaining fluidity – the only way to redirect energy is to flow with the energy, not against it. When redirecting an attack, Taiji practitioners do not attempt to move against the attack, stopping the force of it, but rather move in line with it, taking the energy on its path, and changing its direction.

Katara is the main waterbender in the series. Resilient and adaptive, she perfectly embodies the spirit of Taiji. Despite being a powerful bender by the end of the series, Katara never makes a point to show off or otherwise use her power for her own personal benefit. In the Chinese martial arts, it is said that we have two minds: monkey mind and horse mind.[2] Monkey mind is wild, energetic, and distracting, whereas horse mind is stable, calm, and grounded. The battle between the two is a key focus of Taiji, and to master the art of Taiji one must master the monkey mind, bringing it under control. In short, practitioners must learn to tame the monkey mind to free themselves from its distracting nature.

We see Katara struggle with this in "The Southern Raiders," where she seeks revenge on the firebender Yon Rha who attacked her village and killed her mother. Initially, Katara is certain she wants revenge, but she ultimately determines that revenge would not resolve anything. She states: "I don't know if it's because I'm too weak to do it, or if I'm strong enough not to." This is an excellent example of the cognitive mastery of Taiji, the control of the monkey mind and the recognition that genuine power comes from a passive, internal force.

Here we should consider the concept of *wuwei* in Daoist philosophy, which means "without action." One of the fundamental aspects of Daoist thought, *wuwei* is sometimes confused with not acting, but this is not accurate. In fact, we follow *wuwei* when we do not exert unnecessary resistance against the flow of nature, or in Daoist thought, against the Dao (the "way").[3] In the scene with Katara mentioned above, it is *wuwei* which is showcased.

Earth, Earthbending, and Hong Jia Kung Fu

As an element, Earth is stable, strong, and rooted. While Earth is always shifting and transforming, once it is rooted it is immovable by even some of the strongest forces. This groundedness characterizes the people of the Earth Kingdom and the practice of earthbending.

Iroh says of the Earth Kingdom in "Bitter Work": "Earth is the element of substance. The people of the Earth Kingdom are diverse and strong. They are persistent and enduring." It is this persistence, groundedness, and the enduring nature of Earth, which is exemplified in the practice of earthbending. Earthbending is based on a particular type of Kung Fu, Hong Jia, in which the practitioner takes rooted stances to create a strong sense of balance so that they cannot be moved. This rooted structure of Hong Jia then uses powerful attacks which are rigid, mirroring the rooted nature of the stances.

Although the focus is on rooted stances, the training of Hong Jia stances generates and stores *qi* energy, the vital life energy that exists within oneself and throughout the world.[4] The energy cultivated in Hong Jia is collected and hardened like stone (earth) to give one strength and power, but also stability. Therefore, Hong Jia is not a purely external martial art. The force and strength of the stances in Hong Jia are formed through *qi* cultivation, and so to truly master the forms, the internal side must also be cultivated through the practice of breathwork and meditation, such as through Qigong.

This mixture of internal and external is displayed quite accurately by Toph, the main earthbender of the series. While the strength of stances is evident in all earthbenders in the series, Toph is perhaps the only earthbender who really showcases the internal aspects of Hong Jia. This is partly due to how Toph learned and mastered earthbending. Being blind, she learned to sense vibrations in the earth (a technique the badgermoles taught her). Learning to sense vibrations is akin to learning to sense and cultivate *qi*; it is not always easy to sense, but if you practice and master your mental state, you can feel *qi* energy circulating in your body and harness it. This is precisely what makes Toph's earthbending so powerful – she is not just drawing *qi* from her rooted stances, but is drawing energy from the ground itself and pulling it up through her feet into her body. This mastery of mind is also evident in Toph when she establishes the skill of metalbending in "The Guru." By feeling the vibrations in the metal and recognizing the energy as the same as in earth, Toph creates a hitherto unknown form of bending.

Furthermore, the balance between internal and external is clear in Toph's personality. Although largely impatient, stubborn, and down to earth, Toph also displays characteristics that express the internal side. For example, she almost always remains calm under pressure or when the group finds themselves in precarious situations. Toph also often serves as the voice of reason for the group, especially when they are making plans or thinking about their next move. For example, when Aang needs a firebending teacher and Zuko (once he turns good) offers to assist, only Toph recognizes the necessity of using Zuko, even if he caused them problems in the past. In "The Western Air Temple" Toph informs the group, who all reject Zuko, "you're all ignoring one crucial fact . . . Aang needs a Firebending teacher." Toph can be hot-headed and intense, but she also has moments where the internal aspects of Hong Jia give way to a calmness and rational personality that greatly contributes to the strength of the whole group.

Toph's constant reminder to the others that she can sense when they are lying, makes her an embodiment of one of the central principles of the eightfold path in Buddhism. The eightfold path in Buddhism is the route we must follow if we seek *nirvana* – the release from the constant cycle of reincarnation, of life and death, called *samsara*. Ultimately, each of the eight principles represents some form of balance between extremes. One of these is Right Speech, and Toph is representative of this principle. Right Speech refers to abstaining from lying, and not gossiping or repeating information gained through hear-say, avoiding both harsh and vain language.[5] Although Toph can come across as harsh, her insistence on truth and speaking facts, even those no one wants to hear, reveal the Buddhist influence of the Hong Jia martial art on Toph's personality.

Fire, Firebending, and Northern Shaolin Kung Fu

The element of fire is symbolic of passion; fire is strong, powerful, and energetic. As Aang's first firebending master Jeong Jeong notes about the element of fire in "The Deserter": "Fire is alive. It breathes, it grows." Fire expands and shrinks according to its environment. But unlike the adaptability of water, which finds a path to follow, fire simply creates its own path and if not kept in check will "spread and destroy everything in its path."

Uncle Iroh focuses on the power aspect of the element in his lesson to Zuko in "Bitter Work" – not necessarily its physical power, but the power of mind. He informs Zuko that "The people of the Fire Nation have desire and will, and the energy and drive to achieve what they want." This focus on desire, will, and determination can be recognized as well in the Northern Shaolin Kung Fu styles used by the firebending characters of the show. Quick, energetic, and powerful attacks are at the heart of Northern Shaolin Kung Fu, which is acrobatic, with high-flying kicks and flips.

The high-energy movements should not be interpreted to mean that Northern Shaolin Kung Fu styles are entirely physical in expression. Performing the many feats in the Northern Shaolin Tradition requires an absolute presence of mind. The training undergone by practitioners is as much a test of will as it is of physical strength. Laying one's body across a bed of nails, using a spear tip to hold one's weight by placing it on the stomach, and other such methods of training, are training exercises found at the many temples steeped in the traditional arts. All these training exercises are physically demanding, but also showcase the built-up tolerance of mental exertion – the placing of focus toward the right purpose, a skill equally as demanding as any physical activity.

Zuko, the villain-turned-good-guy of the show, has many of these characteristics. The energetic nature of Northern Shaolin Kung Fu places Zuko in an ongoing hunt to capture the Avatar. The driven nature of firebending, which is fueled by passion in many firebenders, manifests itself in Zuko, who has a strong, driven personality. Once his mind is made up on a goal, that goal is pursued until the end, and nothing dampens that determination. This is clear from the very first episode of Book One, "The Boy in the Iceberg," when Uncle Iroh offers Zuko tea to relax because it is unlikely the latter will achieve the goal of capturing the Avatar – after all, no one has seen the Avatar for 100 years. In response to this offer, which Zuko sees merely as a distraction from his goal, he responds "I don't need any calming tea!"

Like Toph, Zuko's personality is an embodiment of another main aspect of Buddhist philosophy – fittingly, as Northern Shaolin Kung Fu, like Hong Jia, is strongly rooted in Buddhism. Specifically, Zuko's personality and character arc align with the first three of the Four Noble Truths in Buddhism. These four truths are:

1. Life is suffering.
2. Desire is the cause of suffering.
3. Eliminating desire is necessary to cease suffering.
4. Following the eightfold path can remove us from the cycle of suffering.[6]

We know Zuko's childhood featured great suffering at the hands of his father, the Fire Lord, and his sister who, young Zuko says, "always lies" ("Zuko Alone"). By attempting to capture the Avatar, he hopes to regain his honor and end his suffering, but Zuko actually ends up causing more suffering, both for others and for himself. Zuko's suffering comes to an end when he finally gives up chasing the Avatar and instead joins the group to overthrow the Fire Lord. Over the three books, Zuko's character arc and personality-shifts follow the order of the Noble Truths.

Air, Airbending, and Baguazhang

The element of air is a pure representation of freedom; from the way it moves (freely) to the way it takes up space while always seeming empty of it. To embrace this true sense of freedom, the Air Nomads limited their worldly possessions. As Iroh notes in "Bitter Work": "The Air Nomads detached themselves from worldly concerns, and they found peace and freedom."

These characteristics match the martial arts style chosen to represent airbending: Baguazhang (Eight Trigram Palm). In this style, practitioners move in a circular pattern that seemingly follows the flow of air around them, a move that is known as "walking the circle." However free and flowing Baguazhang appears, it nonetheless has firm grounding, much like the stances of Hong Jia. In the case of Baguazhang, the groundedness comes from the unique form of stepping that is used to maintain stability while constantly moving. In proper "mud-walking" – so called because of its appearance of wading through thick mud – the feet glide across the ground and the heel remains flat throughout. By gliding the feet in a half-moon shape, the practitioner always remains firmly on the ground as their steps balance out the quick circularity of the movements. But there are practical purposes to the half-moon shape in mud-walking as well; this shape can be used for hooking one's foot around an opponent's leg in different offensive and defensive techniques. The objective of Baguazhang is to force your opponent to constantly face a moving target that can be in front of them one second and behind them the next.

Baguazhang is rooted in the philosophical traditions of Daoism. Many people in the West are familiar with Daoist symbolism and basic ideas, even if they do not know it. One such example is the *yinyang* symbol, whose proper name is *taijitu* and which represents the unity of polarity, the harmony of opposing forces. Specifically, in Daoist philosophy, the *taijitu* represents *taiji* – the state of lack of differentiation and singularity. But what many do not know is that the *taijitu* symbol forms part of yet another symbol: the *bagua*. The *bagua* symbol features the *taijitu* surrounded by eight trigrams (from which the name *bagua* is derived), representing the fundamental principles at work in the world.[7] These trigrams can be broken into 64 hexagrams and form another commonly known Daoist text, the *Yijing*, also known as the *Book of Changes*.

Aang, as the main character and the Avatar, is also the last of the airbenders after the Fire Nation's genocide. We meet Aang as a carefree child who, over the course of the show, reveals his wisdom and sense of life when the group find themselves in precarious situations. This occurs, for example, when Aang reminds Katara about revenge in "The Southern Raiders," stating that "While you watch your enemy go down, you're being poisoned yourself." In "The Avatar and The Fire Lord," when he considers the best course of action in dealing with the Fire Lord, he notes that "Anyone's capable of great good and great evil. Everyone, even the Fire Lord and the Fire Nation, have to be treated like they're worth giving a chance."

This transition in Aang's character showcases the genuine sense of freedom that airbenders were known to have, and which is characteristic of the practice of Baguazhang. It is freedom not to do what you want, but freedom in the sense of openness to ideas, possibilities, and most importantly, to change. As in the practice of Baguazhang, where change is constant and shifting directions is the norm, this is what freedom means for the airbenders in *ATLA*. Being open to change and to shifting your direction at any moment provides one with the genuine sense of freedom needed to master airbending. Aang displays this sense of freedom in his character development, but also through his willingness to change and to listen to the advice of others as well. We notice this especially when Aang and Uncle Iroh must work together to save Katara and Zuko from Azula in "The Crossroads of Destiny." Aang asks Iroh for advice about his love for Katara (though she remains unnamed in the context), to which Iroh responds "Protection and power are overrated. I think you are very wise to choose happiness and love." Or when, in the same episode, Aang reveals his concern about not being powerful enough to save everyone and considers Iroh's response that "Sometimes life is like this dark tunnel. You can't always see the light at the end of the tunnel, but if you just keep moving . . . you will come to a better place."

But Iroh is not the only one who advises Aang. In fact, there is an entire episode ("Sozin's Comet: Part 3"), in which Aang, struggling to decide how best to handle the Fire Lord, actively seeks the wisdom of past avatars. Although he ultimately does not find their advice useful, his willingness to listen, seek counsel from others, and change his direction when needed, is clear. This openness is genuine freedom and exemplifies airbending as a practice and way of life.

The Power of the Avatar

When we think about what makes the Avatar the most powerful character in the series, the first thing that comes to mind is the ability to use the different bending powers. But when Uncle Iroh teaches Zuko in "Bitter Work" about the different elements and tells him that "It is the combination of the four elements in one person that makes the Avatar so powerful," he is not strictly referring to the bending power of the different elements. Iroh explains the diverse attitudes, personalities, and character strengths that the different elements manifest in the distinct groups of people. He indicates that the power of the Avatar does not come from their bending alone. Instead, the power of the Avatar comes from the combination of the different character strengths of each element, and thus their ability to understand the differences, as well as the similarities between all benders.

The Wisdom of Combination

The personalities of the main characters of the show are derived from their element and bending style, or martial art, which is characteristic of that element. Katara is nurturing and adaptable, Toph is grounded and stubborn, Zuko is driven and passionate, and Aang is fun-loving and free. We can now see that these personalities were not chosen randomly, but are representative of and intertwined with the philosophies from which the selected martial arts were chosen: Daoism and Buddhism. Each personality trait reveals a different central concept in one of these philosophies. In *ATLA*, we can see how they both compliment and differ from one another. In the end, however, the combination of all of them together is what truly makes the Avatar the most powerful bender. It is not the ability to fight using all these elements, but the ability to draw wisdom from and to combine the different characters of these bending styles into one person.

Notes

1. John C. Cox, "Traditional Asian Martial Arts Training: A Review," *Quest* 45 (1993), 366–388.
2. For more on the difference between the two and more discussion of each, see Edward Orem, *Esoteric Martial Arts of Zen: Training Methods from the Patriarch* (CreateSpace Independent Publishing Platform, 2014).
3. To read more about the relationship between *wuwei* and the Dao in Daoist thought, see Edward Slingerland, "Effortless Action: The Chinese Spiritual Ideal of Wu-wei," *Journal of the American Academy of Religion* 68 (2000), 293–327.
4. *Qi* energy is typically seen as the primary life-force, and it is what practitioners of martial arts seek to cultivate; Qigong is a meditative martial art focused on breathing techniques that cultivate *qi*. Being much more "scientific," I did not believe in the mystical nature of *qi* when I first began to practice Qigong. My *sifu* taught me to think of *qi* as bioelectricity, which helped me tremendously. For more on *qi*, its role in martial arts, and the practice of its cultivation in Qigong, see Kenneth S. Cohen, *The Way of Qigong: The Art and Science of Chinese Energy Healing* (London: Random House, 1999).
5. For more on the eightfold path, see Bhikkhu Nyanatiloka, ed., *The Word of the Buddha: An Outline of the Ethico-philosophical System of the Buddha in the*

Words of the Pali Canon, Together with Explanatory Notes (Myanmar, Burma: International Buddhist Society, 1907), 30–31.

6. For more on the Four Noble Truths, see Chris Kang, "Sarkar on the Buddha's Four Noble Truths," *Philosophy East and West* 61 (2011), 303–323.

7. Baguazhang, the main style of my own practice, is complex both in terms of its movement (footwork alone can take years to master), but also in its historical and philosophical roots. Perhaps the best text on Baguazhang is Shou-Yu Liang and Jwing-Ming Yang, *Baguazhang: Theory and Applications* (Boston: YMAA Publication Center, 2008). The first part of the book covers the history, philosophy, and general principles of Baguazhang and the second half provides some explanations of different movements.

4

The End of the World

Nationhood and Abolition in *Avatar: The Last Airbender*

Nicholas Whittaker

"Water. Earth. Fire. Air. Long ago, the four nations lived together in harmony. Then, everything changed when the Fire Nation attacked." These words open every episode of *ATLA*. They make it clear, at the first possible opportunity, that this world is undergoing a crisis: namely, the Fire Nation's offensive war against the other nations. There are all sorts of reasons why the imperialistic, colonial, and warmongering actions of the Fire Nation may be evil and ugly. But one possible reason – one the show frequently suggests – is that they threaten the political division between the four nations. This division is inherently good, *ATLA* seems to propose, and thus Aang's job is to protect this division from the Fire Nation's incursions – to "save the world."

But is a world defined by the existence of four distinct nations the one Aang is meant to save? In this chapter, I'll argue that the answer is no: the existence of the four nations is itself a rotten state of affairs, a crisis that precedes that of the invasions. The world needs to be saved not just from the Fire Nation, but from nations *in general*. In arguing this, I'm not projecting my own ethical judgments onto the show; I intend to show that *ATLA* actually provides us with what I will call an abolitionist philosophical account.

Abolitionism is a theory of justice – derived primarily from the work of Black radicals – built on claims that global and local injustices can be explained by evil institutions or ways of life that cannot be reformed or changed, but that must be abolished. For example, prison abolitionists argue that the various injustices of prisons are not bugs, but features of the very concept of "prison."[1] As a result, they argue, prisons and imprisonment should be abandoned. In characterizing *ATLA*'s philosophical understanding of the four nations as abolitionist, what I'm suggesting is that the

Avatar: The Last Airbender and Philosophy: Wisdom from Aang to Zuko, First Edition.
Edited by Helen De Cruz and Johan De Smedt.
© 2023 John Wiley & Sons, Inc. Published 2023 by John Wiley & Sons, Inc.

show proposes that there's something fundamentally wrong with nationhood, i.e., the separation of the world into different nations.[2] That separation must be abolished.

I will dig into the show's central narrative and philosophical conceit: the four elements. As with the four nations, *ATLA seems* to paint a picture of the world defined by a natural and obvious distinction between the four elements. This seems to justify and explain the difference between the four nations. But we are not, in fact, supposed to simply *accept* either distinction. The divergence between the four elements is *not* obvious, *not* natural, and is misguided; and so, by extension, is that between the four nations. Three of the show's mystical guides – Huu, Uncle Iroh, and Guru Pathik – challenge the apparent distinctions between the elements and the nations.

Naturally *Real* and Socially *Real*

Let's start at the very beginning: "Earth. Water. Fire. Air." The world of *ATLA* is built on a very specific metaphysical picture, the idea that the world is made up of these four elements. They are the building blocks of the world. This kind of metaphysics is common in ancient cultures. The classical Greeks, for example, believed that the world was constructed by the same elements – earth, air, fire, and water – while the *Vedas* – Hindu holy texts – added a fifth element, "void."[3] The essential purpose of such a metaphysics is to break reality down into basic substances that are fundamentally distinct from each other. Discovering these building blocks allows us to isolate and separate them.

Thus, in *ATLA*, the four elements are *distinct* – they can be separated completely – and this distinction is natural. By calling the distinction "natural," what we mean is that it isn't *social*. The distinction between natural and social is an important element of philosophical thought, especially political philosophy. Take, say, the chemical constitution of water and the borders of the country China. Both are real. But there's a crucial difference between the two: the chemical constitution of water is real regardless of what humans do, but the same can't be said for the borders of China. We create or cause the latter through our own actions.

In *ATLA*, the distinction between the four elements seems natural; this schema is like the chemical constitution of water, and not like the borders of China. This seems obvious because, for the majority of the show (we will discuss the crucial exceptions), the distinction between the four elements is accepted without question. There seems to be good evidence for assuming that this assumption is justified. The best example is, in fact, benders! It seems to be an unchangeable and essential fact about the *ATLA* world that some people are naturally born with the ability to bend a certain element and *not* another. (The Avatar, of course, is the obvious exception.) This is a natural, not a social, fact. No human intervention could make

Zuko bend water, or Toph bend air. This seems to indicate that the distinction between the elements is beyond our intervention.

"Thinking Like an Airbender": The Elements and Nations as Naturally Real

Often in life we try to connect the natural and social by making the social reflect the natural. This basic principle could be called "as above, so below," common in much mystical, philosophical, and political thought throughout history. It argues that different planes of existence – say, the physical world and human psychic life, or human social behavior and abstract spiritual entities – fundamentally correspond.

One reason for believing this principle is that the natural can explain and justify the social. The natural causes the social, and so the latter ends up taking the shape of the former. An example is sex and gender. As Simone de Beauvoir (1908–1986) canonically argued, we have built an entire social system of roles and behaviors – called gender – out of the belief that these reflect something fundamentally *natural* about the world, the biological characteristics we call sex.[4]

The metaphysics of the four elements and the politics of the four nations are connected by the principle "as above, so below." The nations mirror the elements in more than just name. "Fire" is not just a mascot for the Fire Nation; their entire society is structured around it. Their clothes are black and red; they reside on volcanic islands; their spiritual and political practices (like the rituals of the Fire Sages and Sun Warriors) gesture toward and employ fire. The show's art style reflects this; scenes in the Fire Nation are often designed with a red, sunset tint, a far cry from the cool blues and whites of the landscapes and backdrops dominating Book One (Water) or the dusty browns and forest greens of Book Two (Earth).

The connection between the nations and the elements is deeper than production design. Benders seem to be proof of the natural distinction between the elements, because benders can bend certain elements and not others, and they have no choice over which element. But this isn't just a fact about metaphysics; being a certain bender becomes grounds for belonging to a certain social-political community. Take the third-season villain Hama, the waterbender (and bloodbender) who becomes stranded in the Fire Nation ("The Puppetmaster"). She ultimately embraces much of the cosmetics of her new home, just as Uncle Iroh does after becoming a fugitive in the Earth Kingdom. But she never *truly* identifies as a member of the Fire Nation.

In our world, immigrants and refugees may continue to strongly identify with their place of origin, even after embracing the language, style, and cultural practices of their new home, due to memories, upbringing, family connections, and so on. But *ATLA*'s metaphysics naturalizes this affiliation. Hama could *never be* a member of the Fire Nation, because she is a waterbender. One can't switch nations any more than one can switch bending abilities; the two reflect each other, because the former explains the latter. Consider what happens when Hama is revealed as a waterbender, or Zuko is revealed as a firebender in the standout "Zuko Alone": both serve as immediate grounds to disqualify the outed individual as a member of the community. Zuko, in particular, is expelled from the Earth Kingdom village without any questions asked, despite the fact that he helps the villagers against their enemies. This is simply because he is known to be a member of the Fire Nation by his bending. That seems to imply that "Fire Nation" is more than just a social category, which can be controlled and changed: it is a *natural* and unchangeable community.

The problem, of course, is that not everyone is a bender. Even if Zuko and Hama are naturally members of their respective nations by way of their connection to the elements, are Sokka and Mai? Notice that benders can have biological family ties to non-benders. Toph's parents are non-benders, for example. Although a non-bender may not have the exact natural connection to an element that a bender has, they must have *some* connection: or else Toph's parents could have given birth to a firebender! The genetics of *ATLA* is a mystery; but it is clear that non-benders have some intrinsic connection to an element, even without access to bending.

One way to explain this is to note that the elements are *not* just physical: they are spiritual, representing certain psychic and mystical features of the *ATLA* universe. Recall when Toph begins to teach Aang earthbending, only to realize he is unable to pick it up as easily as he picked up airbending and waterbending ("Bitter Work"). Toph explains that Aang's problem is that he's "thinking like an airbender" and needs the "attitude of an earthbender." In thinking like an airbender, Aang tries to be reactive, free-moving, evasive, but to be a successful earthbender, he needs to stand firm, meeting the earth head-on, unwilling to be moved. Katara later confirms that there's something important going on here. Air and earth, she explains, are "natural opposites." This might be a physical fact, but the crucial point here is that it's also a *spiritual* fact. "Air" doesn't just describe the name of Aang's nation or the element he can bend. It describes something about his spiritual character. Earth, on the other hand, describes a different spirituality, one that is *distinct and separate* from that of Air. These spiritual characters need not be limited to benders. Perhaps the "intrinsic connection" non-benders have to their elements is to its spiritual character.

So, nations are not purely social, but are natural, and naturally distinct, communities that arise out of the physical and spiritual character of the elements. But, as we'll see, the show frequently suggests that this understanding is *wrong* (despite the fact that the show and its characters often make it seem like it's right). The separation of the world into four nations is *not* natural, because the separation of the world into four elements is not natural.

Resisting Naturalization, Embracing Unity

Huu first appears in "The Swamp," an episode in which the Gaang (minus Toph, who has yet to join) experience visions and become separated and lost. Eventually, Aang, Katara, and Sokka find each other, but cannot find Appa and Momo, who have in fact been captured by swampbenders looking for their next meal. Fortunately, the three friends meet a friendly waterbender – Huu – who reveals that he knows how to find their missing companions. He leads them to a massive banyan-grove tree where, despite Sokka's scoffing, Huu explains that while meditating underneath this tree he connected with the ancient tree and realized that the entire swamp was in fact "just one tree, spread out over miles." The swamp is not just an entire ecosystem, consisting of varied and distinct elements, but is in fact "one big, living organism," a unity. In fact, the swamp is a microcosm for the world itself: the world too is one big living organism, a unity. Addressing Aang, Huu continues: "You think you're different from me or your friends or this tree? If you listen hard enough, you can hear every living thing breathing together. You can feel everything growing. We are all living together, even if most folks don't act like it. We all have the same roots, and we are all branches on the same tree." Huu is not just waxing poetic; he's making a philosophical claim, that the distinctions we imagine between objects and people are not, in fact, *natural*. The "truth" of reality is unity, not division. And he turns out to be right. When Sokka reminds the Gaang that they still haven't found Appa and Momo, Aang realizes how to find them. Placing his hand on the roots of the banyan grove, he states: "Everything is connected." Suddenly, his tattoos glow and we see a sparking current of energy travel from his hand, through the roots, out into the swamp, until Aang sees Appa struggling against his captors. When Aang realizes that everything is connected – that the distinction between himself, and the tree, and Appa is in some sense not real – he is able to "see" past it, to connect fully to the entirety of the swamp. The central lesson is not that there would be *no difference* between Appa – a giant flying bison – and Aang – an airbending boy. The point is that *despite* those differences, the two, like everything else, are fundamentally connected; they are one.

Our second mystic guide is Uncle Iroh. In "Bitter Work," while Toph is teaching Aang to earthbend, Uncle Iroh agrees to teach Zuko how to redirect lightning, a technique Iroh invented. He begins by laying out each of the elements, and explains to Zuko that they each have more than a literal meaning: each element has a psychological or spiritual character. Each nation consists of those individuals who have a particular connection to that character. Iroh is *naturally* a member of the Fire Nation through his spiritual connection to Fire, and this means, according to what we have said so far, that he is *not* and could never be a member of the Water Tribe; after all, they are naturally distinct.

When Zuko asks what Iroh's point is, Iroh says something odd: "It is important to draw wisdom from many different places. If we take it from only one place, it becomes rigid and stale. Understanding others, the other elements, and the four nations, will help you become whole." A still confused Zuko responds "All this four elements talk is sounding like Avatar stuff." To this, Iroh replies: "It is the combination of the four elements in one person that makes the Avatar so powerful, but it can make you more powerful too." He then reveals that he developed the lightning redirection technique not from studying Fire (the physical element, the spiritual force), but water. The technique applies not only to its literal motion, but also to its spiritual character, cohesion, and adaptation through change. When redirecting lightning, Iroh, a firebender, bends fire *like* water. However, if he is naturally connected with fire, and fire is spiritually distinct from water, this should not be possible, hence Zuko's surprised reaction. If Iroh is able to take on the character of another element, then the apparent distinction between them seems to be weaker. If fire can be bended *like* water how separated *are* the two? This also seems to challenge the distinction between two social groups, which, as we have seen, is supposedly grounded in their different natural, physical, and spiritual connections.

Of course, the differences between the elements and the social groups are not completely erased. Fire is still *not* water, physically speaking. And Iroh is not bending water; he is bending fire *as if* it is water. Nonetheless, recall Huu's point: difference does not imply distinction. Two different components can form one whole that connects rather than separates them. Iroh states that the value of incorporating other spiritual forms into one's own life is not purely practical. Rather, it's valuable because it makes one *whole*. As Huu would say, the different spiritual characters of the elements are "all branches on the same tree": only now, the tree isn't just the world in some grand overarching sense, but Iroh, Zuko, and any human being.

But this seems to profoundly challenge the notion that people in the *ATLA* universe naturally belong to communities defined by the inclusion of one element and the exclusion of the other three. Reading Huu and Iroh together allows us to call the supposedly natural basis for the formation of the four nations into question. If difference doesn't necessarily imply a lack of connection, then the apparent differences between elements does not imply that they do not exist in a more primordial unity, that they are not, in a more fundamental sense, *the same*. This is a unity that crucially does not erase physical differences. It does not even erase spiritual differences: being flowing and reactive (like traditional waterbending) is different from being aggressive and active (like traditional firebending). These differences do not result in separation. Iroh is not "naturally" restricted to one spiritual character. And, as Iroh suggests, this is because spiritual characters are merely different aspects of one whole: the whole of human spiritual life, which all people (not just the Avatar or Iroh!) have access to.

If the division between the four nations seems naturalized because it is grounded in the division between the four elements, then what happens when we realize that the latter division is not, in fact, natural? Iroh's insight seems to undermine the idea that Fire Nation citizens *naturally* are spiritually aggressive and active, and the Water Tribe citizens *naturally* have an exclusive monopoly over being spiritually flowing and reactive. But that type of schema was precisely the typical understanding of the four nations as a *natural* order.

These two points – the denaturalization of the four elements and the subsequent denaturalization of the four nations – are made explicit by our third mystical and philosophical guide, Guru Pathik. "The Guru" is one of *ATLA*'s most crucial episodes. It houses a critical spiritual development for Aang, and for our understanding of the cosmology of *ATLA*. Guru Pathik reveals the complex mystical character of chakras, the centers of energy that collectively make up Aang's spiritual being. The sixth chakra – the final one Aang successfully opens – is the Light Chakra, which centers on the dyad between insight and illusion – pulling back illusory notions in order to pierce through to what lies beyond. The guru explains that "The greatest illusion of this world is the illusion of separation." He goes on: "Things you think are separate and different are actually one and the same. *Like the four nations.* Yes, we are one people, yet we live as if divided." As he says this, we see a map of the four nations, divided by the familiar color-coded national boundaries. Those boundaries disappear, and we see the inhabited lands as one undifferentiated mass. The guru continues: "Even the separation of the four elements is an illusion. If you open your mind, you will see that all elements are one: four parts of the same whole." This beautifully sums up everything we have said so far. If there was any doubt that *ATLA* at least considers the possibility that its entire organizing structure is unjustified by "natural fact," let it be put to rest. Guru Pathik here explicitly connects Huu's philosophical account of unity and Iroh's musings on the spiritual character of the elements into the claim that the division between the elements and the nations is not natural. This doesn't mean that there are no differences between them, but that the differences do not naturally result in a separation at a metaphysical, social, or spiritual level.

ATLA and Abolitionism

This picture – that the distinction and separation between the nations is illusory – is an abolitionist picture. Huu, Iroh, and Guru Pathik are in some sense abolitionists. I'm not suggesting that their politics are *no different* from those of the Black abolitionist tradition mentioned earlier. Rather, their basic orientation toward the world is animated by the same kind of raw openness, the same refusal to accept certain social patterns as natural. Huu, Iroh, and

Guru Pathik are willing to at least *entertain* the possibility that the structure of the four nations is one such social pattern. All three accept the possibility that the metaphysical structure underpinning that social pattern – that the four elements are underlying the four nations – ought to be challenged.

All three embrace the notion of "difference without separability," a phrase I take from Denise Ferreira Da Silva that captures the heart of Black abolitionism at its most extreme.[5] Da Silva contends that modern society is grounded on an assumption that the world can be understood through the conceptual lenses of "separability, determinacy, and sequentiality."[6] Modern society seeks to determine what makes things in the world different, and separates them based on those differences into discrete categories (say, a collection of species, or of nations, or of races) that cannot be intermixed.

Black abolitionists argue that this basic way of organizing life results in racism, state violence, capitalism, and so on. Here, I want to emphasize how this understanding illuminates the intuitions that are at the heart of *ATLA's* latent abolitionism. Da Silva opposes the modern grammar of "separability, determinacy, and sequentiality" with "difference without separability." "Difference without separability" seeks to capture the way in which differences can exist within a deeper unity. Understanding that deeper unity reveals that the social, separating lines we draw on the basis of those differences are arbitrary and unfounded. This is how I have characterized the philosophical interventions of *ATLA's* three mystical guides. If the physical and spiritual separation of the elements disappears, such that individuals come to recognize themselves as fundamentally connected to each other, then the social order founded on the principle of natural separation – the four nations – loses that founding principle.

This isn't the end of the discussion. We've seen that the nations aren't "natural," and that the loss of a natural justification could give us grounds to abolish the nations. There may be other, political reasons for nations to continue to exist in *ATLA*. Aang's ability to access all four elements, and thus his transcendence of nationhood, is a hint to the deep philosophical intervention of the series. Aang's task is not to save a world defined by separation and distinction, but to *make it like him*: to serve as a beacon and guide to a future in which difference without separability becomes the foundation of life, and of living together.

Notes

1. Ruth Wilson Gilmore, *Golden Gulag: Prisons, Surplus, Crisis, and Opposition* (Berkeley, Los Angeles, and London: University of California Press, 2017); Angela Davis, *Are Prisons Obsolete?* (New York: Seven Stories Press, 2003). Abolitionism extends beyond prisons; much of Black radical political action takes the form of some kind of abolitionism, such as police abolitionism, wage abolitionism, the more classical example of slave abolitionism, and, as we will see, state abolitionism.

2. Black radical arguments for some form of state abolition can be found in texts like Angela Davis, *Abolition Democracy: Beyond Empire, Prisons, and Torture* (New York: Seven Stories Press, 2005); Marquis Bey, *Anarcho-Blackness: Notes Towards a Black Anarchism* (Chico, CA: AK Press, 2007), as well as in more classical anarchist texts.

3. For an in-depth look at this, see Chapter 2: "Getting Elemental."

4. Simone de Beauvoir, *The Second Sex*, trans. Constance Borde and Sheila Malovany-Chevallier (New York: Vintage Books, 2011).

5. Denise Ferreira da Silva, "On Difference without Separability," in *32nd Bienal de São Paulo: Incerteza Viva – Catalogo* (São Paulo: Fundacao Bienal, 2016), 57–65.

6. Da Silva, 60.

5

The Bending World, a Bent World
Supernatural Power and Its Political Implications

Yao Lin

In the world of *Avatar: The Last Airbender* (*ATLA*) and *The Legend of Korra* (*LoK*) – let's call it the Bending World – some people ("benders") are endowed with telekinetic superpowers to maneuver surrounding objects without physical interaction, by mentally steering ("bending") one of the four classical "elements of nature" composing the objects: air, fire, water, and earth. Perhaps, in a world where the fundamental laws of nature are radically different from those of our world, the fundamental conditions and manifestations of politics should be radically different too. That, of course, is not to deny that political bodies familiar to us are depicted in *ATLA* and *LoK*: tribes, monarchies, autonomous townships, city-states, loose federations, colonial empires, and democracies. Despite those familiar depictions, however, it's worth contemplating how the existence of supernatural power might fundamentally alter the norms and rationales of politics – and how it might in turn help us better understand our own political reality.

Might Is Right, Magnified

In a typical fantasy universe, distribution of supernatural capacities across the population is extremely unequal. The Bending World is no exception. A minority of people are born benders, while the majority are born non-benders. Among benders, a few of them are much more powerful than the rest. Fire Lord Ozai, the "big boss" in *ATLA*, may burn a town to the ground with a single stroke of firebending, whereas numerous "ordinary" firebenders can only bend fire to light candles or do simple tricks ("The Deserter"). Furthermore, while most benders can only bend one element,

Avatar: The Last Airbender and Philosophy: Wisdom from Aang to Zuko, First Edition.
Edited by Helen De Cruz and Johan De Smedt.

there is a successive lineage of rare benders (the Avatars) who can bend all four elements and who, from a certain point on, can also master the art of bending "life energy," a mysterious component of the universe more elemental than the four elements ("Sozin's Comet, Part 4: Avatar Aang").

Given the staggering disparities in bending ability, the few at the top of the superpower hierarchy – such as the avatars and their archenemies – are practically immune from almost all ordinary and "low-level bending" attacks. To be sure, they are still human beings, and can be defeated or killed by "lesser" benders and non-benders at the right moment or with the right method. For example, just like other firebenders, Fire Lord Ozai would lose his power temporarily during solar eclipses ("The Day of Black Sun, Part 2: The Eclipse"); and Ty Lee, a skilled martial artist non-bender, can defeat powerful benders in close combat via "*qi*-blocking," a technique inspired by the notion of *dianxue* ("vital-point striking," sometimes translated as "touch-of-death") popularized in Chinese martial arts novels and movies. Nonetheless, the larger point stands: in the Bending World, it is almost impossible for those who are supernaturally "weak" to physically harm, let alone kill, the few who are supernaturally "strong."

This is in stark contrast to our world. Granted, individual physical strength varies in our world too. But as Thomas Hobbes (1588–1679), one of the founders of modern political thought, famously remarked in his book *Leviathan*, humans are relatively "equal in the faculties of body and mind," in the sense that "the weakest has strength enough to kill the strongest, either by secret machination, or by confederacy with others that are in the same danger with himself."[1] Hobbes further argued that a common knowledge of this fact is crucial to (hypothetically) motivating all of us, the strong and the weak alike, to leave the anarchical "state of nature" that is permeated with the constant fear of being backstabbed to violent death by our neighbors, and to enter a binding "social contract" that forms a "political society" and authorizes a government to adjudicate disputes and enforce law and order.

The specifics of Hobbes's social contract theory have been contested by later philosophers, especially his insistence that extremely draconian restrictions on individual rights and civil liberties are the (rational) price to pay for averting the state of nature. Nonetheless, his core insight that *relatively limited* natural (or supernatural) inequality such as in physical strength (or in deadly superpower) constitutes a basic condition for politics in our world remains illuminating. If that condition changed drastically, our political calculations, behaviors, and expectations would likely change too, and so would political norms, visions, and possibilities.

In a world where some people possess deadly superpower while others don't, it would be natural to expect tensions between those two groups. Those without superpower would understandably be wary of those having it, and under certain circumstances would be able (and may decide) to ostracize the latter from the society. This is indeed a recurring theme across superhero stories. For example, at the outset of the animated film *The Incredibles* (2004), the "supers" were forced to abandon their exploits and go into hiding because public opinion had turned against them because of the collateral damage resulting from their crime-fighting. In the Bending World, non-benders similarly fear, envy, and resent benders, sentiments that culminated in the Anti-bending Revolution during Avatar Korra's time (we'll come back to this later).

But such collective ostracism is possible only when the gap in strength between the two groups is realistically surmountable. After all, how can non-benders ostracize a ruthless Fire Lord if they cannot defeat him as a group? Understandably, when inequality in (super)power passes a certain threshold, most people would simply internalize the conditions and norms of supernatural hierarchy and adapt to it by being resigned and submissive to the rule of the supernaturally mightiest.

In the meantime, the ruling class's calculations and behaviors would also change. For one thing, Hobbes's abovementioned remark – "the weakest has strength enough to kill the strongest" – could not be more apt when it comes to real-world politicians. However powerful they are politically, their lives can easily be lost through targeted assassinations (such as American president John F. Kennedy), by disgruntled bodyguards (such as Indian prime minister Indira Gandhi), or in military coups (such as Chilean president Salvador Allende). In response, various norms, institutions, and strategies have been developed to minimize such danger throughout history – for instance: using patronage or "spoils" to buy the loyalty of security forces; strengthening civilian control of the military; defusing, or exploiting, tensions among ethnic and religious groups; mythologizing the ruling household through legends of divine blessing; regularizing competitive election as a peaceful venue for challenging incumbent politicians; and, above all, forging ruling coalitions and negotiating policy consensuses among relevant stakeholders. Now, imagine a supreme ruler whose supernatural power far surpasses that of their subordinates and subjects, so much so that any attempt at their assassination is futile. Would the supreme ruler still care to, say, bargain with those inferior in (super)power?

Granted, no bender appears to be (super)powerful enough to subdue all other benders at once, and political assassinations do occur in the Bending World.[2] Still, political practices are heavily shaped by the relative strengths of rulers *as benders*. Compare, say, Earth Kingdom politics with Fire Nation politics. The Earth Kingdom has an expansive spy network (the Dai Li) within the walls of its capital city Ba Sing Se, partly because most monarchs of the Earth Kingdom are not powerful enough benders themselves, and have to collaborate with the Dai Li to secure monarchical control over the capital. The supernaturally weakest among the monarchs, such as Earth King Kuei, even became mere figureheads manipulated by the Dai Li ("City of Walls and Secrets"). By contrast, even though Fire Lord Ozai needs ministers and generals to carry out his war plans, he is not depicted as needing to make compromises with them (they are mere executers of his orders), let alone other interest groups such as business owners, local elites, and commoners. Rather, like Prince Zuko and General Iroh, those who dare to confront the Fire Lord would be purged and persecuted at his will.

Political philosopher Hannah Arendt (1906–1975), who narrowly escaped Nazi persecutions in the 1930s, contended that genuinely *political* power is squarely incompatible with *violence*. For Arendt, politics is the process of exercising – and contesting the exercise of – the collective power of decision making by members of a community, whereas violence is imposing one's arbitrary will on others through forceful means.[3] Violence therefore circumvents – and eradicates – politics. As the logic of "might is right" is significantly magnified in the Bending World, its politics is even more threatened by violence than ours. When Sozin's Comet passes across the upper atmosphere of the planet, Ozai's firebending power reaches its height. After coronating himself as the Phoenix King, he proclaims: "It's time for this world to end in fire, and for a new world to be born from the ashes!" ("Sozin's Comet, Part 2: The Old Masters"). In essence, what he wants is a world ruled solely on the basis of violence and terror – a world *devoid of politics*, as Arendt would say.

Energybender Is Coming to Town

In a world where might-is-right is supernaturally exacerbated, how can sheer (super)power – and its threats of violence and terror – be resisted and tamed? More specifically, if Avatar Aang's pacifism impedes him from dueling the comet-enhanced Phoenix King ("Sozin's Comet, Part 1: The Phoenix King"), what hope is there for humankind?

To solve this conundrum, *ATLA* introduces (one might say, *has to* introduce) a previously unknown type of bending toward the very end of the storyline: energybending. Taught to Aang by the ancient, gigantic, and wise Lion Turtle, energybending overturns the notion (assumed up until that point in the story) that the Bending World consists of precisely four "elements of nature," each subject to a corresponding art of bending.[4] Indeed, it turns out that "life energy" is so much more elemental than the four elements that one who masters energybending can simply "confiscate" another bender's ability to bend, however strong it may be, by taking away the latter's life energy (without killing them). Ozai is thereby defeated – and permanently "disarmed," becoming a non-bender. In terms of storytelling, energybending is no doubt a *deus ex machina* (a Latin phrase meaning "god out of the machine"): a plot device whereby a seemingly unsolvable problem in a story is abruptly resolved by an unexpected and improbable occurrence.

Aang the energybender puts a stop to Ozai's plan for world domination. You might wonder: what if future bad guys master the invincible art of energybending? Who's going to stop their evil plans, then? Don't worry! Not only does this *deus ex machina* subvert the four-element cosmology, it's also embedded with a "moral self-destruct" feature, so to speak. The power of bended energy, according to the Lion Turtle, can only be harnessed and wielded by those of "true heart" and "true mind":

> The true mind can weather all the lies and illusions without being lost. The true heart can touch the poison of hatred without being harmed. Since beginning-less time, darkness thrives in the void, but always yields to purifying light.
>
> (Sozin's Comet, Part 2: The Old Masters")

> In the era before the Avatar, we bent not the elements but the energy within ourselves. To bend another's energy, your own spirit must be unbendable or you will be corrupted and destroyed.
>
> ("Sozin's Comet, Part 4: Avatar Aang")

Thanks to their purity, energybenders simply can't – hence won't – do evil, whereas those of "bendable" spirit won't be able to master the art of energybending in the first place. Problem solved.

This surely isn't how things work in our naturalist world. It'd be a nonstarter to expect, say, real-world nuclear weapons to have such built-in moral self-destruct features that only the "truly good guys" can initiate them, while a "bad guy" who attempts to do so would evaporate in a puff of smoke the moment they reach for the button. But this is more than just nuclear weapons or other scary worldly forces versus moralized superpowers. Instead, it should be seen more generally as a metaphor for how crucial characteristics of naturalistic political power, and of naturalistic politics, might get lost in supernatural settings.

"Power tends to corrupt, and absolute power corrupts absolutely," taunted British politician Lord Acton (1834–1902).[5] There is always a danger of abuse of power; that is why it is important in politics to have proper mechanisms for "taming" it, such as democratic elections, checks-and-balances, and other accountability measures. By contrast, because energybending – the invincible super-duper power – does not, and cannot, corrupt the incorruptible few who can master its art in the first place, it is only natural that those incorruptible few become the ultimate guardians of the world, fending off conspiracies and aggressions from various directions. They are not and, let's face it, *should not* be held accountable to anyone else; for who can hold them accountable more effectively than the very fact – the unexplained and probably unexplainable law of (super)nature, written perhaps by some higher supernatural beings – that energybending has a built-in self-destruct safety device, such that an (aspiring) energybender will, by themselves, succumb to the severe adverse impacts of energybending as a punishment if their moral conscience ever goes awry?

This line of thinking is reminiscent of an ancient doctrine called "the divine right of kings," variations of which can be found across cultures. The doctrine asserts that monarchs derive their authority from some higher supernatural being(s) – God, Heaven, or whatever – and therefore cannot be held accountable for their (ab)uses of political power by any earthly authority such as a parliament, the judiciary, or the electorate. If a monarch *really* did something wrong, then the superintending higher being would certainly do something to condemn or punish the ruler: an unforgiving oracle through priests; an instance of *zaiyi* ("natural disasters or abnormalities" that signal heavenly grievances, according to traditional Chinese political thought); a sudden disappearance of the monarch's energybending ability; and so on. According to the naturalist worldview, however, none of those supernatural interventions is available. The sources of political legitimacy cannot be traced to divine ordinances, and the accountability of political power cannot rely on miraculous events or mechanisms that are beyond earthly control by the people.

Martin Luther King Jr. (1929–1968), one of the assassinated leaders of the American civil rights movement, warned us that "freedom is never voluntarily given by the oppressor; it must be demanded by the oppressed."[6] Luckily, as an energybender, Aang *can't* be an oppressor. Rather than becoming a "divine king" himself after Ozai's defeat, Aang remains a "passive guardian" of the world, so to speak, who keeps a watchful eye on potential supervillains or other existential threats to human society, but does not seek or assert political authority over others. Thereby, he opens up room for political participation and contestation by ordinary folk. Indeed, the Aang gang would soon appreciate Arendt's aforementioned insight that politics begins where violence ends: if Aang refuses to be another Ozai who, by threatening violence, imposes his decisions upon others, then everyone would, in the face of policy disagreements,[7] have to (and have the chance to) sit down, talk, persuade, and reach consensuses or compromises.

A Specter Is Haunting the Bending World

So, the passive guardianship of an incorruptible energybender (unavailable in a naturalist world) keeps potential superpowerful autocrats at bay without engulfing politics through the energybender's own rule. Yet, looming over this apparent utopia are two key settings of the Bending World that periodically agitate its politics worldwide: the reincarnation of the Avatar and the stark (super)natural inequality between benders and non-benders. Maybe with the presence of Aang the energybender and his friends, no bender would dare make trouble and bully non-benders. But surely Aang won't live forever, right? What if he is gone, the new Avatar is too young to be of help, the art of energybending is once again lost, and no one is guarding the non-benders against powerful and aggressive benders?

The reincarnation of the Avatar can be seen as an instance of the more general problem of leadership succession (and power transfer), a concern in both our world and the Bending World. When old leaders retire or die, they leave behind power vacuums that the politically ambitious are eager to fill. Reliable processes and institutions must be in place to ensure peaceful successions and transfers of power. For example, monarchies typically determine the order of succession based on primogeniture (the right of the firstborn legitimate child to inherit the parent's title or estate), whereas democracies transfer political office via popular election. Local and national polities in the Bending World have their own rules of succession, too; but the existence of a supernatural guardian of world peace – the Avatar – means that there is an additional layer of recurring power vacuums, unfolded every time the Avatar dies and reincarnates as a baby. The Hundred Year War, for example, endured insofar as Avatar Roku's successor Aang remained a child who had yet to master all four bending arts. Likewise, the post-Aang world is doomed to have another huge political crisis.

Moreover, because the art of energybending has to be learned, rather than passed on automatically to the new Avatar, the Avataric succession this time not only creates a *power* vacuum, but also a *moral* vacuum. Unlike Aang the energybender, his successor Avatar Korra – before she masters energybending – cannot be presumed "true-minded" and "true-hearted" by the people. And if even the Avatar – the greatest bender – cannot be trusted, how can non-benders trust benders as a group, who by (super)nature are much more powerful than non-benders? Though a general strike by the non-bender majority against the bender minority is more or less inevitable in the Bending World given its stark supernatural inequality, the timing of such a strike very much depends on the occurrence of a moral vacuum, made possible by the reemergence of the awesomely pure-spirited art of energybending, destined to be lost again (temporarily at least) following the Avatar's reincarnation.

Hence comes the Anti-bending Revolution, instigated by the Equalists and their scheming, charismatic leader Amon (*LoK*, "Welcome to Republic City"). A top-notch bloodbender disguised as a non-bender, Amon believes – as do other Equalists – that it's unjust for benders to possess supernatural advantages over non-benders and that, overall, bending causes far more harm and suffering than good. In order to "cleanse" bending from the world, the Equalists would kidnap benders, especially children, and use Amon's bloodbending technique to sever ("de-bend") the kidnapped benders' bending abilities. (Unbeknownst to them, such severance can be reversed through energybending, as is explained in *LoK*, "Endgame.")

There surely is a lot to abhor about the Equalists' *tactics*: the kidnappings, the unconsented severances, and the ways in which they stir up hatred and violence against bender minorities among non-bender majorities. But is their *cause* – elimination of bending – misguided too?

Given what we know and don't know about the Bending World, there is good reason to suspect that, even if all current benders were "de-bended" (and there were no energybender around to heal them), future benders would just keep being born. In that case, Amon would never have the luxury to say, "phew, I'm finally done with my job! I shall now de-bend myself – the last bender in the world – and retire and sit in safety under my own vine and fig tree." Instead, he would have to assume the role of supreme guardian for life, performing bloodbending on every newborn bender. What's worse, he really couldn't de-bend *everyone* – because he would need to train some young bloodbender(s), so that upon his death he could pick a successor to carry on the torch of de-bending (most of the) future newborn benders. Now, bloodbending doesn't have a "moral self-destruct" mechanism akin to energybending, so who is to say no future Supreme De-bender would ever become a despotic Phoenix King?

The Communist Manifesto, an 1848 pamphlet penned by German philosophers Karl Marx (1818–1883) and Friedrich Engels (1820–1895), opens with a memorable line: "A spectre is haunting Europe – the spectre of communism."[8] By contrast, we may say a spookier specter is haunting the Bending World – the specter of Equalism. While economic inequality and other social problems also exist in that world (indeed, staggering wealth gaps and class oppressions are portrayed throughout both *ATLA* and *LoK*), the supernatural inequality between benders and non-benders poses a political challenge both unique and uniquely existential.

Unlike wealth, bending ability – as a (supernatural) endowment – is itself *non-redistributable*: whereas we can reduce economic inequality by taxing the rich and transferring part of their wealth to the poor, we can't simply divide up a bender's bending ability and give half of it to a non-bender, making them equal in bending. Wealth may be retained in the absence of wealth gaps, but bending has to be *eliminated altogether* if supernatural equality is the goal. Meanwhile, unlike similarly non-redistributable *natural* endowments (such as intelligence, beauty, height, physical strength, and so on), bending ability is too powerful and potentially destructive a trait to leave as it is. Someone who believes good-looking people enjoy unfair advantages might propose, say, a "beauty tax" to neutralize the advantages, but certainly nobody would think it makes sense to *disfigure* everyone and eliminate beauty itself. After all, beauty doesn't kill. Bending does.

That's why the specter of Equalism will continue to haunt the Bending World long after Amon and his Equalist followers have been defeated, and long after the United Republic of Nations has, in the wake of the Anti-bending Revolution, transitioned from an oligarchic federation ruled by the non-elected United Republic Council to a democracy with regular and competitive presidential elections (*LoK*, "Rebel Spirit"). As long as there are benders and non-benders, the former's bullying of the latter will abound, giving rise to the latter's fear and hatred of the former. Meanwhile, benders' supernatural advantages will certainly intersect with and reinforce class stratification and oppression, as well as erode political equality in the formally democratic United Republic of Nations. In time, democracy will crumble in the face of persistent supernatural inequality – whether giving way to another zealous experiment in support of watchful bloodbending "de-benders," or being overthrown by someone who happens to be the most powerful bender in the world.

All in all, the Bending World is – much more so than ours – a bent world. A world premised on startling inequality in supernatural power, which inescapably conditions and haunts its politics, it is roundly bent toward startling political inequality, oppression, and violence. True, our naturalist world faces those challenges too. But instead of relying on some invincible and incorruptible energybender, we can, and must, make the world better through human endeavor.

Notes

1. Thomas Hobbes, *Leviathan*, ed. Edwin Curley (Indianapolis: Hackett Publishing, 1994), 76–77.
2. For example, as is implied in "Zuko Alone" (and confirmed in the spin-off graphic novel *The Search*), Ozai and his wife Ursa conspired to poison his aging father, then-Fire Lord Azulon.
3. Hannah Arendt, "On Violence," in *Crises of the Republic* (New York: Harcourt Brace, 1972), 155.
4. See Chapter 2: "Getting Elemental."
5. John Emerich Edward Dalberg-Acton, 1st Baron Acton, "Letter to Bishop Creighton," in John Neville Figgis and Reginald Vere Laurence eds., *Historical Essays and Studies* (London: Macmillan, 1907), 504.
6. Martin Luther King Jr., "Letter from Birmingham Jail," April 16, 1963, at https://www.africa.upenn.edu/Articles_Gen/Letter_Birmingham.html.
7. For example, immediately after the war, disputes erupt about the future of the Fire Nation colonies across the Earth Kingdom (see spin-off graphic novel *The Promise*). Many colonizers have settled there for two or three generations, intermarried with local Earth Kingdom residents, and never been to the Fire Nation in their lives. Should they be relocated to the Fire Nation, as part of the postwar decolonization process, or can they stay where they are?
8. Robert Tucker, ed., *The Marx–Engels Reader*, 2nd ed. (New York: Norton, 1978), 473.

PART II
WATER

6

Avatar: The Last Airbender and Anishinaabe Philosophy

Brad Cloud

The last episode of *Avatar the Last Airbender* aired on Saturday July 19, 2008. I remember because I had been seeing commercials for this two-hour special for the past couple of weeks, and it just so happened that I was going to be away that weekend for an Indian Education field trip at a camp and nature center. At the time, I was engrossed in the show – people who could control the elements, warring nations, flying bison, people only a little older than me trying to save the world – it was more than enough to keep a ten-year-old entertained. I had to find out what would happen to Aang during his final showdown with Fire Lord Ozai, so naturally I had my mom tape it for me on a blank VHS.

I was drawn to the familiarity I felt regarding how the characters saw and interacted with the world. From the significance of the four elements, to the spirit world, to the political and historical realities outlined throughout the series, I found a reflection of my own experience and worldview in a piece of media for the first time. As an Ojibwe person growing up in the early 2000s, I hadn't been exposed to many things that accomplished this.

In retrospect, there were three parts of *ATLA* that I connected with the most: The aesthetics of the Water Tribe, the sense of spirituality embedded throughout the show, and the sense that everything was interconnected. By comparing the unique worldview and history presented in *ATLA* with an Anishinaabe worldview, I aim to provide an alternative, Ojibwe-centered lens through which to view the show, as well as highlight the importance of non-Western narratives for youth who come from non-Western traditions.

Avatar: The Last Airbender and Philosophy: Wisdom from Aang to Zuko, First Edition.
Edited by Helen De Cruz and Johan De Smedt.
© 2023 John Wiley & Sons, Inc. Published 2023 by John Wiley & Sons, Inc.

Anishinaabe Philosophy Defined

During my public schooling experience, I didn't once hear the word Anishinaabe in a classroom, despite living in Minnesota, a state that contains both Ojibwe and Dakota Tribal Nations. Because my experience reflects the state of education only six years ago, and because of the purposeful erasure of Indigenous history and presence across Turtle Island[1] by the United States and Canadian governments, I feel it necessary to spend some time explaining who the Anishinaabe are and define what an Anishinaabe philosophy is, or perhaps more accurately, what one version of an Anishinaabe worldview looks like, in order to better understand the similarities between it and the worldview presented in *ATLA*.

Mary Makoons Geniusz defines Anishinaabe as "the self-designation of several American Indian Peoples, including Ojibwe, Ottawa, and Potawatomi."[2] The Anishinaabe were originally one people who lived on the northeast coast around the mouth of the St. Lawrence River around 850 CE,[3] but during their westward migration along the Great Lakes, they eventually split into the three aforementioned groups, with the Potawatomi in charge of keeping lit the *manidoo-ishkode*, the sacred fire that was said to protect the people, the Ottawa responsible for providing supplies for all the nation, and the Ojibwe as keepers of the faith, entrusted with protecting the sacred birch bark scrolls of the Midewiwin, the Anishinaabe religion.[4] Together, they form what is known as the Three Fires Confederacy.

Geniusz goes on to write, "Although these tribes have similar cultures and languages, there are differences between them, and because of those differences one should not assume that everything found in this book [or found in general] about the Anishinaabeg applies to all of these groups."[5] There can also be differences from community to community within the same tribe. Michael Sullivan Sr. writes in the preface of *Aanjikiing: Changing Worlds*, a text detailing traditional Ojibwe funerals, "As with most aspects of traditional ways and spiritual teachings, there are variations to the teachings . . . What appears before you is *Obizaan's* [the author's] version, a version he received from *his* elders."[6] Our customs are gifts given to us by our elders, making the transference of knowledge a very personal endeavor, one that creates a worldview that reflects a lineage of individuals who have passed on information from one generation to the next. As such, my views are representative of those who have taught me, and should be viewed as one shade of Anishinaabe philosophy, rather than a definitive account.

Because of this, I find it important to situate myself in this chapter and outline the communities and individuals that have taught me over the years. My knowledge of Anishinaabe worldview comes from my grandfather, Ron Cloud (Bad River Ojibwe) and the stories he told me growing up, Kathy Eisenschenk (White Earth Ojibwe), my Indian Education advisor and mentor for well over half my life, Randy Gresczyk

(Boise Forte Ojibwe), who was my first Ojibwe language teacher, and James Vukelich (Turtle Mountain Ojibwe) and the teachings he's offered many 'shinaabs around Indian Country. It is through the lens of my own experience and ever-evolving interpretations of the teachings that these individuals have given that I will examine *ATLA*.

The Water Tribe and Indigenous Representation

The beginning of the first episode shows Katara and Sokka floating on a canoe among a myriad of small icebergs, with Sokka trying to spear a fish. They are dressed in what look like parkas with white fur lining their hoods. Katara tries to bend a fish from the water and almost succeeds until Sokka ruptures her water bubble with his spear, releasing the fish back into the ocean.

When I teach Introduction to Creative Writing, I tell my undergraduate students that the beginning of a story should have a good hook, something that grabs the reader's (or in this case, the audience's) attention. I'm sure the hook in this opening scene was intended to be that a person was somehow making water levitate and that there was a boy somehow frozen in an iceberg. What hooked me, though, was that there were two kids who appeared to be, in every way, Indigenous, from their complexions to their attire and mode of transportation. Replace parkas with buckskin clothing and icebergs with stalks of wild rice and they could have been two 'shi-naabs ricing[7] in traditional clothing. At the time, the other shows on Nickelodeon, like *Danny Phantom*, *The Fairly OddParents*, and *The Adventures of Jimmy Neutron, Boy Genius*, showcased primarily white, suburban life. While I enjoyed the storylines of these shows as a kid, I didn't relate to any of the characters the way I did with *ATLA*.

The Northern and Southern Water Tribes are in fact based on the Inuit, a group of Indigenous peoples who occupy the northernmost part of Turtle Island.[8] While the Inuit are a distinct group of peoples who are separate from the Ojibwe in culture, language, and geographic location, there are similar-ities, from a pan-Indigenous[9] perspective, between Native Americans and the Water Tribe that allow Indigenous youths to identify with these characters.

When utilizing the concept of pan-Indigeneity, one runs the risk of turning similarities into stereotypes, such as the use of face paint, feathers, and warriors as mere tokens, a tribal checklist of sorts, instead of valid elements of a culture. However, *ATLA* utilizes pan-Indigenous elements to create a unique people in a way that feels less like appropriation and more like inspiration by imbuing them with a certain level of importance that is often missing in more reductive examples. When Sokka is preparing for the oncoming Fire Nation ship ("The Avatar Returns"), he is seen applying war paint and holding a war club. If the scene had been crafted differently, it could have come off as superfluous, a mere transitional scene to get from one conflict to the next. However, the slow, methodical side-by-side shots of Zuko and Sokka preparing for battle, along with the rather intense-sounding drum and flute in the background cues the audience to recognize the significance of this moment.

When I was younger, my grandfather used to show me pages of a book called *The Indians (The Old West Time-Life Series)*,[10] a terribly outdated text by today's standards, but the first I'd ever encountered about Native Americans. There was an entire chapter dedicated to "Woodland Indians" that shows illustrations and photos of Ojibwe clothes, lodges, and tools. One of the illustrations that has remained in my memory depicted a Great Lakes-style war club, the kind I'd later see some men's traditional dancers hold while attending powwows. Seeing Sokka prepare for an upcoming fight not with the more common contemporary instruments of war like guns and bulletproof vests, but with war paint and what appeared to be a Great Lakes-inspired war club was an affirming experience, one that validated my history and identity.

Aside from the cultural artifacts of the Water Tribe, the manner in which members of the Water Tribe are presented resists the myth of the "vanishing Indian"[11] and instead highlights their resilience and potential for cultural and political renewal. Peter Wood reaches this conclusion when comparing the Northern and Southern Water Tribes – the Southern Water Tribe is depicted as impoverished and barely hanging on, while the Northern Water Tribe has grand architecture and a traditional culture that is still very much intact.[12] The cause of this distinction is based on the colonization experienced by the Southern Water Tribe, the attacks that Katara mentioned to Aang that happened 80 years prior ("The Boy in the Iceberg").

The extent of my public-school education regarding Native Americans was learning about the friendly relations between the pilgrims and "Indians" and watching the movie *Dances with Wolves* in high school. After that, Native Americans were apparently gone, and students were left to come to their own conclusions as to why. Of course, we're still here as sovereign[13] peoples with distinct cultures, languages, and political systems. That didn't mean, though, that I didn't grow up hearing things like, "All the Indians were wiped out," "This is our land now," or "Get over it" from my classmates. Seeing Indigenous people represented with agency, self-autonomy, and resilience played an important role in how I saw myself as a young Ojibwe person.

Spirituality: Similar Ways of Seeing the World

A recurring theme in *ATLA* is the sense of balance, spirituality, and interconnectedness in the world. These three elements form the foundation of the worldview presented throughout the series, and also overlap in several ways with my understanding of an Anishinaabe worldview. As I watched the show during its original three-year run (as well as the many afternoons I spent watching reruns), I noticed many similarities in how I was taught to view and operate in the world.

In "Winter Solstice: The Spirit World, Part 1" the Aang Gaang are flying on Appa when Katara spots something on the ground. They look down and see a large black patch surrounded by trees. Sokka says, "It's like a scar." The scene progresses to show ash and the remainder of burnt trees sticking out of the ground. "Listen," Sokka goes on to say. "It's so quiet. There's no life anywhere." Footprints are found and it's revealed that the Fire Nation are behind this mass burning and desecration of land. Aang is understandably hurt by what he sees, and he feels responsible due to his absence for 100 years.

As Anishinaabe, we're taught to respect the rest of creation. At my senior honoring when I graduated high school in 2015, James Vukelich came and conducted a pipe ceremony, and spoke at length about the Anishinaabe people. He described us as "pitiful beings," but not in a negative way. He mentioned that, according to the Ojibwe creation story, humans were the last to be created on Earth. It was the elements (earth, wind, fire, and water), the plant beings, the animal beings, and only then the humans. If humans were removed from this equation, the plants and animals would get along just fine without us. Vukelich said that the plant and animal beings know this, and take pity on us by acknowledging our dependence and offering themselves to us to ensure our survival. So from an Anishinaabe perspective, to see such a disregard for life elicited a similar response to Aang's in me.

Basil Johnston, an Ojibwe author, writes that, in an Ojibwe worldview, natural places like valleys, mountains, and woods each have a particular mood that reflects that location's "soul-spirit," the community of souls that reside there.[14] He goes on to write that removing some or all of the plant beings from that location will alter its mood. From a standard Western perspective, a field or valley without any human occupants would be considered unpopulated, but from an Anishinaabe perspective, we recognize that it's those plant and animal beings who populate that place and create a community of living beings – take someone away, and you disrupt that community.

It wasn't surprising to me, then, when Hei Bai, the spirit who watched over the newly scorched forest, was upset. Not only was his community destroyed, but he was the one responsible for protecting them. Hei Bai's mood and physical appearance, from a panda to a monstrous four-armed creature, had been changed because of the removal of that place's inhabitants. Had the Avatar not explained to him that the forest would grow back, that it too would follow the naturally cyclical pattern of life, Hei Bai would have continued to enact his anger by kidnapping villagers.

Johnston describes the roles and relationships of spirits, noting how they are guardians of certain places and can affect the physical world in various ways.[15] In "The Siege of the North, Part 2," Aang learns that the koi fish circling one another in the Spirit Oasis are actually the physical manifestations of the Moon and Ocean spirits, Tui and La, who are responsible for creating the ability to waterbend. Admiral Zhao, having learned of their existence from Wan Shi Tong's Library, intends to kill Tui in order to destroy waterbending itself and conquer the Northern Water Tribe. In this, we see that spirits are an integral part of our world. Their presence, as well as their absence, has real-life effects on the other inhabitants of this world and can often mean the difference between life and death.

The mere existence of spirits in *ATLA* and the normalcy with which they're treated was another element of the show that I could relate to. As Johnston writes about manidoog (spirits) and their role in the Ojibwe worldview: "The manitous [manidoog] were just as much a reality as were trees, valleys, hills, and winds."[16] For *ATLA*, this was a significant step away from the majority of other media around at the time – ghosts and ghouls were something to be feared and seen as separate from our reality. For Anishinaabeg, manidoog simply are.

Another definition of manidoo that I've heard is *mystery*. This understanding of the word is, for me, one of the underlying principles of an Anishinaabe worldview – that the throughline of creation is, in fact, mystery. Ask "Why?" enough times and eventually you reach the ultimate answer: I don't know. Some call it fate, destiny, cosmic forces. Some give a name to whomever pulls the strings of reason and reality in our universe – God, Allah, Yahweh. We call it mystery, and it's something to be respected.

This is why I was so interested in the episode where the Aang gang went to the swamp ("The Swamp"). Mystery seems to be at the heart of the episode. When they land, odd things begin to happen – vines move on their own, people have visions, and swamp monsters attack them. By the end of the episode, we realize that Huu, one of the inhabitants of the swamp, was responsible for moving the vines with waterbending (as well as acting as the swamp monster), and Sokka explains away the visions that the group had. However, there's no explanation for the vortex that pulled them down. It remains a mystery. And to top it off, the episode ends with a vine moving by itself and swatting away a small bird, suggesting that there's more to the swamp than Sokka thinks. This episode seems to grapple with the unknown and, ultimately, the unknowable, arriving not at a definite answer, but a certain comfort with a lack thereof.

In the same episode, after it's revealed that the swamp monster is actually Huu, the Aang gang ventures to the top of a rather large tree with him and it's revealed that the entire swamp is in fact offshoots of this tree, and that it, like the entire world, is really "one big living organism." Aang sees the logic of the swamp being one organism, but seems to have doubts about it being applicable to the entire world, to which Huu replies, "Sure. You think you're any different from me or your friends, or this tree? If you listen hard enough, you can hear every living thing breathing together. You can feel everything growing. We are all living together, even if most folks don't act like it. We all have the same roots, and we are all branches of the same tree." Here, Huu reveals the throughline of the entire series: despite our differences, we are all people who deserve to be treated with humanity.[17]

I've written elsewhere on this topic,[18] but I see the inherent interconnectedness of creation being accurately represented by the dreamcatcher. Originating with the Ojibwe, the dreamcatcher is created using only one strand of thread or sinew. Even though it appears disjointed, having multiple intersections and knots, the web only consists of one strand. Our relation to one another is like this. We each represent an intersection on this pattern, and although we appear to be separate from the rest of the design, we are part of it because there is only one thread. That the Avatar is meant to bring balance back to the world means to restore this understanding of creation, that although there are four nations, they, like the swamp, make up one organic whole.

Notes

1. Turtle Island is the name given to the continent of North America by many Indigenous peoples, coming from several creation stories involving the turtle.
2. Mary Makoons Geniusz, *Our Knowledge Is Not Primitive: Decolonizing Botanical Anishinaabe Teachings* (New York: Syracuse University Press, 2009), 3.
3. *Ojibwe History* (PBS documentary, 2000), https://www.pbs.org/video/wpt-documentaries-ojibwe-history.
4. Edward Benton-Banai, *The Mishomis Book: The Voice of the Ojibwe* (Minneapolis: University of Minnesota Press, 2010), 99.
5. Geniusz, 4.
6. Lee Obizaan Staples and Chato Omishkebines Gonzalez, *Aanjikiing: Changing Worlds – An Anishinaabe Traditional Funeral* (Winnipeg: Algonquian and Iroquoian Linguistics, 2015), xiii.
7. The practice of harvesting wild rice with tools called rice knockers.
8. Peter Wood, "Reframing Sympathy for Indigenous Captives in *Avatar: The Last Airbender*," *Undergraduate Review* 14 (2018), 176–181.
9. A pan-Indigenous perspective focuses on what separate tribal nations have in common, such as shared historical experiences, similar customs, and contemporary realities.
10. Benjamin Capps, *The Indians* (Old West Time-Life Series; New York: Time Life Books, 1973).
11. This refers to the concept that Native Americans were destined to slowly die out due to our supposed inferiority. The inaccuracy of this concept is apparent in the fact that I'm currently writing this chapter.
12. Wood, 178.
13. My use of sovereign here stems from the understanding that tribal nations are autonomous political entities in relation to the United States government.

14. Basil Johnston, *Ojibwe Heritage* (New York: Columbia University Press, 1976), 33–34.

15. Basil Johnston, *The Manitous: The Supernatural World of the Ojibway* (New York: HarperCollins Publishers, 1995), xx.

16. Johnston (1995), xx.

17. See also Chapter 1: "Native Philosophies and Relationality in *Avatar: The Last Airbender*."

18. Brad Hagen, "On Dreamcatchers," *Transmotion* 5 (2019), https://journals. kent.ac.uk/index.php/transmotion/article/view/868/1647.

"Lemur!" – "Dinner!"
Human–Animal Relations in *Avatar: The Last Airbender*

Daniel Wawrzyniak

One of the awesome things about *Avatar: The Last Airbender* is the attention given to non-human animals in their different relationships to humans. It's tempting to write an entire chapter just about Momo or Appa as full-fledged non-human characters with their very own perspectives, but here we'll focus more broadly on what interactions with animals in *ATLA* can tell us about humans. Just as we all learn and develop our personality and moral character through contact with other beings and through our decisions while dealing with them, so do the protagonists of *ATLA*. Character development and personal growth are key features of *ATLA*, and the best example of constant learning is definitely Sokka, though Aang has something to teach us too.

Sokka the Hunter

As we watch Sokka throughout the adventure, confronting new situations and reflecting upon his beliefs and attitudes, we can observe and learn with him about the treatment of (non-human) animals. In the very first scene of the series we watch Sokka and Katara trying to catch some fish for dinner. Sokka's relation to animals here is simple: he's a hunter and animals are food. This is quite understandable given the fact that Sokka lives in a small Water Tribe community near the South Pole surrounded by water and ice, where other food sources are scarce and hunting is crucial for survival. Sokka is only concerned with animals insofar as they are useful to him: he eats them or wears their fur to stay warm.

Using animals as means to human ends is just as natural for Sokka as it is for many people in our world. However, throughout history (and especially since the second half of the last century) some philosophers have started to

Avatar: The Last Airbender and Philosophy: Wisdom from Aang to Zuko, First Edition.
Edited by Helen De Cruz and Johan De Smedt.
© 2023 John Wiley & Sons, Inc. Published 2023 by John Wiley & Sons, Inc.

question our practices and attitudes toward animals. Sokka doesn't seem to trouble himself with such reflections in the beginning. But this changes as soon as he leaves the comfort zone of his small home village to join Katara and Aang on a journey that confronts him with a myriad of adventures and encounters with human and non-human individuals.

Human Ends and Animals as Means

Humans use animals for several ends, and for most of us that sort of interaction with animals seems perfectly fine, just as it does for Sokka. But is such carefreeness justified? One person who definitely thought so was German philosopher Immanuel Kant (1724–1804). Kant distinguishes humans from non-human animals by claiming that humans as rational beings possess a unique kind of worth, or dignity, which stems from our ability to understand and follow moral rules and duties toward other humans. Instead of being powerlessly controlled by our whims and urges, we can critically reflect upon our actions and let our actions be governed not by instinct but by reason. This power is what, according to Kant, makes every human a uniquely valuable individual, or "person." Because of their unique worth, it is immoral to use other humans as mere ends for the purposes of others. For Kant, humans are "ends in themselves" and we must respect that status while dealing with one another.[1] Kant thus sees all humans as equal partners in a mutual moral contract obligating all humans to treat each other with care.[2]

However, Kant sees no foundation for such dignity and respect in the case of non-human animals: since animals lack the cognitive capacities to understand abstract moral rules and the self-control to be guided by them, they cannot be our equal partners in a moral contract. So, for Kant, there is no reason to act respectfully toward them. In this regard non-human animals are "things" for Kant "with which one can do as one likes."[3]

Kant famously stresses one restriction: we mustn't let our interactions with animals be guided by cruelty. While this principle surely saves animals from some serious suffering, it's worth noting that Kant bases this rule on the respect he regards as purely owed to human beings. By performing cruel actions on animals, Kant claims, we risk corrupting our sense of morality and becoming insensitive toward our fellow humans.[4] Such a position is called *anthropocentrism*, meaning that human beings are at the center of all considerations. If other "things" in nature deserve any kind of consideration, it's only because of humans being directly or indirectly affected by it. While many people today would certainly agree with Kant that cruelty to animals is a no-go, it is pretty controversial to say that this has absolutely nothing to do with the animals themselves, who are directly affected by what we do to them. At least, this is not what Sokka comes to think eventually.

Sokka-style: Meat, Sarcasm, and Empathy

Sokka isn't a cruel guy who enjoys tormenting animals. In fact, he gradually grows in empathy for the animals he meets – at least sometimes. An iconic example is his encounter with the saber-tooth moose lion cub ("Bitter Work"). While Sokka is lurking in a tree waiting for the perfect moment to jump down on his prey he muses, "You're awfully cute. But unfortunately for you you're made of meat." At this moment, he begins to see the animal in front of him as more than just food. As Sokka spends more time with the cub he slowly starts to bond with it and becomes more empathic. "Look, I'm sorry I hunted you, but that's just the natural order of things. Big things eat smaller things. Nothing personal." He clearly starts to think that killing an animal requires justification, and the justification is owed to the animal he plans to eat, not to other human beings. Slowly the "meat-creature," as Sokka called the cub before, becomes a unique individual for him. He even names the cub Foo Foo Cuddlypoops.

Sokka gives animals more credit than Kant, who regards any form of justification toward the affected animals themselves as needless and nonsensical. But while it is understandable to eat other creatures if you live in an area where other food sources are scarce, why should this provide you with a justification to use animals as food sources when other options are available, for example, when you travel to other places as Sokka does?[5]

He knows he can change his eating habits and that this would in fact be a more virtuous choice, as he promises while still being stuck in the ground: "If I get out of this alive, it's a karmically correct vegetarian existence for me. No meat ... even though meat is sooo tasty." Sokka hereby implies that using animals for food is the result of our socialization, past choices, and tastes that we can reflect upon. "If I can just get out of this situation alive," he states, "I'll give up meat and sarcasm. Okay? That's all I got. It's pretty much my whole identity. Sokka, the meat-and-sarcasm guy. But I'm willing to be Sokka, the veggies-and-straight-talk fellow. Deal?" Sokka shows that we can reassess our beliefs and habits and that we can change if we find that there are good reasons for doing so. Unfortunately, Sokka is not a good role-model for sticking to resolutions. Within the same episode, when he's about to get rescued, he exclaims: "Aang? Thank goodness! Have you got any meat?" Still, Sokka shows that when we allow empathy toward animals it becomes hard to see them as mere means to our ends. And eating Foo Foo Cuddlypoops is definitely off the table.

Sokka's attitude toward Momo is similar. When Aang, Katara, and Sokka visit the Southern Air Temple and meet the winged lemur, Aang regards him[6] as a specimen of an animal species he associates with his lost home and as a possible pet ("The Southern Air Temple"). Sokka, however, regards him as a meat source. While Aang excitedly shouts: "Lemur!," Sokka drools and decides: "Dinner!" When Sokka later finds Aang sobbing, he tries to comfort him by saying: "Aang, I wasn't really gonna eat the lemur, okay?" Sokka doesn't know at that point that Aang's grief is really caused by Aang finding the dead remains of his mentor Gyatso, but Sokka's reaction shows that compassion and empathy are important to him. Here we have an example of Kant's indirect moral duties to animals for the sake of other humans. Sokka decides that it would be wrong to eat the lemur, not because he owes it to that animal, but because it would hurt the feelings of his friend, Aang, to whom he owes consideration directly. By the end of the episode Momo brings Sokka some fruit, which Sokka instantly accepts as an alternative option to satisfy his hunger. And as the two further interact in the many chapters that follow, Momo becomes a cherished companion for Sokka. Eating Momo would no longer enter Sokka's mind, simply because he owes it directly to his winged lemur friend. Aang naming the lemur Momo also expresses that he has become a unique individual for the group.

What makes Sokka so interesting as a character is his perpetual willingness to re-think his views. Just consider how Sokka changes his old gender stereotypes about women being less skilled fighters once he meets the all-female Kyoshi warrior band ("The Warriors of Kyoshi"). As American ecofeminist and activist scholar Marti Kheel (1948–2011) points out, stereotypes of meat-eating and masculinity are in fact closely connected in our society – for example, when men are regarded as effeminate for not eating meat.[7] By re-thinking his views on gender and animal ethics Sokka becomes an admirable example of self-criticism.

Aang's Relations to Animals: Harmless Entertainment?

When it comes to living a life guided by balance, self-reflection, and self-improvement, Aang seems to be the perfect role-model (next to Uncle Iroh, of course). Aang is a committed vegetarian and believes all living beings should be treated with respect, as he explains to the King of Omashu and his armed guards: "Love each other. Respect all life. And don't run around with your spears" ("The King of Omashu").

Aang believes that killing animals or causing them pain is wrong. Even in situations of self-defense he only attacks animals as far as is needed to scare them off. He fights the protective mother of the saber-tooth moose lion cub ("Bitter Work") to protect Sokka but never deliberately injures any animal – even fierce giant sea creatures like the Unagi off the coast of Kyoshi Island are no exception ("The Warriors of Kyoshi").

Still, Aang seems to think that animals can be used as means to human ends, as long as we don't harm them. Right after waking up from his

100-year-long hibernation Aang asks Katara to go otter penguin sledding. He sees these animals as living beings that shouldn't be harmed but that are also perfectly usable as sleds. For Aang, every animal is perfectly suited to be used for some sort of prank or sporting activity, or other form of pastime (which may include animal companions) – even if you have to invent a purpose for which this particular animal seems perfectly suited. Through this attitude Aang is actively instrumentalizing animals for his ends (mostly playing and entertainment). Singing groundhogs become organ pipes ("The Library"), elephant koi become windsurfing boards ("The Warriors of Kyoshi"), and so on.

Kant sees no need for justification in using animals. By contrast, Aang's animal uses seem funny and unproblematic for many viewers because of an underlying assumption that no animals were harmed during this adventure. Singing groundhogs can go on running through their tunnels after popping up and singing their notes. Otter penguins can stand up and walk on without a scratch after being used as sleds. All these examples build on the assumption that it is principally possible to use animals without harming them, at least in Aang's view. If there's no harm, there's no need to worry. This sort of using others would even be justified if we applied Kant's prohibition of instrumentalizing humans to animals. Importantly, Kant allows the use of humans as means as long as we also treat them as ends in themselves, which means behaving toward them in ways they can "possibly agree to." So, we have to make sure we don't harm them in the pursuit of our goals, and we should not put their will completely under our control.[8] Accordingly, as long as Aang doesn't use animals as mere means to his ends, one might claim he does nothing wrong.

There may be justified cases for using animals, as when Aang uses the water-spitting unagi as a giant fire extinguisher to save the burning village on Kyoshi Island ("The Warriors of Kyoshi"). Saving villagers from a big fire seems a strong enough reason to outweigh stressing out the unagi for a few minutes. But this example for an emergency doesn't show that it would be justified to stress out animals for fun. As Aang, Katara, and Sokka start their journey to the North Pole, Aang has a whole to-do list ready with some questionable items: "and finally we'll ride the hog monkeys. They don't like people riding them. But that's what makes it fun!" Aang knows he'll stress out those animals, but he is apparently convinced that this won't cause any damage to them. The trouble is that we can't be sure that our riding animals or using them for other ends won't have negative effects on their life quality. Animals are complex beings with complex needs. Making sure they lack nothing vital while keeping them as pets or for sports can be extremely demanding. Our resources are often limited, and animal keepers will often make trade-offs between the life quality of "their" animals and their own financial means and comfort.

No Harm, No Problem?

Aang's easy-going spirit and Sokka's growing empathy for animals may be adorable, but someone might say this offers no reason for why others should follow their example or even go beyond it. Why should we give any consideration to animals?

A number of philosophers have challenged Kant's view that only humans require respectful consideration. For those philosophers what makes individuals worthy of consideration is their capacity to feel pleasure and pain, and to experience those feelings as happening to them. This view is called *pathocentrism* – all individuals who can feel pain and have at least a minimal level of consciousness need to be treated thoughtfully. One proponent of pathocentrism is contemporary American philosopher Christine Korsgaard, who, despite being a Kantian scholar herself, has challenged Kant's position toward animals. She agrees with Kant that humans possess special rational and moral capacities, but she doesn't think this give us an exclusive protection from being used as mere ends for the means of others. Rather, our rational and moral abilities make us capable of critically thinking about how we treat other living beings and whether we have reasons to treat them with care.[9] We can understand that many animals are also able to consciously experience their own lives and that they do care whether they can enjoy life or are constrained in fulfilling their needs – for example, by humans limiting their mobility through confinement or deciding that it is time for them to be killed and eaten.

Korsgaard points out that, "What is special about us is the empathy that enables us to grasp that other creatures are important to themselves in just the way we are important to ourselves."[10] We can see this kind of empathy at work when Aang looks after Appa, or when Sokka starts bonding with Momo. They recognize that when they are dealing with these non-human individuals they are dealing with someone, not just something. That's why we shouldn't harm animals, because animals can – and reasonably should – mind for their own sakes being harmed, whereas "things" cannot mind anything at all.[11] Admittedly, we mostly feel empathy toward those animals we bond with. Think of Sokka and Foo Foo Cuddlypoops. But following Korsgaard's argument, we can reasonably expand this empathy toward all other animals that can mind for their own sakes how they get treated by humans – therefore we should.

If we follow Korsgaard, the reason why we shouldn't harm animals is that what happens to them matters to them. We as rational and moral beings are able to be concerned for their well-being for their own sakes. Ignoring the perspective of the animals we interact with means being deliberately insensitive – which would be a sign of bad moral character. Even Kant emphasizes that in order to nurture our sense of morality, we need to develop a disposition to "love something" without "any intention to use it."[12] This imperative gets even stronger when we regard an animal not as something (Kant), but as someone (Korsgaard). If it is important to us to be sensitive moral people, it should also matter to us to regard animals not just as self-moving toys, nor as tools only waiting for us to use them.

Instead, we should regard animals as beings that exist for their own sakes. So, if we meddle with their lives, we should at least have sufficiently strong reasons to justify doing so. We shouldn't just ask: "Does using these animals for this end cause them any harm?" We should also wonder: "Are we treating these animals as beings with a life of their own or simply as 'made for us'? And what reasons do we have for using them?" Aang's use of the unagi to save a whole village has better chances of passing this test than using otter penguins as sleds for a fun afternoon. We should also be skeptical about whether otter penguins truly don't mind being grabbed all of a sudden, used as sleds, and having to find their way back to their colony afterward – even if they weren't physically harmed in the process.

Questioning Our Attitudes, Sokka-style

In short, we can learn from *ATLA* that when it comes to human–animal relations we should think more critically about our interactions with animals. An important key for scrutinizing our habits and views is a willingness to show empathy for other living beings. Sokka demonstrates how contact with animals can encourage one to develop such empathy and thereby re-think how "natural" it really is to use animals as we please. But we can also learn that learning never stops. While Aang is already empathic toward all animals and takes care not to harm them, he still at times uses them for questionable ends. Just as Sokka starts questioning the casualness of killing animals for food, Aang would be well-advised to re-think his casualness of using animals for killing time.

While we might be able under perfect circumstances to meddle with other individuals' lives without making their lives less enjoyable, we should ask ourselves what it says about us, if we decide that our personal happiness justifies taking control over the lives of others. Using animals for our ends and merely trying to avoid cruelty and harm may seem completely unproblematic at first. But as we can learn from Sokka, we can call a lot of things we've previously taken for granted into question and change our views if we find compelling reasons for doing so. We can find those reasons by having new experiences and keeping an open mind. We don't have to go on an epic journey like Sokka does, but we do have to step out of our comfort zone once in a while and start putting our habits and convictions to the test. The many ways in which we use animals for food, clothing, entertainment, even pet keeping, are among those things we should scrutinize – precisely because many of us take them for granted. Let's check our dearly held views Sokka-style: with empathy and open-mindedness toward new perspectives – and just a tad of sarcasm.[13]

Notes

1. Immanuel Kant, *The Metaphysics of Morals*, trans. and ed. Mary J. Gregor (Cambridge: Cambridge University Press, [1797] 1996), 6:462. For Kant's works I use the page numbers according to the standard German edition, *Kant's Gesammelte Schriften*, edited by the Royal Prussian (later German) Academy of Sciences which has become standard to allow other reputable editions to be consulted.
2. Christine M. Korsgaard, *Fellow Creatures: Our Obligations to the Other Animals* (New York: Oxford University Press, 2018), 148.
3. Immanuel Kant, *Anthropology from a Pragmatic Point of View*, ed. L. Zöller and R.B. Louden, trans. R.B. Louden (Cambridge: Cambridge University Press, [1798] 2007), 7:127.
4. Kant ([1797] 1996), 6:443.
5. For some interesting thoughts on this idea, see Gary Comstock, "Subsistence Hunting," in Steve F. Sapontzis ed., *Food for Thought: The Debate Over Eating Meat* (Buffalo: Prometheus Books, 2004), 359–370.
6. As many other scholars, I avoid using the pronoun "it" for animals, to stress that they are not "things." For example, in *Fellow Creatures,* Korsgaard uses "she" as the default pronoun for animal individuals to simultaneously address feminist issues.
7. Marti Kheel, "Vegetarianism and Ecofeminism: Toppling Patriarchy with a Fork," in Sapontzis, 327–341.
8. Immanuel Kant, *Groundwork to the Metaphysics of Morals*, trans. and ed. Mary J. Gregor (Cambridge: Cambridge University Press, [1785] 1996), 4:429–430.
9. Korsgaard, 141–145, 168–169.
10. Korsgaard, 169.
11. Admittedly this argument becomes debatable for animals with no or only very limited cognitive and emotional capacities such as jellyfish or insects. But many animals we interact with – mostly mammals – can be said to possess those qualities.
12. Kant ([1797] 1996), 6:443.
13. I am greatly indebted to Juliane Bettin, Oliver Lauenstein, and the philosophical colloquium of Holmer Steinfath for critical feedback on earlier drafts.

8

On the Moral Neutrality of Bloodbending

Johnathan Flowers

In *Avatar: The Last Airbender* and its sequel, *The Legend of Korra* (LoK), we encounter bloodbending, a subset of the fictional martial art of water-bending. It is a collection of techniques that allows the user to control the body of a target through manipulation of the water inside it. Bloodbending is treated as one of the most dangerous bending techniques, due to the corrupting effect that it has on its user. Indeed, it can endanger the mental health of its practitioner because of the risks associated with possessing this power over another person (Avatar Extras: "The Puppetmaster").[1] Perhaps, though, the mental health risks of bloodbending are not essential to the style, but instead are the result of the intentions of the person performing the martial art.

Bloodbending is sometimes referred to as the "puppetmaster technique" because it is the only bending art whose focus is on the direct manipulation and control of a target. This facet of bloodbending is in contradiction to the philosophy of waterbending, its parent style, and healing, its parallel art. At the core of waterbending lies harmonious cooperation and redirection of attacks without dominating an opponent. Waterbending and healing use flowing, wave-like motions which emphasize the fluidity of water and the push and pull of the tides. Bloodbending, by contrast, requires a more rigid, structured form of movement as befitting its "darker" nature. However, is still a subset of waterbending, an art which emphasizes compassion and harmony. Because of this, it might be the case that the mental health risks of bloodbending are not essential to the style, but rather the result of the intentions of the person performing the art. In other words, it is people that make bloodbending evil, and not bloodbending that makes people evil: bloodbending simply gives them an outlet for what was already there. If this is the case, is it possible that bloodbending is neutral?

In our world, most martial arts styles incorporate a guiding philosophy aimed at cultivating not only the physical techniques of the practitioner, but

Avatar: The Last Airbender and Philosophy: Wisdom from Aang to Zuko, First Edition.
Edited by Helen De Cruz and Johan De Smedt.

also their moral and emotional character. As a student of the martial arts for over 20 years, I have encountered this philosophical orientation in various ways. While my practice centers on the Japanese martial arts (Aikido, Shotokan Karate, and Shinkendo), I have also encountered this philosophy in my practice of Chinese martial arts (Taiji and Baguazhang). All of these practices are neither good nor evil in themselves. Rather, they help express what the student brings to them. Maybe the same is actually true for bloodbending.

The Origins of Bloodbending

We are first introduced to bloodbending through the history of Hama, a waterbender of the Southern Water Tribe who was captured during the Fire Nation's rise to power. Incarcerated in a maximum-security prison designed specifically to hold waterbenders, Hama was powerless to resist her captors due to their restriction of any liquid that could be used to bend. Moreover, Hama describes how Fire Nation jailers would restrain the arms of their Water Tribe prisoners in iron chains, as waterbending relies on arm movements. This restraint, according to Hama, was particularly cruel because it served to remind the waterbenders of their powerlessness. Despite the conditions of her imprisonment, Hama's captors could not fully restrain the source and origin of waterbending, the full moon, nor could they fully eliminate all the sources of liquid in the prison. As Hama explains, "The rats that scurried across the floor of my cage were nothing more than skins filled with liquid and I passed years developing the skill that would lead to my escape" ("The Puppetmaster"). Here the origins of bloodbending, as a specific application of waterbending to the blood inside an individual, become clear: each month, during the full moon, Hama tested her bloodbending on these animals without regard for their safety or well-being. Her initial experiments with bloodbending are shown to cause discomfort, if not outright pain, to the elephant rats, as she commands their bodies through bending the blood in their veins. Here is where we might note the "dark" origins of bloodbending. Unlike other substyles of bending presented in *ATLA*, such as metalbending, bloodbending is grounded in the direct domination and control of another person (or animal). All other styles of bending were developed through refinement and control of elements that are "cousins" to the primary element.[2] While Hama's bloodbending shares this process of refinement, it is the application to people and other living things that makes it dark.

Aside from the presence of blood in elephant rats' bodies, the other critical element for the development of bloodbending is the presence of the full moon, which greatly enhances the powers of waterbenders (see also "The Siege of the North, Part 2"). The full moon provided Hama with the power to sense the blood in the elephant rats as she sensed other liquids through her bending, but it also provided her with the power to manipulate it. This point is worth thinking about because it implies that bloodbending requires an enhancement of the abilities of the waterbender to be successful. In other words, bloodbending is a more difficult technique to perform without assistance, a fact that remained the case in the *ATLA* and *LoK* universe until the introduction of Yakone, Tarrlok, and Noatak's ability to bloodbend without the aid of the full moon in *LoK*. Further, the requirement of the full moon to enhance a waterbender's powers aligns with other ways bending is enhanced, refined, or repurposed in more advanced techniques. For example, Toph's development of metalbending is a refinement of her "seismic sense" which she learned from the badgermoles who taught her earthbending.

Bloodbending as Advanced Waterbending?

Bloodbending shares many features with other advancements of bending styles. Like "seismic sense," lightning bending, and waterbending's own healing and spiritbending, bloodbending is a refinement of elements in the bending style, in this case, the ability to sense and manipulate liquids. This similarity, while generally assumed, is most clearly demonstrated when both Katara and Hama manipulate and draw forth the sap in plants, their "blood" so to speak, and use it as part of their attacks ("The Swamp"). Bloodbending bears some similarity to Foggy Swamp-style plantbending, which uses sap to manipulate and move plants. In fact, we might call plantbending a kind of bloodbending, as it also manipulates living organisms. Indeed, when Katara explains Foggy Swamp style to Hama, the latter doesn't seem surprised at its existence.

The similarities between Foggy Swamp-style plantbending and blood-bending do not end there: Foggy Swamp style's movements are more rigid and solid than either Southern- or Northern-style waterbending, though they do not have the same kind of rigidity as bloodbending. This point is more interesting when we think about Foggy Swamp-style plantbending as the manipulation of the "blood" of a plant: the rigidity of plantbending might reflect the necessary rigidity needed to manipulate living organisms like plants and animals. We can see this when Aang and Katara first encounter Huu, the plantbender. Even the description that Huu provides of how he uses plantbending, "I just bend the water in the plants" ("The Swamp"), parallels Hama's more ruthless description of bloodbending: "Controlling the water in another body, enforcing your own will over theirs" ("The Puppetmaster"). The crucial difference between plantbend-ing and bloodbending lies in Hama's emphasis on enforcing the will of the bender on their opponent. Put another way, bloodbending is not simply bending the blood in another person, it is dominating their will through bending.[3] However, is this truly necessary for bloodbending?

One further point about bloodbending as simply an advanced collection of techniques is worth mentioning. Hama states, "Once you perfect this technique, you can control anything, or, anyone" ("The Puppetmaster"). She seems to imply that the control developed through bloodbending is through domination. But we should pay special attention to her emphasis that the bloodbender could control anything, by which we can assume she means "anything with water." Again, the parallels between bloodbending and plantbending become apparent: both techniques involve the manipulation of an organism through the liquid within it. Both can be performed without injuring their target.

In "The Puppetmaster" and "The Southern Raiders," Katara bloodbends another person. In "The Puppetmaster," she bloodbends Hama herself, suppressing her peaceably, though not necessarily comfortably, and preventing her ongoing bloodbending of Aang and Sokka. Hama's discomfort does not seem any greater than either Aang's or Sokka's, nor does it seem any greater than the discomfort experienced by other individuals restrained by bending. Katara's bloodbending during this scene is caused by fluid motions more reminiscent of her bending style, though slightly more rigid, visually indicating that Katara's bloodbending is a more gentle application of the technique. In contrast, in "The Southern Raiders," Katara's bloodbending results in a more violent contortion of the Fire Nation commander, in line with Hama's techniques. Accordingly, the commander appears to be in more discomfort than either Aang, Sokka, or Hama when they were subject to the technique. Finally, in *LoK*, Tarrlok first restrains, and then renders unconscious, the Republic City officials sent to arrest him.

What are we to make of this? From the examples of Katara and Hama, as well as the parallels between bloodbending and plantbending, we can rethink bloodbending as a parallel art to plantbending. We can understand the painful nature of bloodbending as an intentional choice on behalf of the bender. As Katara demonstrates in her use of the technique, a bloodbender does not need to cause pain or anything more than mild discomfort in their target. Alternatively, the bloodbender can choose to use the technique to cause extreme discomfort. This point, the malleability of bloodbending to gently restrain or suppress, is confirmed in the commentary for "When Extremes Meet" (*LoK*), where Brian Konietzko, the co-creator and executive producer of *ATLA* and *LoK,* states the following concerning bloodbending: "There's no lasting damage if it's done right. You know, it's just uncomfortable."[4] In other words, bloodbending need not dominate an opponent, nor does it need to painfully immobilize them. Bloodbending can be used just as easily to suppress as to cause harm.

The Martial Arts Basis of Waterbending and Bloodbending

The bending styles in *ATLA* draw their inspiration from real-world Chinese martial arts. Waterbending is based upon the Yang and the Chen styles of *taijiquan*. Often known as Taiji, *taijiquan* is an "internal" martial art where the focus is placed on connecting with and redirecting an opponent's attacks such that they are suppressed or disrupted with minimal harm caused to either the attacker or the defender. Waterbenders' flowing, spinning, suppressing, and trapping motions are all examples of the ways that *taijiquan* and its related arts emphasize not meeting force with force. In fact, one of the staple techniques of waterbending, the water whip, uses identical motions to a Taiji movement called "single whip," which is one of the most iconic movements in Taiji and emphasizes the fluidity of the art ("The Waterbending Scroll").[5] Like waterbending, *taijiquan* treats conflict as a meeting of interacting forces rather than as a meeting of opponents. To this end, both waterbending and *taijiquan* seek harmonious resolutions to conflict as opposed to simply crushing or battering an opponent into submission.

This emphasis on harmony extends beyond the execution of technique and into the philosophical orientations of this martial art, specifically the emphasis on "softness" grounded in a philosophical need to preserve the harmonious interaction between individuals in combat. Put another way, *taijiquan* emphasizes not meeting force with force. In principle, when two forces meet, the stronger of the two forces will overcome the weaker, or two equal forces will cancel each other out. Recognizing this, *taijiquan* structures its techniques to yield to oncoming force such that the practitioner can entrap, suppress, or flow with an oncoming attack, rather than meet the attack with opposing force. This principle is represented by yin and yang, two complementary forces which make up the *taiji* or supreme principle from which all things emerge. In Chinese philosophy, the alternation of yin and yang brings the world into being as a result of constant motion. Visually, this alternation is represented by the traditional *yinyang* symbol, two interlocking teardrop shapes of black and white which emphasize the transition of complementary forces into one another in an unceasing cycle.

In *ATLA* the *yinyang* symbol is formed by the Moon and Ocean spirits, two koi fish which circle each other in an ongoing dance that balances their complementary powers. Tui, the Moon spirit, with its white coloration and black dot, represents yin as the receptive principle in the *taiji*. La, the Ocean spirit, is a black koi fish with a white spot, representing yang, the active principle. As Koh the face stealer explains to Aang during a visit to the spirit world ("The Siege of The North, Part 2"), Tui and La translate to "push" and "pull," terms which mirror the active and receptive elements of yin and yang. These are also crucial terms in *taijiquan* training. For example, *tuishou* or "pushing hands" is a primary mode of practice in *taijiquan* which instructs the student in how to avoid meeting force with force and to develop the sensitivity necessary to flow with an opponent's energy, rather than to respond instinctively with an opposing force.

Taijiquan students are expected to learn defensive suppression techniques prior to the more offensive striking techniques or the more advanced joint locks and breaks referred to as *qinna*, or "the technique of catch and hold."[6] A body of techniques which involves the redirection of energy into an opponent to cause discomfort, harm, or eventually dislocation, *qinna* techniques as practiced in *taijiquan* all aim at the harmonious suppression of an opponent. In these techniques, the very structure of the opponent's body, combined with their own momentum, is used to create a situation where relieving this discomfort requires them to follow the redirection of their energy or risk potential further injury. To this end, *taijiquan* training in *qinna* emphasizes using progressively more pressure to redirect the opponent into a position desired by the practitioner such that the conflict ends on the latter's terms. In doing so, the amount of pain caused to the opponent is relative not only to the technique applied, but also to the relative skill level of the practitioner. Since many *qinna* techniques can seriously injure an opponent, the training in these techniques comes only after the practitioner has mastered the basics.

If this sounds familiar, it should: just as Katara needed to master the basics of waterbending and receive a little help from the moon in order to learn bloodbending, *taijiquan* practitioners need to learn the fundamentals of their martial art before they can learn the *qinna* techniques, which, like bloodbending, are refinements of basic techniques in *taijiquan* through focus on a specific application. Just as Katara could choose not to cause harm through bloodbending, so too does *qinna* offer *taijiquan* practitioners the option not to harm.

The Nature of Bloodbending as Depending on the Character of a Person

Qinna, like *taijiquan* itself, is intimately related to waterbending in *ATLA*: its rigid trapping and locking motions supply the visual basis for the movements of Hama and Katara's bloodbending techniques. Its description in *ATLA* mirrors its use in *taijiquan*: as mastery of bloodbending gives a waterbender the potential to control anything with water in it, so *qinna* allows the *taijiquan* practitioner to control an opponent in a measured way through the redirection of momentum. Many of the locking techniques and holds within *qinna* can be used to cause pain. But just as bloodbending can be done without causing lasting harm to an opponent, so can *qinna*.

In my own martial arts practice, there is an analogous difference between waterbending and bloodbending in the Japanese martial arts Aikido and Aikijutsu, which draw heavily on the philosophical and technical systems of Chinese martial arts. Both are joint locking and suppression martial arts that rely on the redirection of momentum like *taijiquan*. In Aikido and Aikijutsu, the *kotegaeshi*, or outward wrist twist is a technique that redirects the momentum of an opponent's arm by rotating their wrist perpendicularly to the direction of the strike. While this sounds simple, relatively small changes in how the technique is applied can result in large changes in the responses of the opponent. A more progressive motion results in a gradual suppression of an opponent with minimal pain, whereas a faster motion can result in a sudden sharp application of pain to the joint, and even lasting damage. In Aikido, the varieties of *kotegaeshi* taught in the dojo tend toward progressive suppression, or redirections that preserve the option for increased pain and lasting damage, but do not take it immediately. In contrast, Aikijutsu tends toward more sudden or immediate applications that result in pain or damage to the opponent. Neither application is better or worse, and both leave open the option not to harm. In fact, the main difference between the two is how the techniques are used. While an Aikijutsu-style *kotegaeshi* might be more painful than an Aikido-style *kotegaeshi*, this does not make the technique inherently evil, nor does it leave the Aikidoka more open to "madness," as they are both mere techniques.

In the context of Japanese martial arts, what matters is the intention behind the technique, whether it proceeds from *satsujinken* or *katsujinken*, from the sword that takes life or the sword that gives life. The "sword that takes life" and the "sword that gives life" aren't really talking about a literal sword. These terms were popularized by Yagyu Munenori in *Heiho Kadensho*, one of the central texts of the Japanese sword style Yagyū Shinkage Ryu, that is also an influential text in the development of Japanese martial arts philosophies.[7] A seventeenth-century samurai, Yagyū Munenori wrote the *Heiho* as a manual for students of Yagyū Shinkage Ryu. It offered philosophical advice on the use of martial arts to preserve a harmonious society. It also taught students to cultivate the discipline necessary to ensure that one does not fall prey to the desire to use martial arts for greedy purposes. If Hama or Fire Lord Ozai[8] had read the *Heiho Kadensho*, and had followed its directions, they might not have become the villains they did.

In the *Heiho*, the sword is a metaphor for any martial arts technique. To this end, the "sword that takes life" and the "sword that gives life" refer to how these techniques are used. In this sense, *satsujinken*, the sword that takes life, refers to the use of martial arts with the express intention to kill or to harm. In essence, this is a person who goes looking for a fight. Karl Friday describes *satsujinken* in a more complicated way: "When a combatant uses force of will to overpower, immobilize, and strike down an opponent before he can react, this is called 'setsunin-tō' (i.e. 'sword[smanship] that transfixes,' or 'swordsmanship that kills response')."[9] This should sound familiar; it could be a perfect description of bloodbending as practiced by Hama: a use of already established and morally neutral techniques for the domination and overpowering of a person for egoistic aims. In contrast, *katsujinken* is the use of martial arts techniques to subdue or control an opponent with an eye toward the smallest amount of injury to both practitioner and opponent. Friday expresses this difference as follows:

"Katsujin-ken, by contrast, involves a sophisticated manipulation of the opponent and his actions by means of utter selflessness; properly conducted, it is virtually undefeatable."[10] Here, he may as well be describing Katara's gentler bloodbending, as well as her compassion toward Hama.

Bending That Saves Life

What can we learn about bloodbending from looking at the real-world martial arts and philosophies that inspired it? Plenty! Beyond grasping that Hama's bloodbending and Huu's plantbending aren't so different, we can understand that the rightness or wrongness of a martial art like bloodbending isn't something inherent to that art. It is a product of the practitioner as much as it is a product of the practice. Hama might have developed bloodbending out of her desire to hurt those who hurt her, what we might call "bending that takes life." However, in the hands of Katara, bloodbending can be "bending that saves life," through the responsible and compassionate use of its techniques.

Notes

1. Joshua Hamilton, "The Puppetmaster," June 13, 2010, at https://www.amazon.com/gp/video/detail/B00VE6G2V0/ref=atv_yv_hom_c_unkc_1_1.
2. See Chapter 2: "Getting Elemental."
3. See Chapter 9: "On the Ethics of Bloodbending."
4. Michael Dante DiMartino, Bryan Konietzko, Janet Varney, and Seychelle Gabriel (July 9, 2013), "When Extremes Meet" commentary. Book One: Air Blu-ray.
5. A good example of the prevalence of single whip is in Yang Chengfu's *The Essence and Applications of Taijiquan*, trans. Louis Swann (Berkeley, CA: Blue Snake Books, 2005). The move is so common that it is often used as the logo for many Taiji associations. It was reproduced in Ju Ming's sculpture "Tai Chi Single Whip," in the Citygarden Sculpture Park in St. Louis, MO.
6. Liu Jin Sheng, *Art of Seizing and Grappling: Instructor's Manual for Police Academy of Zhejiang Province*, original ed. (Shanghai, 1936); translated from Chinese in 2005 by Andrew Timofeevich.
7. Yagyū Munenori, *The Life-giving Sword: Secret Teachings from the House of the Shogun*, trans. William Scott Wilson (Boston, MA: Shambhala, 2013).
8. This point bears mentioning as one of Munenori's students was Tokugawa Iemitsu, the third Tokugawa Shogun of Japan.
9. Karl F. Friday, *Legacies of the Sword: The Kashima-Shinryū and Samurai Martial Culture* (Honolulu: University of Hawai'i Press, 1997), 31.
10. Friday, 31.

9

On the Ethics of Bloodbending
Why Is It So Wrong and Can It Ever Be Good?

Mike Gregory

We only learn of bloodbending in "The Puppetmaster," at the end of Book Three of *ATLA*, and it is never used again. However, in *The Legend of Korra* (*LoK*), bloodbending is banned by the United Republic of Nations through the efforts of Katara. Why is bloodbending so objectionable? Why does Katara take it to be so bad, despite its minimal impact in the four nations before Republic City was formed? This prompts a further question: if bloodbending does violate some moral principle in a particularly serious way, can there be an instance of morally *permissible* bloodbending? And finally, does this mean that Katara was wrong to advocate for the ban on bloodbending?

We need to first establish what it is that bloodbending is, according to its treatment in the *ATLA* series. Then we can point out why this is particularly bad in ways that other forms of bending are not. Then, we will try to answer the question about potentially permissible forms of bloodbending and whether this affects or does not affect Katara and the Council of Republic City's decision to ban bloodbending in *LoK*.

What Is Bloodbending?

Bloodbending was discovered by Hama, a southern waterbender who was held in captivity by firebenders in a prison where waterbenders were deprived of water. Hama discovered that she could create her own water by pulling the liquid out of plants and controlling the bodily fluids in rats, and eventually humans. In bending the bodily fluids of an organism, bloodbenders can take hold of and move its muscles in order to manipulate its body according to the bloodbender's wishes. Importantly, the victims of

Avatar: The Last Airbender and Philosophy: Wisdom from Aang to Zuko, First Edition.
Edited by Helen De Cruz and Johan De Smedt.
© 2023 John Wiley & Sons, Inc. Published 2023 by John Wiley & Sons, Inc.

bloodbending remain cognitively aware, as in the case of Aang and Sokka, who were being bloodbent by Hama, but still retained enough awareness to speak and object to what she was doing to them.

However, Hama understood the practice not only as controlling the bodily functions of a person, but also as *overriding the person's willpower*. Hama describes the act of bloodbending to Katara as, "Controlling the water in another body, enforcing your own will over theirs" ("The Puppetmaster"). The person under the control of a bloodbender is not only physically controlled but also deprived of their ability to will for themselves.[1] This means two things. First, the person under the grip of a blood-bender is able to form intentions of their own, and so possesses a will of their own. Second, the bloodbender, in order to control their subject, *knowingly overrides* the will of their victim. They impose their own will in order to use the subject toward their own end.

Therefore, bloodbending is the act of controlling the bodily fluids in a person in order to enforce your own will on them for your own purposes. This means that to bloodbend someone is to intentionally override the will of whoever you are bloodbending. In other words, bloodbending someone is to use them for your purposes while ignoring what they want.

Let's assume that Hama's definition is correct. Indeed, every instance of bloodbending in both *ATLA* and *LoK* conforms to her definition of bloodbending as *indifferent to* the will of the subject. In principle, Hama could be wrong and there could be an alternative *cooperative* model where the bloodbender bends in cooperation with the will of the subject. As a hypothetical example, imagine that Katara bloodbends Sokka in order to launch him onto Appa to retrieve her an apple, after Sokka's enthusiastic agreement. Here Sokka agrees to be used for Katara's purposes and so this might be done in cooperation with Sokka's will. However, we don't see this cooperative model in either series. This is either because bloodbending is unable to work in this cooperative way, or because instances of the cooperative model are almost always made redundant by the subject's ability to perform actions herself.[2] Besides, there are actions that aren't morally permissible even if someone were to agree to them, as in agreeing to be a slave. Thus, we are given no reason here to think that the cooperative model is possible.

What Makes Bloodbending Bad?

What makes bloodbending more objectionable than other forms of bending? The practice of bloodbending has brought about objectionable consequences, but in *ATLA* the consequences are miniscule compared to almost all other forms of bending at the end of the Hundred Year War. Particularly, we can think of fire-bending as an obvious example of a form of bending that has brought about horrific consequences.

Firebending was a tool for oppressive violence for a century, either directly or indirectly harming individuals and entire communities of benders and non-benders alike. If the consequences were what mattered, then firebending would surely be the most morally objectionable form of bending. However, Avatar Aang only took away the bending of one fire-bender, Phoenix King Ozai, and only because the Fire Lord himself was unable to reform ("Sozin's Comet, Part 4: Avatar Aang"). The problem here is not the particularly destructive properties of *firebending* but the particularly destructive practitioners of this form of bending. This is highlighted in *ATLA* when the Sun Warrior Chief says that "Fire is life, not just destruction" ("The Firebending Masters").

Yet, in the case of bloodbending, the entire form of bending is banned by Katara in *LoK* despite causing little *actual* harm and being a rare skill. This might mean that there is something morally objectionable about blood-bending *itself*. In order to show what makes bloodbending particularly objectionable, let's turn to the philosopher Immanuel Kant (1724–1804). As we'll see, Kant's "Formula of Humanity," and more particularly, his prohibition on using other persons merely as means, can explain what is bad about bloodbending.

Kant and Using as Mere Means

Kant argues that there is a universal principle, called the Categorical Imperative (CI), that dictates morality. One formulation of CI, the "Formula of Humanity" (FOH), instructs us, "So act that you use humanity, whether in your own person or in the person of any other, always at the same time as an end, never merely as a means."[3]

It is important to note that this is a principle about the way we think about pursuing our ends or goals. Kant took this principle not to be directly about the actions we do, but about the reasoning we take to perform the action. So, taking up goals and ends for myself also requires that I adopt certain means to get there. This principle is a prohibition on the *kinds* of means that I can use to pursue my ends: I can use persons as means, but not *mere* means.

Think, for instance, about sitting in Uncle Iroh's tea house as you order from Zuko and he brings your tea. I take it as my end or goal to have a cup of tea and in order to get that tea, I order it from Zuko who, begrudgingly, brings me my tea. You are indeed using Zuko as a means to get some of Iroh's delicious tea ("The Drill"). However, your use of Zuko is conditional on his consenting to be used in this way (because he wants to make Iroh happy). Here you use Zuko as means but not as a mere means.

Kant contrasts "using as an end" with "using as a thing." I can use a thing that I own as I want. However, human beings are persons; they exist not merely as a means to my end, but they are "ends in themselves."[4] Kant takes

nonhuman animals to be things and not persons because they lack
"humanity." According to Kant, the principle above, and the prohibition on
using as mere means, does not apply to animals:[5] animals can be used as
things, in a similar way to how I use a hammer or a toy. Yet, because human
beings are persons and not things, they cannot be used or owned as property.
Persons have freedom and the freedom of others limits my own free action.[6]

Judging whether I use a person for my ends is then not completely up to
me, it depends on the consent of the other person involved. Thus, the relevant difference between using others *merely* as a means and *permissibly*
using others as means, is that when you use someone as a *mere means* you
use them as a means to your own end while not making this conditional on
the person's consent. By contrast, you can use people as means, but not as
mere means, if, as a matter of moral principle, you make the use of these
people conditional on their consent. Contrast our earlier case of Zuko in
the teahouse with Azula's use of Long Feng in the coup of Ba Sing Se ("The
Earth King"). Azula uses Long Feng for her own end as a means. However,
as we find out when the Dai Li ultimately swear allegiance to Azula, her
use of Long Feng was not conditional on his consent to being used this
way. Indeed, she deceives him so that he *cannot* consent to her use of him.
Azula uses Long Feng as a *mere* means. What is the nature of the consent
needed to make use of another person?

Kant states that making false promises uses the person as a mere means
because the person I want to use "cannot possibly consent" to being
deceived.[7] This suggests that the nature of the consent needed is the *merely
possible* consent of the person being used. In this interpretation, what is
wrong in the false promises example is that deception, in virtue of the sort
of action it is, *cannot possibly* be consented to, as when Long Feng could
not possibly consent to Azula's coup because he wasn't fully aware of it.
This initially seems like a plausible interpretation.[8] However, if the only
criterion is that the person used *could possibly* consent to the action, then
there are problems. For example, imagine a case where a doctor harvests
the organs from a healthy patient in order to save patients with organ
failure. Obviously the patient *could possibly* consent to the action, but
does he actually? It seems problematic to suggest that harvesting organs
from a person who didn't actually consent isn't using them as a mere
means. In a similar way, couldn't Azula just imagine that Long Feng *could
possibly* consent to her plan to rule Ba Sing Se if he could only see that she,
as she says, has the "divine right to rule" ("The Crossroads of Destiny")?
Indeed, according to Kant, the relevant type of consent is the *actual* consent of the person being used. So, the use of a person is permissible only if
using them is subject to their actual consent.

To recap, to use someone as a mere means is to: (i) Use them as a means
toward my end, (ii) without making using that person conditional on the
consent of the person being used, (iii) where "consent" is understood as the
actual consent of the person to the way they are being used.

Does Bloodbending Violate Kant's Principle?

Now we can evaluate bloodbending. Above, we briefly identified the main characteristics of bloodbending. It is the act of controlling the bodily fluids in a person in order to enforce your own will on them for your own purposes. If we pair this definition of bloodbending with the definition of using merely as a means, we will see that bloodbending uses a person as a mere means. Let's go through the recap one step at a time as it relates to bloodbending:

1. The bloodbender uses a person *as a means* if they feature in the practical reasoning of the bloodbender as a means toward the bloodbender's end. Whenever a bloodbender bloodbends a person in order to achieve her own end, she uses that person in service of her own end, whatever that may be.
2. The bloodbender *necessarily* makes the subject a means *without* making this use dependent on the consent of the subject. As Hama describes bloodbending, it is the act of imposing your own will on the other through the manipulation of their bodily fluids ("The Puppetmaster"). We can infer, then, that the bloodbender does not make the bloodbending of the subject conditional on the actual consent of the subject.
3. The bloodbender does not make the genuine *actual* consent of her victim a factor in her action. In fact, as mentioned above, the subject of bloodbending remains able to give her consent even while being bloodbended and is often seen objecting to being bloodbended, as when Sokka protests to being bloodbent by Hama ("The Puppetmaster"). However, the actual consent of the subject is either ignored or not taken into account when bloodbending.

One might object that surely it is *possible* to bloodbend without using a person merely as a means if they *do* provide their genuine actual consent to be used. However, this misses the focus on the moral reasoning of the bloodbender. The bloodbender, through her bending, adopts the maxim that she will impose her will on another *regardless* of their consent. This means that a bloodbender *already* uses another merely as a means even if they *do in fact* consent. In order to see this point, imagine a scenario where Fire Lord Ozai selects several individuals from the Southern Water Tribe, which he is annihilating, in order to subject them to dangerous medical experiments that promise to yield valuable medical insights that would benefit all four nations. Now suppose that one of the selected individuals, who is convinced of the experiment's overwhelming benefits for large numbers of humans in the long run and who believes that these benefits vastly outweigh his own agony, happens to genuinely consent to the medical experiments. Fire Lord Ozai does not care one bit whether any of the selected individuals give consent. It would be odd to say that he treats all the other individuals except the one that happens to consent as a mere means. After all, he treats each of them in the same way, for the same reason, in the service of the same end and regardless of whether they give consent. Likewise, the moral reasoning of the bloodbender does not make the pursuit of her ends contingent on the consent of those she uses as a means, and so uses them as a *mere means*. Here the emphasis is not on the particularly bad or good consequences that the bloodbending brings about, nor on the pain that it inflicts as such.[9]

Thus, bloodbending *necessarily* uses others as a mere means and so violates Kant's principle. Notice that this means only that bloodbending uses other as a mere means, if they are, in fact, used as a means to the bloodbender's end. If the bloodbender uses another as a means, she necessarily uses this person as a *mere* means. That bloodbenders necessarily use persons as mere means explains the particular status of bloodbending within *ATLA* and *LoK*. Bloodbending, unlike other types of bending, *necessarily* violates a moral principle.

Can Bloodbending Ever Be Permissible?

The above claim, that bloodbending *necessarily* violates a moral principle by using persons as mere means, immediately raises the question about whether it is *ever* permissible to bloodbend. In *ATLA,* we see Katara bloodbend twice: she bloodbends Hama in order to save Sokka, Aang, and herself, and in a fit of vengeance, she bloodbends the firebender she erroneously believed killed her mother ("The Southern Raiders").

The second case is clearly a case of impermissible bloodbending where Katara's bloodbending highlights her feelings of vengeance toward the firebender. These feelings cloud her moral judgment so that she bloodbends the firebender, using him as a means, and therefore as a mere means, toward her own vengeful end.

In the first case, where Katara bloodbends to save the lives of Sokka and Aang and herself, her bloodbending seems to be permissible. How can this be the case, given that bloodbending *necessarily* uses persons as mere means? In this case, Katara does not use Hama as a *means* to her end. Recall that when bloodbending someone, if they are used as a means, they are used as a *mere* means.

By contrast, if someone is not used as a means at all, they cannot be used as a *mere* means. This seems to be the case when bloodbending is used in self-defense as in this case. Katara does not *use* Hama in service of her own end, but is preventing Hama from violating Katara's own rights (the right to not be used as a mere means) and the rights of Sokka and Aang. In this situation, Katara does not aim to further some end *by means of* Hama, but rather aims only to stop Hama from harming her and her friends. Katara, in other words, bloodbends *only in order to end* Hama's wrongful action, which is immediately resolved when Hama stops her bloodbending. Katara's maxim, in this case, was to stop Hama's harmful actions and not to use her for some further end. As a result, Katara's bloodbending of Hama is not an instance of using a person as a mere means because she is not using Hama as a means *at all*.[10]

What if Hama Was Wrong?

Thus far, we have assumed that Hama's definition of bloodbending is correct. If Hama is correct that bloodbending uses someone by overtaking their own will with the will of the bloodbender, then bloodbenders necessarily use persons as means. In *LoK*, it seems that Katara, as well as the leaders of Republic City, agree with Hama in her assessment of bloodbending and so banned the practice of bloodbending completely.

Yet, there is still the possibility that Hama is wrong about bloodbending. What if, for example, Sokka asked Katara to lift him up onto Appa using her bloodbending in order to retrieve her an apple? Katara uses Sokka as a means, but does so without making Sokka into a mere means because her bloodbending him up to Appa is subject to his consent (if he objects at any point, she will stop). I earlier called this the cooperative model.

It seems that there are still two reasons that, despite the possibility of the cooperative model of bloodbending, Katara was right to ban bloodbending. First, the mere potential to engage in morally impermissible bloodbending is enough to justify a ban on the practice. Even if I never bloodbend anyone without their consent, and so only engage in the cooperative model of bloodbending, the potential power that the bloodbender has over others makes bloodbending a dangerous practice. Think of, for instance, driving around in a tank, while respecting all the traffic laws and respecting the other drivers. Even if the driver of the tank remains perfectly within the law, she still poses a danger to those around her, because she is always in a position to use her disproportionate power to use people as mere means toward her end. So, a ban on tanks, like Katara's ban on bloodbending, does not need to assume that Hama was right about every possible instance of bloodbending. All we need to assume is that bloodbenders have an unequal power to overpower another's will. That, in and of itself, is a problem.

A second and related option for explaining Katara's ban is the potential for even moral permissible instances of bloodbending to have corrupting effects on its practitioners. As Kant has also argued, practices that are not themselves morally impermissible can lead to a corruption in our moral reasoning. Indeed, *ATLA* suggests that bloodbending might lead to the madness of its practitioners who are corrupted by their potential power over others.[11] However, bloodbending here, though strictly permissible, degrades the practitioner's commitment to the Kantian principle by damaging the repulsion we feel when using persons as things. Noatak and Tarrlok's bloodbending of the wolves and other animals degraded their own intuitions about bloodbending human beings (*LoK*, "Skeletons in the Closet"). When asked to bloodbend each other, Noatak's commitment to the Kantian principle is obviously gone, while Tarrlok's resistance suggests that he understood the difference in bloodbending animals and his own brother. However, despite Tarrlok's resistance to bloodbend his brother, Tarrlok's bloodbending has clearly degraded his own commitment to the principle, as exhibited in his later manipulations (even if it ends in regret). This is what is meant by bloodbenders opening themselves up to going crazy with power: even strictly permissible uses of bloodbending corrupt a commitment to the Kantian principle to not use persons as means, and so leads directly to abuses of bloodbending.

Therefore, despite the potential existence of permissible moments of bloodbending, bloodbenders still have the potential to dominate the wills of others and their commitment to the moral principle to not use persons as mere means might be degraded even by permissible instances of blood-bending. Thus, even if Hama's definition of bloodbending is not strictly true, and the cooperative model is possible, Katara might have still had good reasons to ban bloodbending as a bending practice.

Notes

1.]nt[This is complicated by exceptions where powerful benders break out of bloodbending, such as Katara being able to break the grip of Hama's blood-bending. However, the vast majority of those subjected to the effects of blood-bending are unable to free themselves. Furthermore, the fact that Katara can break the grip of the bloodbender is not, by itself, morally significant. A momentary controlling of my body, as we shall see, is morally problematic, even if I can easily escape.

2. Another exception to this might be in the case where the subject lacks the physical ability to perform some action but does in fact will it. For example, if the sexual partner of the bloodbender suffers from erectile dysfunction, and so the bloodbender bloodbends their partner in order for them to be able to have sex, then the bloodbender bloodbends their partner to do something which they wanted to do (presumably) but lacked the physical ability to do. While I am not overcoming the will of my partner, I am bloodbending them. However, this example might still be problematic for bloodbenders depending on the practical reasoning involved, as we will see below. If the bloodbender adopts the maxim that they will cause an erection when they want, or when they presume I want to have sex, then their use of bloodbending, even when I do in fact consent, is problematic. I would like to thank Patricia Spronk for this example.

3. Immanuel Kant, *Groundwork for the Metaphysics of Morals* [1785], ed. and trans. Mary Gregor and Jens Timmerman (Cambridge: Cambridge University Press, 2012), 4:429. All quoted passages follow the more widely available English translations cited below.

4. Kant (2012), 4:428–429.

5. See Chapter 7: "'Lemur!'— 'Dinner!'" See also Christine M. Korsgaard, "Kantian Ethics, Animals, and the Law," *Oxford Journal of Legal Studies* 33:4 (2013), 629–648, for an argument that develops Kant's person/thing distinction to include nonhuman animals.

6. Immanuel Kant, "Natural Right Course Lecture Notes by Feyerabend" [1784], in Frederick Rauscher and Kenneth R. Westphal eds., *Kant: Lectures and Drafts on Political Philosophy* (Cambridge: Cambridge University Press, 2016), 27:1335.

7. Kant (2012), 4:429.

8. This interpretation is presented in more detail in Christine M. Korsgaard, *The Sources of Normativity* (Cambridge: Cambridge University Press, 1996), 137–140.

9. See Chapter 8: "On the Moral Neutrality of Bloodbending." According to my perspective, then, the moral wrongness of bloodbending is not directly affected by its ability to be performed without hurting the subject.

10. In addition to self-defense cases, this line of reasoning can also be applied, for instance, to cases of saving unconscious people who are in imminent danger. In bloodbending a drowning child to safety, I do not use the child as a means to my end, and so do not use the child as a mere means. See also Pauline Kleingeld, "A Kantian Solution to the Trolley Problem," *Oxford Studies in Normative Ethics* 10 (2020), 204–228.

11. Avatar Extras (Book Three: Fire) "The Puppetmaster" #73 and 74. "Fact: Those who practice this technique open themselves up to madness . . . In other words, they go crazy with power."

10

Mystical Rationality

Isaac Wilhelm

The main characters in *Avatar: The Last Airbender* often deliberate in empirically informed ways. When Katara and Sokka start criticizing each other's abilities to perform various tasks around camp, for instance, Aang solves the dispute by carefully observing what everyone's unique talents are. Ultimately, he suggests that they all switch jobs ("The Great Divide"). When Toph, Aang, and Sokka start scamming Fire Nation villagers in order to obtain food, Katara weighs the potential benefits of such activities against the risks involved. Ultimately, she recommends that they stop the scamming ("The Runaway").

The main characters also let mystical, spiritual sources influence their deliberations. When trying to decide whether to kill Fire Lord Ozai, Aang consults with mystical individuals – specifically, past Avatars and a Lion Turtle – to hear their wisdom ("Sozin's Comet, Part 2: The Old Masters"). Though a firebender by birth, Iroh studies all four nations' spiritual bending practices in order to learn the defensive art of redirecting lightning ("Bitter Work").

In this chapter, we will explore some ways in which reasoning based on mysticism can be rational, focusing on the episode "The Fortuneteller," in which Aang, Katara, and Sokka save a village from a volcanic eruption. In this episode, Sokka advocates a purely empirical approach to reasoning. The villagers, however, believe that no source of knowledge is more reliable than Aunt Wu, the local fortuneteller. At several points in the episode, Sokka claims that the villagers' reliance on Aunt Wu is irrational. The villagers claim otherwise: since Aunt Wu has never led them astray, it is rational to rely on her.

As we will see, the villagers are right. Their approach to reasoning – based on Aunt Wu's fortunetelling – is more rational than it initially seems to be. Roughly put, despite their belief in the mystical, the villagers behave

Avatar: The Last Airbender and Philosophy: Wisdom from Aang to Zuko, First Edition.
Edited by Helen De Cruz and Johan De Smedt.
© 2023 John Wiley & Sons, Inc. Published 2023 by John Wiley & Sons, Inc.

in accord with a standard philosophical theory of rational decision-making, a theory of what makes some decisions rational and other decisions not. So Sokka is wrong to claim that the villagers' reliance on Aunt Wu is irrational. The villagers behave quite rationally.

Sokka, the Villagers, and Aunt Wu

In "The Fortuneteller," Sokka finds the villagers' behaviors frustrating. He claims that believing Aunt Wu's predictions is irrational: there is no good reason for thinking that Aunt Wu's predictions will come true. The villagers disagree: they strongly believe in the accuracy of Aunt Wu's predictions. What Sokka finds most frustrating, however, is that Aunt Wu's predictions *do* come true – but only because the villagers believe whatever Aunt Wu predicts.

In particular, the following pattern appears throughout "The Fortuneteller." Because the villagers believe Aunt Wu's predictions, they behave in certain ways. Those behaviors bring about the very things that Aunt Wu predicted would happen. Consequently, the villagers take Aunt Wu's predictions to be confirmed. Of course, in a sense, the villagers are right: Aunt Wu's predictions are constantly coming true. But the villagers are only right because they *make* the predictions come true. And Sokka finds that extremely irritating.

Consider an event that occurs in the middle of the episode. Sokka approaches a villager who is wearing red shoes. The villager says that Aunt Wu made the following prediction.

(1) When the villager meets their true love, they will be wearing red shoes.

Sokka asks how often the villager wears red shoes. "Every day," they respond. Sokka becomes furious: "Then of course [the prediction is] gonna come true!" The villager, seemingly unaware of Sokka's anger, becomes elated: "Really? You think so? I'm so excited!"

At the end of this exchange, Sokka thinks that the villager's behavior is irrational. To understand why, note that, in all likelihood, the villager will fall in love with someone at some point or other. So if they are always wearing red shoes, then (1) is true. But the truth of (1) has nothing to do with any special connection between wearing red shoes and meeting true loves. If the villager wears red shoes all the time, then for any action X which they will perform, the following holds.

(2) When the villager does X, they will be wearing red shoes.

For instance, the villager will be wearing red shoes when they *fail* to meet their true love. So it is irrational, Sokka thinks, for the villager to constantly wear red shoes: doing so has no impact whatsoever on whether the villager will find true love or not.

As we will see, contrary to Sokka's claims, the villager's behavior is rational. Given that the villager believes (1), it follows from a standard philosophical theory of rational decision-making that in order to be rational, the villager should always wear red shoes. Let us see why.

Expected Utility Theory

The standard philosophical theory of rational decision-making is called "expected utility theory." This theory states the conditions under which someone is rationally required to take a particular action. In other words, expected utility theory says what is – and is not – rational for people to do.

Expected utility theory is based on a particular view of the actions that people perform: for any given person and any given action, there is a certain amount of value – called the "expected value" – which that person can expect to get from performing that action. In other words, the expected value of doing something is what you can reasonably expect to gain or lose by doing that something.

For example, suppose that Katara is playing poker. She is trying to decide between the following two options. First, she could call a bet, and so either gain or lose money depending on who has the better hand. Second, she could fold, and lose all the money she has bet so far. The expected value of calling the bet is the amount of money that Katara can expect to win – or maybe lose – by calling. The expected value of folding is the amount of money that Katara can expect to lose by folding.

There is a formal, mathematical definition of expected value. Because it is fairly complicated, it is presented in the appendix for this chapter. Roughly put, according to that definition, the expected value of an action is a special kind of sum. In particular, the expected value of an action equals a weighted sum of the values of each possible outcome of that action. For example, recall Katara's poker game. The expected value of calling, for Katara, is the sum of two amounts of money. The first amount is how much she expects to get, if she calls and wins. The second amount is how much she expects to lose, if she calls and loses.

Suppose that a person faces exactly two choices: perform an action, or do not perform that action. Then expected utility theory says the following.

Expected Utility Theory

The person is rationally required to perform the action if and only if the expected value of performing the action is greater, for the person, than the expected value of not performing the action.

In other words, the person should perform that action whenever they expect to get more value from doing so than from not.

Once again, consider Katara playing poker. According to expected utility theory, Katara is rationally required to call the bet if and only if the expected value of calling is greater than the expected value of folding. To put it another way: Katara should call the bet if and only if she can expect to get more money by calling than by folding her hand.

That seems like the right result for a theory of rationality – like expected utility theory – to deliver. For intuitively, if a person expects to get more money by calling, then that is what they should do. So expected utility theory delivers the correct verdict regarding Katara's poker-playing. And that is not a coincidence. Expected utility theory is extremely popular in philosophy because it often gives the right results. That is, expected utility theory often agrees with our intuitions about what agents are rationally required to do.[1]

The Rationality of Wearing Red Shoes

Expected utility theory can show that the villager, discussed earlier, is rationally required to wear red shoes. It follows that Sokka is wrong to suggest that the villager is irrational. For given expected utility theory, the villager is doing exactly what they should.

Recall that according to expected utility theory, an agent is rationally required to perform a particular action whenever the expected value of performing that action is greater than the expected value of not performing that action. So according to expected utility theory, the villager is rationally required to wear red shoes whenever the expected value of wearing red shoes is, for that agent, greater than the expected value of not wearing them. And so, to determine whether the villager's behavior is rational, it suffices to determine whether one of these expected values is greater than the other.

The appendix contains a formal proof which shows that the expected value of wearing red shoes is greater, for the villager, than the expected value of not wearing red shoes. The proof is somewhat complicated, and relies on some mathematical theorems. For now, a summary of the basic ideas underlying the proof will suffice.

The proof relies on just two pieces of information. First, for the villager, we can assume that the value of meeting their true love is greater than the value of not meeting their true love. In other words, the villager values finding love more than not finding it. Second, because the villager believes in Aunt Wu's predictions, they are completely confident that (1) – reproduced below – is true.

(1) When the villager meets their true love, they will be wearing red shoes.

In other words, the villager is completely confident that if they do not wear red shoes, then they will not meet their true love.

With just these two pieces of information, we can show that according to expected utility theory, the villager should always wear red shoes. Very roughly, here is why. Because the villager is so confident in (1), it can be shown that the expected value of not wearing red shoes equals the value, for the villager, of not meeting their true love. That, along with some mathematics, implies the following: the expected value of wearing red shoes is greater than the expected value of not doing so. Therefore, according to expected utility theory, the villager should always wear red shoes.

In other words, according to expected utility theory, wearing red shoes is rational. Sokka is wrong to criticize the villager for behaving in that way. Given the villager's confidence in Aunt Wu's predictions, wearing red shoes is the right thing to do.[2]

Generalizing to Other Cases

This theory of rationality illuminates other situations in "The Fortuneteller." Time and again, the villagers act in accord with Aunt Wu's predictions. Initially at least, those actions appear to be irrational; they appear that way to Sokka, for instance. But those actions are perfectly rational for the villagers to perform, according to expected utility theory.

Take the very first villager that Aang, Katara, and Sokka encounter, the one being attacked by a platypus bear. Earlier, Aunt Wu predicted that this villager's journey would be safe. Because of their trust in Aunt Wu, the villager is completely certain that this prediction will come true. So despite the platypus bear's ferocious attacks, the villager remains unfazed. They happily dodge the platypus bear's sharp claws until Appa arrives, roars, and scares the attacker off.

The villager and Sokka have a brief dispute over whether or not it was rational for the villager to remain calm during the attack. Sokka, unsurprisingly, suggests not, for Sokka thinks that Aunt Wu's prediction was wrong: "You didn't have a safe journey; you were almost killed!" Clearly, Sokka thinks that remaining calm was irrational: the villager's calm behavior, Sokka suggests, was motivated by Aunt Wu's false prediction. But as the villager points out, Aunt Wu's prediction was not false at all: it actually came true. So their journey was safe. Remaining calm, the villager implicitly suggests, was the rational thing to do.

According to expected utility theory, the villager – and not Sokka – is right. Given that the villager is completely confident in the truth of Aunt Wu's prediction, it was rational to remain calm throughout the attack: the expected value of remaining calm is, plausibly, greater than the expected value of panicking.

Wrapping Up

We can draw a general conclusion about the nature of rationality from all this. Sokka assumes that only empirical approaches to reasoning are rational. But given a standard theory of rational decision-making – namely, expected utility theory – that is not so. Mystical approaches to reasoning, such as approaches based on Aunt Wu's fortunetelling, can be rational too.[3]

Because of this, I see "The Fortuneteller" as advancing an argument for the claim that there is no great difference between empirical kinds of reasoning and more mystical kinds of reasoning. At the very least, these two kinds of reasoning do not always differ with respect to how rational they are. Both kinds of reasoning can be rational; and both kinds of reasoning can be irrational too. So rationality is, by its nature, compatible with both reasoning based on empirical considerations and reasoning based on mysticism.

Appendix

In this appendix, I present the fully formal definition of expected value. Then I use that definition to formulate a mathematically precise version of expected utility theory. Finally, I use all this to prove that the expected value of wearing red shoes is, for the villager, greater than the expected value of not wearing red shoes.

Expected value is defined using propositions and functions. Propositions are represented by lower-case letters: "x," "y," and so on. In addition, some propositions are represented using a combination of letters and the negation symbol "$\neg$." Expressions like "$\neg x$" should be understood as shorthand for "It is not the case that x."

Two different types of functions will be relevant here. One type is used to regiment claims about agents' credences – that is, how confident agents are – in various propositions, given that various other propositions occur. These are called "credence functions": a credence function is a function Cr which maps pairs of propositions to real numbers between 0 and 1. So if x and y are propositions, then $Cr(y|x)$ is a real number in that numerical range. And the expression "$Cr(y|x)$" should be understood as saying "The agent in question has credence $Cr(y|x)$ in the following: given that y occurs, x occurs too."

For example, recall Katara's poker game. Let x be the proposition that Katara calls the bet. Let y be the proposition that Katara wins. And suppose that $Cr(y|x) = 0.5$. Then "$Cr(y|x) = 0.5$" says the following: Katara has degree of confidence 0.5 – in other words, Katara is 50% sure – that given that she calls the bet, she will win.[4]

The other type of function is used to regiment claims about what agents value. These are called "valuation functions": a valuation function is a function which maps propositions to real numbers. So if y is a proposition, then V(y) is some real number or other. And the expression "V(y)" should be understood as saying "The agent in question places V(y) amount of value in the occurrence of y."

For example, let y be the proposition that Katara wins. And suppose that V(y) = 2. Then this equation says the following: $2 is how much Katara stands to win.

Now to define expected value. Let x be a proposition which describes an action that an agent might perform. Let y be a proposition which describes a possible outcome of that action. Let Cr be the agent's credence function, and let V be the agent's valuation function. Then the "expected value" of x – written "EV(x)" – is defined below.

$$EV(x) = Cr(y|x)V(y) + Cr(\neg y|x)V(\neg y)$$

Roughly put, this equation says that to determine the value which an agent can expect to get from performing the action described by x, you must do the following. First, take the agent's credence that the possible outcome described by y will indeed occur, given that the agent does the action described by x. Multiply that credence by how much the agent values that outcome. The result is, roughly put, the expected value of the specific outcome which "y" describes. Second, take the agent's credence that the outcome described by y will *not* occur, given that the agent does the action described by x. Multiply that credence by how much the agent values the *non*-occurrence of that outcome. The result is, roughly put, the expected value of the specific outcome which "¬y" describes. Third, add those two numbers together. According to the equation above, that sum is the overall value which the agent can expect to get, if they perform the action described by x.

Now for the mathematically precise version of expected utility theory. Suppose that an agent faces exactly two choices: perform an action, or do not perform that action. Let x be the proposition that the agent performs that action; so "¬x" expresses the proposition that the agent does not perform that action. Then according to this version of expected utility theory, the agent is rationally required to perform the action if and only if

$$EV(x) > EV(\neg x)$$

In other words, the agent should perform the action if and only if the expected value of doing so is greater than the expected value of not doing so.

Now let us prove that, according to this version of expected utility theory, the villager is rationally required to wear red shoes. Let r be the proposition that the villager wears red shoes, and let m be the proposition that the villager meets their true love. Let Cr be the villager's credence function, and let V be the villager's valuation function.

According to the mathematically precise version of expected utility theory, the villager should wear red shoes if and only if EV(r)>EV(¬r). So to determine whether the villager should wear red shoes, we need only determine whether EV(r) is greater than EV(¬r) or not.

In the main text – in the section called "The Rationality of Wearing Red Shoes" – I mentioned that in order to determine whether or not EV(r)>EV(¬r), just two pieces of information are needed. The first piece of information is expressed by the formula below.

$$V(m) > V(\neg m)$$

In other words, the villager values meeting their true love more than not meeting their true love. The second piece of information is expressed by the following equation.

$$Cr(\neg m | \neg r) = 1$$

In other words, the villager is completely confident that if they do not wear red shoes, then they will not meet their true love.[5] Both pieces of information are, in fact, true: the villager really does value meeting their true love more than not, and the villager really is completely confident that if they do not wear red shoes, then that meeting will not occur. So in the proofs to come, it is reasonable to assume both that V(m)>V(¬m) and that Cr(¬m|¬r) = 1.

Now to prove that EV(r)>EV(¬r). A standard theorem of probability, in conjunction with the fact that Cr(¬m|¬r) = 1, implies that Cr(m|¬r) = 0.[6] Therefore,

$$EV(\neg r) = Cr(m | \neg r) V(m) + Cr(\neg m | \neg r) V(\neg m)$$

$$= 0 \cdot V(m) + 1 \cdot V(\neg m)$$

$$= V(\neg m)$$

It follows that EV(r)>EV(¬r) if and only if EV(r)>V(¬m). So to complete the proof, it suffices to show that "EV(r)>V(¬m)" holds.

Toward that end, multiply both sides of the inequality "V(m)>V(¬m)" by "Cr(m|r)." The result is below.[7]

$$Cr(m | r) V(m) > Cr(m | r) V(\neg m)$$

By the theorem of probability mentioned earlier, Cr(m|r)+Cr(¬m|r)=1; in other words, Cr(m|r) = 1 − Cr(¬m|r). Substituting "1 − Cr(¬m|r)" for "Cr(m|r)" in the right side of the above inequality yields

$$Cr\left(m|r\right)V\left(m\right) > \left(1 - Cr\left(\neg m|r\right)\right)V\left(\neg m\right)$$

By some straightforward algebra, it follows that

$$Cr\left(m|r\right)V\left(m\right) + Cr\left(\neg m|r\right)V\left(\neg m\right) > V\left(\neg m\right)$$

And since EV(r) = Cr(m|r)V(m) + Cr(¬m|r)V(¬m), it follows that EV(r)>V(¬m). This completes the proof.

Notes

1. For a thorough introduction to expected utility theory, and philosophical theories of decision-making more generally, see Martin Peterson, *An Introduction to Decision Theory* (New York: Cambridge University Press, 2017) and Katie Steele and H. Orri Stefánsson, "Decision Theory," in *The Stanford Encyclopedia of Philosophy*, Winter 2020, at https://plato.stanford.edu/entries/decision-theory.

2. It is worth pointing out that expected utility theory has a striking implication: if a person happens to be extremely confident in a liar, or a quack, or a conspiracy theorist, then it is often rational for that person to believe whatever that liar, or quack, or conspiracy theorist, says. Though this is clearly a problematic implication, philosophers often disagree over what exactly the problem is. Some philosophers take this to be a theoretical problem. It shows that the theory of expected utility is wrong, because the correct theory of rationality would not have this implication. Other philosophers take this to be a practical problem. Rather than showing that expected utility theory is wrong, it shows that in order to avoid being misled, people need to be taught more than just how to think rationally: the practical problem is the problem of determining what else to teach people, and how to teach it.

3. One might claim that the villagers' reasoning should actually count as empirical. The reasoning itself is not mystical, one might claim: rather, mysticism only enters the villagers' reasoning insofar as the source of their information – namely, Aunt Wu – is mystical (thanks to William Irwin for suggesting this). This approach to the villagers' reasoning is compatible with my own. For this approach still draws a distinction between two kinds of reasoning: namely, reasoning on the basis of empirical sources only, and reasoning on the basis of at least some mystical sources. Understood in this way, "The Fortuneteller" can be interpreted as advancing an argument for the claim that there is no great difference between these two kinds of reasoning. Rationality, in other words, is compatible with reasoning based on mystical sources.

4. Functions like these are often called "conditional credence functions." For more details about credence functions, and other notions from probability theory

formulated over spaces of propositions expressed using logical symbols like "¬," see E.T. Jaynes, *Probability Theory* (New York: Cambridge University Press, 2003).

5. This equation is a formal representation of the fact that the villager is completely confident in the truth of (1) from the section called "Sokka, the Villagers, and Aunt Wu" in the main text. That is, the villager is completely confident in the truth of Aunt Wu's prediction.

6. It is usually assumed that credence functions like Cr obey the axioms of probability theory. That is why a probability theorem can be used here; and that is why facts about probabilities are used elsewhere in this proof. For an explanation of why credence functions like Cr are often assumed to obey the probability axioms, see Alan Hájek, "Dutch Book Arguments," in Paul Anand, Prasanta K. Pattanaik, and Clemens Puppe eds., *The Handbook of Rational and Social Choice* (New York: Oxford University Press, 2009), 173–195.

7. To obtain this result, I assumed that $Cr(m|r)>0$. This assumption is definitely reasonable for the villager in question. They definitely have non-zero credence that if they wear red shoes then they will meet their true love.

11

"I will never, *ever* turn my back on people who need me"

Repairing the World Through Care

Nicole Fice

When describing the sixth chakra to Aang, Guru Pathik says "it deals with insight and is blocked by illusion. The greatest illusion of this world is the illusion of separation. Things you think are separate and different are actually one and the same." Aang is quick to catch on to what Guru Pathik is talking about and gives the example of the four nations. Guru Pathik nods and says that the Fire Nation, the Earth Kingdom, the Water Tribes, and the Air Nomads are all one people. Aang insightfully responds, "We're all connected. Everything is connected" ("The Guru").

What is the significance of Guru Pathik's lesson? One possible interpretation comes from care ethics, a feminist moral theory that emerged in the late twentieth century. Care ethics begins with a relational understanding of personhood, which holds people are fundamentally situated in complex webs of chosen and unchosen relationships to other people, social institutions, and communities.[1] We are connected through these relationships.

Care Ethics

Care ethics holds that, to live a good life, one should work to create and maintain healthy relationships.[2] This is because healthy relationships are of central importance in our lives. Additionally, to be a morally good person, one should try one's best to care well for others, as our relationships can further give rise to weighty moral duties.[3] What it means to care well is contextual. It depends on the relationship in question and the social and political circumstances in which caring takes place, as well as who or what we are caring for.[4]

Avatar: The Last Airbender and Philosophy: Wisdom from Aang to Zuko, First Edition.
Edited by Helen De Cruz and Johan De Smedt.
© 2023 John Wiley & Sons, Inc. Published 2023 by John Wiley & Sons, Inc.

Care ethics also holds that our relationships extend beyond the ones we have with other individuals. The feminist orientation of care ethics also reminds us that care isn't a personal matter, but that it is entrenched in social and political contexts. We exist in complex webs of relationships with entities such as social groups, our communities, and nation-states.[5] We also stand in relation to historical contexts, social circumstances, and systems of oppression.[6] These wider connections, much like our interpersonal relationships, influence us in profound ways. As in personal relationships, one should aim to care about and for one's wider communities in a way that promotes healthy relations. For example, to be a good member of our community, we should help our neighbors and ensure our societies are structured such that the needs of our community members are met, both on local and global levels. In this way, care can act as a guide to structure a good society and can motivate social change.

Importantly, the feminist orientation of care ethics calls for us to challenge the myth that care is something that is essentially feminine. Just like feminism, care ethics is for everyone – it shouldn't be mistaken for a strictly feminine ethic.[7] Everyone is capable of learning to care well.

The philosopher Joan Tronto defines care as: "a species activity that includes everything that we do to maintain, continue, and repair our 'world' so that we can live in it as well as possible."[8] Care is a practice that works toward some end, namely, to repair our world so that we can thrive in it with others. Caring includes both attitudes and actions. Caring attitudes are the ways we think about the world and the well-being of other people. Acts of care include concrete steps we take toward helping others or our communities.

Care ethics appears in *Avatar: The Last Airbender* in at least two ways. First, the practice of caring is deeply rooted in the moral lives of some of the characters in the series. This chapter will focus on Katara, although similar arguments could be made about Iroh, Aang, and others. Second, care motivates the political goal of the Gaang (Aang and his friends, Katara, Sokka, Toph, and later, Zuko) which, ultimately, is to repair their world so people can live well. This requires the Gaang to address local and global harms caused by Fire Nation imperialism and industrialization.

Katara, a Master of Care

Katara is a strong, compelling character. We see this in her ability to master waterbending in a short time after successfully challenging Master Pakku's sexist tradition of refusing to train women ("The Waterbending Master"). She also masters the sub-skills of healing (see "The Crossroads of Destiny") and bloodbending ("The Puppetmaster"). Katara's powerful waterbending is not the only thing that makes her such a good character. Morally speaking, her greatest strengths include her sensitivity to the needs of others and her ability to take responsibility for those needs to ensure that they are met. These are central aspects of caring according to care ethics. To further explain what it means to care well, let's explore three phases of caring that Tronto identifies: "caring about," "taking care of," and "care-giving."

For Tronto, the first stage, "care about" someone or something requires recognition that there is a need and that this need should be met. For example, caring about social causes – like providing asylum to refugees – means that the person who cares about these issues recognizes that there are people who have needs, like needing to be safely sheltered away from danger. Further, the person concerned about this issue has the conviction that the needs of others *ought* to be met. Caring about someone or something requires one to be sensitive to the needs of others and to believe these needs ought to be met in order for others to live well. "Caring about" involves a kind of empathy which can be understood as being able to appreciate someone else's situation from their perspective and being motivated to help them because of that perceived perspective.[9]

Katara's sensitivity toward others is clear throughout the series. For example, when the Gaang travels to Ba Sing Se ("The Serpent's Pass"), they see a large number of refugees fleeing to the city. Katara is shocked: she empathetically remarks she "can't believe how many people's lives have been uprooted by the Fire Nation." Here, she cares about those whose lives have been uprooted by Fire Nation imperialism. We also see her care about Zuko for the first time when they are imprisoned in the Crystal Catacombs beneath Ba Sing Se ("The Crossroads of Destiny"). She offers to try to heal his scar with water from the Spirit Oasis. Even though, ultimately, she does not heal his scar, Katara is still able to recognize Zuko may have a need that she could meet, despite the fact that he is an enemy at that point in time.

The second stage of caring is "taking care of." This involves helping to ensure that others have their needs met. A person who "takes care of" sees that they can do something to help others. It also requires making judgments about how we ought to respond to those needs. Consider, for example, when Katara and Sokka discover Aang in the iceberg ("The Boy in the Iceberg"). Upon realizing that someone is trapped inside, Katara cries "He's alive! We have to help!" Before Sokka can stop her, she rushes forward to free the person trapped in the ice. Katara recognizes that there is something that ought to be done to help Aang – as surely, it would be bad for anyone to be stuck in an iceberg!

The third stage of caring is "care-giving." Care-giving builds on "caring about," since to care for someone or something we need to be sensitive to the needs of others and think that these needs should be met. It also builds on "taking care of," where agents take responsibility for meeting the needs of others. "Care-giving" is the direct action of providing care to someone to help meet their needs so that they can live well. It involves physical and emotional labor on the part of the care-giver to ensure that others have their needs met.

Katara rarely hesitates to take direct action to help others in need.[10] "The Painted Lady" focuses explicitly on Katara's care-giving. The fishing town the Gaang encounters in this episode suffers from pollution by a Fire Nation factory, and the villagers struggle to survive. Katara insists the Gaang must help, but her pleas are dismissed by Sokka who reminds them of the impending invasion. Katara knows that she should help the village, otherwise the villagers will continue to suffer. In this way, she takes up the first stage of "caring about," as she is sensitive to the needs of the towns-folk. She also knows that she *can* help and takes responsibility for helping them. In this way she adopts the second stage of "taking care of." In the night, she disguises herself as the Painted Lady, the benevolent spirit of the Jang Hui river, and returns to the village to deliver much-needed food. She goes so far as to trick the Gaang to stay another night by feeding Appa purple berries and insisting that he is sick. When they return to the town to get medicine, they find out that all medicine is redirected to the factory. The next night Katara heals those who are sick in the town using her waterbending. On the final night, she and Aang team up to destroy the factory that is polluting the river. Delivering food, healing the sick, and destroying the polluting factory are all acts of Katara's "care-giving."

Destroying the factory, at first, doesn't go down well. The factory workers attack the village, assuming the townsfolk are responsible for its destruc-tion. Katara returns in the disguise of the Painted Lady and fights off the factory workers with the rest of the Gaang. As a final act of care-giving, Katara and the Gaang help the citizens help themselves to clean the polluted river. Katara's efforts are recognized at the end of the episode by the real river spirit, who thanks Katara for what she has done to help the village. The episode provides a great example of care as a practice which works to repair our world so that we and others can live in it as well as possible. In this case, Katara acted to repair the village so that the townsfolk could thrive again.

"The Painted Lady" is perhaps the most obvious example of how Katara progresses through the stages of care. Practicing care well, however, can be an intense and challenging task. Caring well, like learning to bend, takes time to master. To be a good person, from the perspective of care ethics, one must have a habit of caring and an ongoing commitment to help others. While Katara certainly has the habit and commitment, sometimes her care goes awry or comes into conflict with other members of the Gaang. This doesn't make her a bad person, nor do these conflicts mean that we must abandon care ethics. In fact, care ethics acknowledges that conflicts are bound to arise because our relationships and our world are complicated. For example, caregivers sometimes make incorrect judgments about when and how to help others. Consider the following example. In "Imprisoned," Katara encourages Haru to earthbend to help an old man trapped under a collapsed mine, despite knowing earthbenders will be imprisoned. Katara recognizes that they need to help the old man, but getting Haru to earthbend backfires. The old man tells the Fire Nation soldiers occupying the town that Haru is an earthbender and gets him arrested. Even though the Gaang later saves Haru and the other imprisoned earthbenders, we may think that Katara's moral judgment is misguided, as it puts Haru in jeopardy.

In "The Runaway," we also see how Katara's care can cause disputes between characters. Katara scolds Toph for using earthbending to win money from a street gambler. Toph retorts and angrily accuses Katara of being "motherly." This accusation is meant to be derogatory. It is significant that Toph accuses Katara of being motherly, as mothering is often a paradigmatic example of caring. Toph's accusation reinforces the myth that caring is something essentially feminine. We should avoid this, because in sexist societies this myth works to devalue care by labeling it as "women's work" which is deemed inferior or trivial. But it should be clear now that care is not trivial: it is necessary for survival and living well. Nor is it something exclusively feminine. Care should be supported as a practice available to everyone, allowing responsibilities for caring to be shared, rather than disproportionately falling on the shoulders of marginalized individuals. We should recognize, however, that Toph may have good reason to be skeptical of caregivers, as her own parents were paternalistic and overbearing, while delegating the actual care to servants. But Katara's care is not paternalistic. She simply tries to keep the Gaang out of trouble, since they are, after all, undercover in the Fire Nation.

ATLA presents conflicts between characters in nuanced ways so that it leaves room for contemplation and reconsideration. While Katara's care is resisted by Toph, the story doesn't end there. Later in that episode when Sokka talks with Toph, he reveals that, while Katara can be motherly, it is something that he relies on. Sokka says that "When our mom died, that was the hardest time in my life . . . She stepped up and took on so much responsibility. She helped fill the void that was left by our mom." Toph goes on to say, "The truth is, sometimes Katara does act motherly, but that's not always a bad thing. She's compassionate and kind, and she actually cares about me." Sokka and Toph recognize the ways Katara's care helps them survive and thrive. Although care is hard work, Katara shows us throughout the series how important it is to care and how, if we are committed to caring well, we can make the world a better place.

In contrast to Katara, who may sometimes misdirect her care, consider Azula. One of the things that makes Azula such a frightening villain is her lack of concern for others, even for her friends Mai and Ty Lee. For example, in "Return to Omashu," Azula tries to convince Ty Lee to join her team to track down Iroh and Zuko, and later also the Avatar. Initially, Ty Lee declines: she says she is happy as a performer in the circus. Azula fails to appreciate Ty Lee's choice and when watching her tight-rope performance that evening, she intimidates Ty Lee by setting the net beneath her on fire. Azula disregards her friend's desires and puts her in danger to get what she wants. Her lack of care makes her particularly evil.

Care and Political Goals of the Gaang

Care is not only a moral characteristic of individuals like Katara. In *ATLA*, it is also a political force that motivates change. Care has important implications for political life and can motivate radical societal changes to ensure that the needs of others are prioritized.[11] Caring involves repairing the world, and this kind of repair sometimes necessarily involves large-scale political action. This is precisely what the Gaang is doing in *ALTA*, working together to repair their world and remedy the harms of Fire Nation imperialism.

One of the critically acclaimed aspects of *ATLA* is that it intelligently explores themes like imperialism and oppression.[12] Examples include the genocide of the Air Nomads, Sokka and Katara losing their mother, and refugees displaced by Fire Nation invasions in the Earth Kingdom. Through their experiences and travels, the Gaang see the world in peril and out of balance. As Zuko warns his father, "We've created an era of fear in the world. And if we don't want the world to destroy itself, we need to replace it with an era of peace and kindness" ("The Day of Black Sun, Part 2: The Eclipse"). The Gaang knows that they must act to stop the Fire Nation. So, how is this goal motivated by care?

Let's recall Tronto's definition of care as a practice aimed at repairing our world so we can flourish within it. Caring can be performed by groups of people like the Gaang, and maybe even the Order of the White Lotus. The actions of these groups are caring ones: they *care about* and *take care of* the people and communities they help along their journey. Their journey to defeat the Fire Nation is one of *care-giving*, as they are taking direct action to repair the circumstances of the world by stopping the Fire Nation's invasion of it. To see how stopping the Fire Nation is motivated by care, let's think of the needs of humanity: the Gaang knows that people have suffered and will continue to suffer if the Fire Nation takes over. They also know that the four nations are connected and interdependent: if the Fire Nation succeeds, the well-being of the entire world, including the Fire Nation's inhabitants, will be in peril. Because the Gaang cares about the well-being of the world itself, they take responsibility for defeating the Fire Nation. Their goal to restore balance to the world is one of repairing it so that people can live better lives.

The overarching political story told in *ATLA* depicts Aang, Katara, Sokka, Toph, and Zuko (and their allies) repairing their world. This repair is only possible because the Gaang see the world as woven together by relationships of interdependence, and because they care about, and take responsibility for, addressing the needs of those in the world.

Repairing Our Worlds

Both Katara and the Gaang are motivated to repair their world so that people can live better lives within it. Throughout *ATLA* we see that characters like Katara are deeply committed to helping people, whether they are friends or strangers. This is what makes Katara so admirable: she cares about people and does whatever she needs to do to help them. Further, we see that care lies at the center of *ATLA*'s political story. Because they care about the world and the people in it, the Gaang take responsibility for saving the world. Ultimately, their ability to see how the world is interconnected allows them to end Fire Nation imperialism.

Notes

1. Also see Chapter 19: "Not Giving Up on Zuko" on relationality; Chapter 1: "Native Philosophies and Relationality in *Avatar: The Last Airbender*" on an Indigenous conception of relationality.
2. Joan Tronto, *Moral Boundaries: A Political Argument for an Ethic of Care* (New York: Routledge, 1993), 126; Virginia Held, *The Ethics of Care: Personal, Political, and Global* (Oxford: Oxford University Press, 2006), 135.
3. Stephanie Collins, *The Core of Care Ethics* (New York: Palgrave Macmillan, 2015), 47.
4. Fiona Robinson, *The Ethics of Care: A Feminist Approach to Human Security* (Philadelphia: Temple University Press, 2011), 115, 117–118.
5. Joan Tronto, "Creating Caring Institutions: Politics, Plurality and Purpose," *Ethics and Social Welfare* 4 (2010), 161.
6. Held, 133.
7. bell hooks, *Feminism Is for Everybody: Passionate Politics* (South End, MA: South End Press, 2000), 118.
8. Tronto (1993), 103.
9. Held, 24.
10. The quote from Katara in the title of this paper is said in "The Painted Lady."
11. Tronto (1993), 192; Held, 159–160.
12. Nicole Clark, "'Avatar: The Last Airbender' Is Still One of the Greatest Shows of All Time," *Vice*, July 20, 2018, at https://www.vice.com/en/article/5943jz/avatar-the-last-airbender-is-still-one-of-the-greatest-shows-of-all-time.

12

Spirits, Visions, and Dreams
Native American Epistemology and the Aang Gaang

Justin Skirry and Samuel Skirry

The world of *Avatar: The Last Airbender* is composed of four nations that are profoundly out of balance. The creators of the show put a lot of care into designing each nation with its own culture. For example, Ba Sing Se, the Earth Kingdom's capital, reminds us of the Chinese capital of Beijing and the Forbidden City. The Earth Kingdom brings to mind the authoritarian Ming and Qing dynasties in China. The Air Nomad's meditative practices and quest for detachment indicate a more Tibetan-Buddhist influenced way of life. The drive for domination and control found in the Fire Nation is reminiscent of Imperial Japan. Finally, the reliance on animals for sustenance and warmth, the architecture, and even Katara's "hair loopies" (as Sokka calls them) are all indicative of an indigenous culture like the Inuit.[1]

At the beginning of the series, Aang, the Last Airbender, finds himself alone and without a people. After discovering him in an iceberg, Katara and Sokka bring him home to the Southern Water Tribe where he receives a skeptical reception. The villagers are unsure if Aang should be allowed within their makeshift and war-torn walls. In fact, a village elder, Kanna (Sokka and Katara's grandmother) initially sends Aang away, fearing he may cause more harm. Even Sokka is initially apprehensive. But this doesn't last long, for after discovering the massacre of his people at the Southern Air Temple, Katara comforts Aang by welcoming him into their Water Tribe family: "Monk Gyatso and the other Airbenders may be gone, but you still have a family. Sokka and I, we're your family now." Twelve episodes later, Bato officially declares Aang an honorary member of the Southern Water Tribe and the tribe's acceptance of him is complete. Aang now has a people ("Bato of the Water Tribe").

Aang's acceptance into the Southern Water Tribe is an example of *pijitsirniq* – serving and providing for family and the community – found within Inuit Traditional Knowledge or *Inuit Qaujimajatuqangit*. These

Avatar: The Last Airbender and Philosophy: Wisdom from Aang to Zuko, First Edition.
Edited by Helen De Cruz and Johan De Smedt.
© 2023 John Wiley & Sons, Inc. Published 2023 by John Wiley & Sons, Inc.

values are crucial to the Inuit way of life. In 2013, the Government of Nunavut in Northern Canada released an official document providing a definitive list of these principles, including: respecting animals, the land, and the environment (*Avatittinnik Kamatsiarniq*); decision making through discussion and consensus (*Aajiiqatigiinniq*); and respecting others, relationships, and caring for people (*Inuuqatigiitsiarniq*).[2] Like many traditions among Indigenous peoples of the Americas, this knowledge is intended to provide a guide for life. These values exhibit the belief that all things are intimately connected and deserving of respect.[3] The newly formed Aang Gaang, anchored in Katara's and Sokka's Southern Water Tribe values, follow *Inuit Qaujimajatuqangit* as they travel the world in search of the necessary knowledge for defeating Fire Lord Ozai and restoring balance to the world.

"Knowledge . . . is priceless"
(Professor Zei, "The Library")

The Gaang set off on their journey to find masters to teach Aang water-, earth-, and firebending. But this is only the tip of the proverbial iceberg. They must obtain knowledge of all sorts of things along the way in order to build a picture of their place in the world and how to act in it. Of course, how different people create "world pictures" varies from culture to culture. Inuit Traditional Knowledge is one way, while the Fire Nation takes a more imperialistic approach that ignores the close connections amongst people and their environment.

Brian Burkhart (a contemporary Cherokee philosopher) uses the stories of Thales and Coyote to shed light on the difference between Western and Native American ways of knowing. The story of Thales is found in *Theaetetus,* one of Plato's (428–348 BCE) dialogues on knowledge. It recounts a story about the early Greek philosopher Thales (624–548 BCE), who fell into a well while studying the stars. Similarly, Coyote is described in Native American cultures as losing his way because he is too busy figuring out how things work. Notice that both Thales and Coyote lose track of what's at their feet. Yet, in the Western tradition, the story of Thales is commonly used to show the nobility of philosophical and scientific quests for knowledge with little regard for the usefulness of that knowledge. By contrast, the Coyote stories are used in Native American cultures as cautionary tales – you should not lose track of your connections with the world around you.[4]

The Fire Nation is much like Thales and Coyote, because they have lost track of their interconnectedness with the rest of the world. Like Coyote, the Fire Nation has spent a lot of time figuring out how things work. For example, its members have harnessed nature to make war machines, like airships, tanks, and the drill. These technologies indicate a disconnect with the natural environment in that they seek to control nature for their impe-rialistic purposes. In "The Painted Lady," the Aang Gaang come across a fishing village where a Fire Nation factory has heavily polluted the river, and the villagers living nearby can no longer rely on the river for suste-nance. The Fire Nation's imperialist war machine considers nature as something conquerable and does not appreciate the interrelatedness bet-ween nature and the people in their community. Unlike Professor Zei's belief that knowledge is priceless, the Fire Nation's approach to knowledge is expensive, and the environment and the people must foot the bill.

In contrast, the Aang Gaang's Southern Water Tribe or Inuit approach to knowledge avoids the mistakes of Thales and Coyote. Their approach to knowledge emphasizes relations with the rest of the world. For example, Katara acts in accordance with *pijitsirniq* when she provides food and medicine to the ailing fishing village in "The Painted Lady." Furthermore, the Aang Gaang follows the principle of *Avatittinnik Kamatsiarniq*, or respecting the land and the environment, when they destroy the Fire Nation factory so that the environment can heal. This principle is also displayed in "The Spirit World: Winter Solstice, Part 1." Aang calms the spirit, Hei Bai, by reminding him that the forest will grow back, which will reestablish the connection between the forest and Hei Bai as well as between Hei Bai and the villagers. In line with their Southern Water Tribe or Inuit values, the Aang Gaang strive to preserve connections.

The different world pictures held by the Fire Nation and the Southern Water Tribe promote very different kinds of behavior. On the one hand, the Fire Nation's world picture is one of domination and control without any concern for preserving connections and with no regard for the ethical implications of their actions. On the other hand, the Southern Water Tribe's world picture promotes practicing *Inuuqatigiitsiarniq*, to care for and respect all things while also being mindful of the ethical components of their actions. Furthermore, this world picture does not represent knowledge in some detached and impractical, "knowledge for knowledge sake's" way, as with Thales. Rather, as John DuFour (a contemporary Nakota philoso-pher) points out: the Native American approach to understanding is likely based on a practical concern for a life well lived.[5] In other words, this world picture acts as a kind of "map" for ethically guiding behavior.

"You have no idea where you're going, do you?" (Sokka, "The Warriors of Kyoshi")

Maps are an essential part of travel, especially when riding a sky bison. The Aang Gaang's map of the world is incomplete in more ways than one. More literally, a complete map of the Fire Nation is virtually impossible to find. But, in terms of knowledge, or epistemologically, each member of the Aang Gaang begins their journey with their own map to guide them through life. Over time, their individual maps will integrate and evolve based on their discoveries along the way. For instance, the continuous power shifts as the Fire Nation takes more Earth Kingdom territories, like the fall of Omashu and later of Ba Sing Se, make for changes in both literal and epistemological maps. As the Aang Gaang learn more about themselves, the world, and their place in it, they will together create a map that becomes more and more complete and, therefore, an ever-improving guide to action.

There are fundamental differences in Native American and Western approaches to building epistemological maps. Lee Hester (a contemporary Choctow philosopher) and his Euro-American co-author, Jim Cheney, express the difference this way: "It is a world built on the basis of an ethical-epistemological orientation of attentiveness (or, as Native Americans tend to put it, *respect*) rather than an epistemology of control. Such ceremonial worlds . . . are not developed piecemeal but are synthetic creations adjusted holistically to all the concerns that arise."[6] This indicates a holistic approach to knowledge, with ethics woven into it. In contrast, the Fire Nation's imperialist approach promotes an epistemology of control that severs relations into bite-sized, isolated pieces, while leaving ethics off to the side.

Another important aspect of literal maps is that they are intended to represent a geographical territory. Ethical-epistemological maps may differ from culture to culture, but they are also supposed to represent the same ethical and epistemological "terrain." Native Americans recognize that their ethical-epistemological maps will never be complete and are, therefore, always open to change as the ethical-epistemological "terrain" changes. However, the Fire Nation believes their map is complete and so their map is not open to change: they think their map is 100% correct. This could lead to many ethical wrong turns.[7] For instance, in "The Avatar and the Fire Lord," we see Avatar Roku confronting Fire Lord Sozin about his plans for world domination. Here, Roku and Sozin's ethical-epistemological maps conflict. But rather than change, Sozin believes Roku is just wrong, so he unethically allows Roku to perish in a volcanic eruption. Notice that Sozin's map is entirely epistemological, without an ethical component. The Fire Nation has become blinded by its quest for world domination. Much like Coyote, they have forgotten their attentiveness and interrelatedness with the world.

V.F. Cordova (1937–2002), a Jicarilla Apache philosopher, points out that our maps (or "matrices" as she calls them) are "exposed when two people from different cultures come together."[8] For example, in "Avatar Day," the Aang Gaang visit a village where the people hate the Avatar due to Avatar Kyoshi's "murder" of Chin the Conqueror. This attitude is entirely inconsistent with the Aang Gaang's ethical-epistemological map, on which the Avatar is not a murderer but a beloved symbol of hope. Instead of writing off the villagers as "wrong," as Sozin did to Roku, Katara proposes investigating things further. Sokka, with his special hat and bubble pipe, leads the investigation into the remaining physical evidence. Aang also contacts Avatar Kyoshi to learn her perspective. They discover that in separating what is now Kyoshi Island from the mainland, the earth gave way from under Chin who fell to his death. This reconciles the inconsistency between the Aang Gaang's and the villagers' respective ethical-epistemological maps: the Avatar is both kind and merciful, as well as the unintentional cause of Chin's death.

Two approaches to ethical-epistemological map-building are evident. The Fire Nation takes an imperialist approach of domination and control, while the Aang Gaang, in line with its Southern Water Tribe or Inuit values, takes a more ethical-epistemological approach. The latter look at the bigger picture: how all people are connected in accordance with *Inuuqatigitsiarniq*. The Aang Gaang see the world as connected, and so their ethical-epistemological map evolves and flows like the waves. These relationships contribute to the perpetual transformation of their ethical-epistemological maps. Although Sokka and the rest of the Aang Gaang start out not knowing where to go, their various experiences help them find their way, both ethically and epistemologically.

"It's important to draw wisdom from many different places. If we take it from only one place, it becomes rigid and stale" (Uncle Iroh, "Bitter Work")

Ethical-epistemological map-building, however, does not occur in a vacuum but is a group effort. Burkhart points out that Western approaches to knowledge tend to be individual, while Native American approaches focus on the individual's place within a larger community. He references René Descartes' (1596–1650) book, *Meditations on First Philosophy*, which provides a first-person account of a lone meditator locked inside a stove-heated room. The Meditator's first absolutely certain belief is "I am, I exist." This is expressed in Descartes' other work as the famous statement, "I think, therefore I am." This proposition is emblematic of the West's assumption that knowledge is properly obtained individually. However, for Native Americans, the statement should read "We think, therefore I am." It is the collective "thinking" or knowledge of the community that shapes the individual.[9] People should consider the experiences of the entire community, especially the experiences of their elders, when building their ethical-epistemological maps.

Similarly, the Aang Gaang, both individually and as a community, develop their ethical-epistemological maps through their own experiences *and* those of the group. While they travel, their personal maps are changed and reshaped based on new experiences. Sokka's sexism is an early example of a disruption and change of an individual's map. In "The Boy in the Iceberg,"

Sokka discounts Katara's bending abilities not for being useless, but because they are being handled by a girl: "I knew I should have left you home. Leave it to a girl to screw things up." This is tackled soon after in "The Warriors of Kyoshi," in which the Aang Gaang is captured by Suki and her fellow female Kyoshi Warriors, who mistake them for Fire Nation spies. Sokka discounts their capture by claiming he was unprepared. After getting beaten a second time, Sokka reluctantly has a change of heart and asks them to train him. When the Aang Gaang is forced to leave, Sokka tells Suki, "I should have treated you like a warrior." Sokka's ethical-epistemological map has been disrupted and changed for the better through his experiences with the Kyoshi Warriors.

Likewise, the group's ethical-epistemological map is reshaped in "The Headband." While trying to blend into their Fire Nation surroundings, Aang accidentally disguises himself as a student. He is promptly picked up for truancy and thrown into a classroom. Aang's class is subject to heavy Fire Nation propaganda. Students are not allowed to question their daily lessons, because the Fire Nation believes their epistemological map is complete and 100% correct. When Aang returns to the group, noodle portrait of the Fire Lord in hand, they are initially apprehensive about opening themselves up to Fire Nation citizens. But Aang insists, saying, "Those kids at school are the future of the Fire Nation. If we want to change this place for the better, we need to show them a little taste of freedom." Aang holds a school dance against the rules and teaches them traditional Fire Nation moves. The party is a big hit, and the students enjoy expressing themselves through dance. As a result, the Aang Gaang sees how the war has affected these students as well.

Both examples show how ethical-epistemological maps can be changed and adapted to new experiences in the physical world. Human experience, however, is not limited to just the physical for Native Americans. Vine Deloria Jr. (1933–2005), a Standing Rock Sioux philosopher, states "The Indian understands dreams, visions and interspecies communication . . . as a natural part of human experience."[10] This contrasts with typical Western philosophical approaches to knowledge. For example, Descartes uses dreams to cast doubt on his day-to-day physical experiences. For how do I know that I'm really sitting here at this desk when I could be dreaming and, therefore, really in bed asleep? From this perspective, dream experiences are not "real" experiences. They are not eligible building blocks for ethical-epistemological maps. This can also be expanded beyond dreams to include any experience that does not occur during our waking, day-to-day life, like trips to the spirit world. But, to rely solely on waking experiences in the physical world would be to take knowledge from only one place.

Aang, in fact, has several dreams, most of which are expressions of guilt or anxiety. Two such examples are his guilt for abandoning his people and disappearing for 100 years in "The Storm" and his anxiety just days before the invasion on the Day of the Black Sun in "Nightmares and Daydreams." But, at the beginning of "The Avatar and the Fire Lord," Roku contacts Aang in a dream with specific instructions to travel to his island. The difference is that this dream is not an expression of Aang's feelings, but a means by which a spirit communicates with him. Earlier in the series, in "The Swamp," Aang has a kind of "daydream" or vision of a girl in a white dress and of a flying boar. Two episodes later, in "The Blind Bandit," Aang uses this vision to identify Toph Beifong as his earthbending teacher. Visions like this are rare. But Aang's journeys to the spirit world, and especially his communication with his past selves, are very important for building his ethical-epistemological map.

"The past can be a great teacher" (Aang, "The Firebending Masters")

Aang has access to the spirit world and his past selves throughout the series. Like elders, these past selves are part of his community and contribute to his ethical-epistemological map. However, Aang's first communication with the spirit world happens by accident. In "The Spirit World: The Winter Solstice, Part 1," Aang tumbles into the spirit world while flying after Hei Bai in search of Sokka. He meets Roku's animal guide, the dragon Fang, who brings him to the Fire Temple. Through this spiritual experience, Aang gets his first glimpse of Sozin's Comet and receives instructions to visit Roku's temple on the Winter Solstice. When he returns to the physical world, Aang acts on this information. Once at the temple, the spirit of Roku explains how Sozin's Comet was used to start the war and could be used again to finish it at summer's end. This gives their mission a new sense of urgency.

Aang does not usually reach the spirit world by accident, but does so intentionally through the ritual of meditation. Gregory Cajete (a contemporary Tewa philosopher) highlights the role of ritual and ceremony as ways of coming to know and understand things.[11] Even though Aang's meditation is a Tibetan-Buddhist practice, it is still a ritual or ceremony for preparing himself to enter the spirit world and communicate with his past selves. For example, in "The Siege of the North, Part 2," Aang, despite some interruptions, meditates to enter the spirit world in hopes of finding the moon and ocean spirits. He learns from Koh the Face Stealer that the moon and ocean spirits have manifested themselves in the physical world as the two koi fish in the Spirit Oasis at the North Pole. Aang returns to the physical world to save them from General Zhao, but, unfortunately, Zuko thwarts him.

Aang uses meditation to enter the spirit world on a few other occasions as well. Recall, in "Avatar Day" when he contacts Avatar Kyoshi to learn why Chin Village holds the Avatar in such contempt. Avatar Roku and Aang also communicate regularly over the course of the series.

Perhaps the most serious communication with his past selves occurs on the cusp of Aang's fated confrontation with the Fire Lord (now the Phoenix King). At this time, Aang faces an ethical dilemma. As the Avatar, he must bring the world back into balance by defeating the Fire Lord. Yet, his Air Nomad values forbid him from killing any living thing. So, the question becomes: how can he defeat the Fire Lord without killing him?[12]

At the end of "Sozin's Comet, Part 1: The Phoenix King," a mysterious force beckons Aang to a strange island. In the beginning of "Sozin's Comet, Part 2: The Old Masters," Aang finds a spot on the island where he cannot bend, indicating a connection to the spirit world, and decides to meditate. He turns toward the elders of his community – his past selves – for help. Aang poses his question to many of them. Roku tells him to be decisive. Kyoshi states, "Only justice will bring peace." Avatar Kuruk of the Water Tribe tells him to shape his own destiny and that of the world. Another Air Nomad Avatar, Yangchen, states that he must put the needs of the world over his own spiritual needs. All their advice seems to lead to the same conclusion: the Fire Lord must die.

Aang is not satisfied with this advice because it doesn't allow him to reconcile these inconsistent aspects of his ethical-epistemological map. Soon after, Aang discovers that he's not on an island at all but on the back of a spiritual being living in the physical world. This is the Lion Turtle who then bestows further knowledge and power on Aang that allows him to integrate the inconsistencies in his map and to guide his actions. Aang now knows what to do. He ultimately defeats the Fire Lord, but instead of killing him, Aang takes his firebending away, effectively preventing him from acting on his burning desire for world domination.

"I knew I'd know it when I knew it" (King Bumi, "Sozin's Comet, Part 2: The Old Masters")

Throughout the series, the Aang Gaang uses Inuit Traditional Knowledge, *Inuit Qaujimajatuqangit*, found within Southern Water Tribe culture to build their ethical-epistemological maps. These maps were built step by step from a wide variety of experiences. Luckily, they didn't limit themselves to just their day-to-day experiences in the physical world. The Aang Gaang would've missed out on a lot of useful knowledge and guidance had they ignored dreams, visions, and spiritual experiences. Their use of all aspects of human experience created an ethical-epistemological map for leading a useful and ethical life imbued with respect for their relationships with others and their environment. The Avatar's re-establishment of these relationships is what ultimately returns harmony to the world.

Notes

1. Josh St. Clair, "The Real-world Inspirations Behind *Avatar: The Last Airbender*," *Men's Health*, May 21, 2020, at https://www.menshealth.com/entertainment/a32627235/where-is-avatar-the-last-airbender-set; For pictures of Inuit people with Katara's hair style, see https://pbs.twimg.com/media/Dn1OpLfXoAI-sEf.jpg.
2. Government of Nunavut, "IQ Principals," *Incorporating Inuit Societal Principals* (2013), 4, at https://www.gov.nu.ca/sites/default/files/files/incorporating_inuit_societal_values_report.pdf.
3. Adam Arola, "Native American Philosophy," in Jay L. Garfield and William Edelglass eds., *The Oxford Handbook of World Philosophy* (Oxford: Oxford University Press, 2011), 555.
4. Brian Burkhart, "What Coyote and Thales Can Teach Us: An Outline of American Indian Epistemology," in Anne Waters ed., *American Indian Thought: Philosophical Essays* (Oxford: Blackwell, 2004), 15–16.
5. John DuFour, "Ethics and Understanding," in Anne Waters ed., *American Indian Thought: Philosophical Essays* (Oxford: Blackwell, 2004), 39.
6. Lee Hester and Jim Cheney, "Truth and Native American Epistemology," *Social Epistemology* 15 (2001), 320.
7. Hester and Cheney, 329.
8. Kathleen Dean Moore, Kurt Peters, Ted Jojola, and Amber Lacy, eds. *How It Is: The Native American Philosophy of V.F. Cordova* (Tucson: The University of Arizona Press, 2007), 62.
9. Burkhart, 25.
10. Barbara Deloria, Kristen Foehner, and Sam Scinta, eds., *Spirit and Reason: Vine Deloria Jr. Reader* (Golden, CO: Fulcrum Publishing, 1999), 67–68.
11. Gregory Cajete, "Philosophy of Native Science," in Anne Waters ed., *American Indian Thought: Philosophical Essays* (Oxford: Blackwell, 2004), 54.
12. For a different look at this problem, see Chapter 26: "Ahimsa and Aang's Dilemma."

PART III
EARTH

13

Time Is an Illusion
Time and Space in the Swamp

Natalia Strok

Pants are an illusion, and so is death.
(Huu, "The Day of Black Sun, Part 1: The Invasion")

When the Avatar and his friends visit a mysterious and mystical swamp, they have visions that call into question our ordinary understanding of time and space. As it turns out, the knowledge Aang gains in this adventure will be key to his ultimate success. The Avatar must master the four elements and bring balance to the world, but he must also understand the illusion of time and the interconnection of all beings.

Calling from the Swamp: A Mystical Place

In "The Swamp," Sokka, Katara, Aang, and Momo are flying on Appa when, without even noticing it, Aang makes Appa descend. A strange light that can be seen through the trees hypnotizes him. "I think the swamp is calling to me . . . I am actually hearing the earth," he says. Suddenly a tornado attracts them to the swamp. Notably, three of the four elements are involved. The attraction comes from the Earth (calling Aang), using the Air (the tornado), to a watery place. They fall from Appa into the swamp and are separated from Appa, who is entangled in the vines, and Momo, who bites the vines in order to free his friend.

After a terrifying first part of the night, Appa and Momo are chased by some tribal waterbenders in canoes. Meanwhile the three human friends separate because of mysterious vines that drag them in different directions. When separated, each starts to hallucinate. Katara sees her mom, Sokka sees Yue, and Aang sees and follows a giggling young girl he has never seen before. Their different visions lead them all to the same big tree in the center of the swamp.

Avatar: The Last Airbender and Philosophy: Wisdom from Aang to Zuko, First Edition.
Edited by Helen De Cruz and Johan De Smedt.
© 2023 John Wiley & Sons, Inc. Published 2023 by John Wiley & Sons, Inc.

The three human friends fight with a monster made of plants that turns out to be manipulated by a tribesman, Huu – the wise man of the water-bender tribe who protects the swamp. Huu explains that this sacred place is one big tree, which expands itself and creates this "whole world," where everything lives together as a unity. This includes the perception of time and space: "everything is connected."

Past, Present, Future: Soul, Mind, and Time

Katara sees a figure, which she thinks is her mother until she reaches and touches her, only to discover a tree instead. For a moment she really believed that her mother was there, and so she cries in disappointment. Sokka sees a glowing Yue but, unlike Katara, he first mistrusts his senses and thinks it is a hallucination. The bright Yue approaches and says: "you didn't protect me." Perhaps this is a manifestation of Sokka's feelings of guilt. Aang finds a young girl and a flying pig. The giggling girl doesn't answer Aang's question about who she is. Instead, she runs away, and he is unable to catch her. When the three friends reunite, Sokka explains Katara's and his visions as memories or recurrent thinking, but there is no reasonable explanation for Aang's.

The pagan philosopher Plotinus (204/5–270 CE) and the Christian philosopher Augustine (354–430 CE) may be able to help us explain these visions. According to both these philosophers, time is "the life of the soul."[1] Plotinus explains time in terms of cause and effect, telling us that the effect is the image of the cause. Time is the image of eternity, because eternity is the cause of time.[2] The same causal relationship applies to the Soul of the world, which is the image of the Intellect. This Intellect dwells in eternity, but the Soul is intimately linked to time.

In Plotinus' worldview, what comes after is the image of what comes before. Every step further down the levels of reality in this hierarchy is more material than the previous one, following this order: (i) the One, (ii) the Intellect, (iii) the Soul of the world, and (iv) the natural world. The Intellect is the image of the One; the Soul of the world is the image of the Intellect; and the natural world is the image of the Soul. In the natural world there are particular souls in every animated creature, which participate in the Soul of the world. Clearly, the swamp is a spiritual place. With Plotinus, we can think of the spiritual world or Soul of the world as producing the friends' visions in the natural world.

For Plotinus, time is the life of the Soul. What kind of life is this? The Soul is a bridge between the eternal Intellect and the natural world and, because of that, it is transitional. If eternity is a simultaneous whole, time is a successive whole: "instead of a complete unbounded whole, a continuous unbounded succession, and instead of a whole all together, a whole which is, and always will be, going to come into being part by part."[3]

According to Plotinus, the succession of visions of the three friends would be reunited in the intelligible realm. Why? Because in the intelligible realm there is no succession. Everything occurs at once in eternity, without time and succession. This helps explain how the visions can involve people who did not live at the same time. Katara's and Sokka's mother was already dead before Sokka and Katara met Yue.

Plotinus explains that time is not something extrinsic to every soul, but of everyone. He states that the individual souls in the natural world participate in the Soul of the world that reunites them.[4] And time cannot be separated from the soul, as it is a consequence of its descending from the realm of the resting Intellect, eternal, to the world of the succession, which is life of the soul and, we can say, our life as particular souls. In this episode of *ATLA*, every vision has to do with the life of those experiencing the visions. It is life that has a temporal development, but it can be thought of from a different point of view. If it is seen from eternity, it is not successive but simultaneous. Katara sees her mother as present, but she is not living at the present time, she was alive in the past. Might Katara's mom live presently in her soul?

This interpretation of time as linked to every soul needs some clarification. It is not possible to speak of particular times for everyone, a kind of private time, because in Plotinus' philosophy all souls are united in some way: "Is time, then, also in us? It is in every soul of this kind, and in the same form in every one of them, and all are one. So time will not be split up, any more than eternity, which, in a different way, is in all the eternal beings of the same form."[5] The individual souls are reunited in the Soul of the world, and in the same way, time is reunited as the life of the Soul. It makes sense, then, that the swamp visions and related events are all linked to their mutual journey of restoring balance to the world.

We can say without any problem that Katara and Sokka are remembering when they see their mother or Yue, but it is a bit more complicated when analyzing Aang's case, because his vision is not a memory. In Book 11 of his *Confessions* Augustine presents his concept of time, which is linked to his theory of memory. In Augustine's Christian frame, God, who is eternal, creates time. Speaking of God, he says, "Your years do not come and go. Our years come and go, so that they all may come; your years stand all at once because they stand still, and those that go do not give way to those that come, for your years do not pass away."[6] God is motionless and eternal, like the One and the Intellect in Plotinus.

Within this framework, Augustine argues that past time no longer exists and future time does not yet exist, so there is only present time, which, as soon as we speak, is no longer present. Analyzing his own experience, Augustine finds that past and future exist when they are present to him, when he is thinking about past or future events. He concludes that, "There are three times: the present of things past, the present of things present, and the present of things future."[7] These three presents are: memory, attention, and expectation, because time is a "distention" of the mind, that is, the unfolding of the soul that remembers, pays attention, or expects.[8] With Augustine, we can say that Katara is having a memory of her mother, that Sokka is perceiving an attention of Yue, who is no longer the girl he knew but the bright Moon, and Aang is having an expectation of his future earthbending master and friend, Toph Beifong, whom he will meet two chapters later, in "The Blind Bandit." Thus, different events can be reunited in this present time of the swamp; they happen in a way that is linked to the mind and soul of the human members of Team Avatar.

Huu explains that in the swamp we see visions of people who we think are gone, but the swamp tells us that they are not. We are still connected to them: "Time is an illusion and so is death." Past events are present when we remember or think about them, because they are connected to us and we are connected to them. Aang understands that if time is an illusion, his vision is of someone he will meet, because he is already connected to that person. To be clear, time is not a fiction – it is a real thing for Huu as well as for Plotinus and Augustine. Rather, Huu explains, the illusion is the misperception of past as just past, or future as just future. Our connection with events or people in the past or future makes it possible to think of everything as present. From this point of view, the point of view of eternity, all these events are present. Katara's mom is present in her, Yue is present in Sokka, and Toph is present in Aang.

Everything Is Connected: From Unity to Multiplicity

The visions lead the three friends to the center of the swamp, an enormous tree. "It's the heart of the swamp. It's been calling us here," says Aang. Huu, the protector of the swamp, explains to Aang that in fact the swamp was calling them. In contrast to Sokka, who always emphasizes that there is a rational explanation for any phenomenon, Huu says: "Oh, the swamp is a mystical place all right. It's sacred. I reached enlightenment right here under the banyan-grove tree. I heard it calling me, just like you did."[9] This place seems to be a metaphysical key to understanding the world. Huu explains that the swamp is this one big tree spread out over miles: "Branches spread and sink, take root, and spread some more. One big, living organism. Just like the entire world."

Related to Plotinus, Neoplatonism can shed light on Huu's claims about the tree and the swamp. In Neoplatonic metaphysics the multiplicity has an original cause, the One, which produces everything from its own nature by emanation. The first cause or principle produces from itself; it uses nothing from outside, like a lake that overflows into rivers. In our case, a tree from its trunk produces its branches, and from these branches, its leaves. Also from these branches (when they sink in the swamp), new trees take root. This means that everything is related, and all has a unitary and singular origin.

Aang listens attentively, but he has some doubt concerning Huu's assertion that the whole world is like the swamp. He understands that in the swamp everything is this huge tree, but is the world one big organism? Huu answers: "Do you think you are any different from me or your friends or this tree?" Huu affirms that when listening hard enough, you are able to hear every living creature breathing together, and that everything grows together, because we are all living together, in spite of what some people think. "We all have the same roots and we are all branches of the same tree." Huu explains that all living creatures form a unity. So this tree, which connects all the swamp, is a metaphor for the whole world.

Aang uses his new knowledge to find Momo and Appa. By touching the roots of the tree he expands himself in space, through the branches, until he finds his animal friends. His attention flies as an electrical current until he sees them being captured by the tribesmen. At that moment, this seems to be something that only the Avatar can do, but we later discover that Toph has a similar ability. Through her earthbending, she can sense if someone is around; she can feel every movement around her.

This connection is also found in *The Legend of Korra*. When Toph is living in the Foggy Swamp, she can always "see" where her daughters and relatives are and how they are doing.[10] While training with Toph, Korra says that the grumpy old lady seems to enjoy having someone around to beat up, and asks her why she has left everything and wants to be disconnected from the rest of the world. Toph answers: "I'm more connected to the world than you have ever been. The roots and vines, they run all over the world." In fact, she can see her daughters and the cities where they live: "you are blind compared to me." Toph explains to Korra that she needs to be in balance in order to defeat her enemies of the past and the future. Thus she leads her to the banyan-grove tree where she can reconnect to everything again. Much as Aang did previously, Korra expands herself through the roots and sees her loved ones.

The examples of Huu and Toph make clear that this ability to connect everything and see miles away isn't restricted to the Avatar. Anyone can potentially gain this ability and achieve this enlightenment under the banyan-grove tree of the mystical swamp.

Avatar: The Reunion of Multiplicity

His experience in "The Swamp" teaches Aang about the nature of the world, the unity of time, and the connection of space. All knowledge from the past is, in fact, present, but all knowledge of the future is present as well. It makes sense, then, that Aang has the knowledge of all the other Avatars of the past and the future, yet in spite of that he is Avatar Aang and needs to make his own decisions.[11]

One might object that Aang cannot speak with his future selves, although he can consult his past lives. This is the case as long as the Avatar is alive. As a matter of fact, after death, Aang will be able to communicate with Korra (or Korra with him).[12] This is a mystical lesson learned in a mystical place, the swamp. The unity of past, present, and future selves belongs to the Intellect, which dwells in eternity and does not function in a rational way. In fact, Aang as the last Airbender does not speak with past or future selves in his daily life. Rather, it is Aang the Avatar who does so when he enters a spiritual state. Aang is a bridge between these two metaphysical realms, the natural and the spiritual.[13]

When thinking about the connection that all creatures have, as branches from the same tree, it is easy to feel bad about what Aang seems to be obligated to do – defeat the Fire Lord in order to bring balance to the world. War and destruction are against this lesson of the swamp. Because Aang is already concerned about causing harm (for instance, he is a vegetarian), he continuously thinks about how to stop the Fire Lord. Killing the Fire Lord is not a solution, because death, just like time, is an illusion. Appreciating that everything is connected can help us accept the past, the present, and the future. The world is a unitary whole, and we coexist with different kinds of beings. Aang will find a way to modify reality, without causing the death of the Fire Lord.[14]

"The Swamp" shows that bringing balance to the world requires more than mastering the four elements. It also requires understanding the connection of all time and all space, and the connection of all creatures as well.

Notes

1. Plotinus, *Enneads* III 1–9, trans. A.H. Armstrong (Cambridge, MA: Harvard University Press, 1967), III 7 11 (45). See Augustine, *Confessions*, trans. Thomas Williams (Cambridge, MA: Hackett, 2019), 11 20.26, where he explains that time is related to the soul.
2. Originally from Plato, *Timaeus* 37 d5.
3. Plotinus, *Enneads* III 7 11 (55).
4. Andrew Smith, "Eternity and Time," in Lloyd Gerson ed., *The Cambridge Companion to Plotinus* (Cambridge: Cambridge University Press, 2006), 213–214, 209.
5. Plotinus, *Ennead* III 7 13 (65).
6. Augustine, *Confessions* 11 13.16.
7. Augustine, *Confessions* 11 20.26.
8. Augustine, *Confessions* 11 23.30; 26.33.
9. See also Chapter 10: "Mystical Rationality."

10. *The Legend of Korra*, "The Coronation"; "The Calling."
11. See also Chapter 12: "Spirits, Visions, and Dreams," which looks into these visions.
12. *The Legend of Korra*, "Endgame."
13. See also Chapter 1: "Native Philosophies and Relationality in *Avatar: The Last Airbender*."
14. See also Chapter 26: "Ahimsa and Aang's Dilemma."

There Is No Truth in Ba Sing Se

Bald-faced Lies and the Nature of Lying

Nathan Kellen

Lying and deception are everywhere in *Avatar: The Last Airbender*.[1] Almost constantly on the run from the Fire Nation, the members of Team Avatar use all manner of deception to avoid capture, including lying about their identities and dressing up in disguise. Even Avatar Aang is not above lying; his mischievous nature often has him engage in more playful forms of deception, for example, in "The Southern Air Temple" he wakes Sokka up by tricking him into believing there is a prickle snake in his sleeping bag.

Lying is occasionally an essential plot device. Consider "The Great Divide": in this episode Team Avatar attempts to cross the Great Divide – the world's largest canyon. Accompanying them are two competing tribes, the Gan Jins and the Zhangs, who have been locked in a feud for a century. The Gan Jins believe that their ancestor Jin Wei was responsible for transporting a sacred orb from one gate to another, and that the Zhang forefather Wei Jin stole the orb from him. The Zhangs believe that their ancestor Wei Jin was merely returning the orb, and was unjustly accused of theft and falsely imprisoned for his good deed.

The two tribes bicker and fight with each another, and while they temporarily make peace and work together during the trip, they jump right back into conflict after leaving the canyon. At this point, Aang attempts to dissolve the conflict in a way that many fans find narratively unsatisfying, or perhaps even immoral: by lying.[2]

Sick and tired of the constant bickering, Aang tells the people of the warring tribes that he personally knew both Jin Wei and Wei Jin, but that the real truth is different from the stories passed down to the Gan Jins and Zhangs: the two tribal forefathers were twin brothers, engaged

Avatar: The Last Airbender and Philosophy: Wisdom from Aang to Zuko, First Edition.
Edited by Helen De Cruz and Johan De Smedt.
© 2023 John Wiley & Sons, Inc. Published 2023 by John Wiley & Sons, Inc.

in a game as children, and the stories have been greatly exaggerated. Accepting Aang's testimony, the two tribes make peace and travel together to Ba Sing Se.

After the tribes' departure, Sokka remarks that they are all lucky that Aang knew the two brothers and was thus able to solve the hundred-year conflict. With a wry smile, Aang replies "You could call it luck . . . or you could call it lying! I made it all up." The lesson? A hungry and fed-up Avatar is not beyond lying to solve problems.

While the story told in "The Great Divide" is a clear case of lying (even if it is a morally acceptable lie), not all examples in *ATLA* are so clear cut. When Team Avatar first arrives in Ba Sing Se in "City of Walls and Secrets," they are immediately approached by Joo Dee, a persistent guide assigned to show the heroes to their new quarters and cater to their every need. Despite their best efforts, Team Avatar are unable to explore the city on their own, as they can't shake off Joo Dee. Everywhere Joo Dee goes, the inhabitants of Ba Sing Se are afraid to speak the truth. The animal trader denies any knowledge of illegal markets, the university student denies any knowledge of political turmoil, and Joo Dee herself denies that there is a war with the Fire Nation.

These denials frustrate Team Avatar not just because they lead to dead ends in their investigations into the whereabouts of Appa and the city's war preparations, but because they know that the denials are false. These are not simple lies, at least not as "lying" is colloquially understood. Most people, including many philosophers, have held that lying requires an intention to deceive. But the animal trader knows that the heroes will not believe his denial, and Joo Dee knows that they have seen the war with the Fire Nation with their own eyes. So what is going on here?

The lies propagated by the Dai Li, the Earth Kingdom's cultural ministry and secret police, are what philosophers call "bald-faced lies," undisguised lies which lack an intent to deceive the audience. This chapter examines the nature of deception and lying by attempting to find an understanding of lying which can make sense of the Earth Kingdom citizens' behavior.[3] We will primarily be concerned with analyzing the concepts of deception and lying, rather than explaining when they are and are not morally right and wrong, though we will briefly discuss what makes them such a dangerous and problematic phenomenon.[4]

Fire Nation Disguises and False Statements: Deception, Misleading, and Lying

Let's first distinguish lying from the more general phenomenon of deception. Deceptive practices, like lying, are attempts at causing others to have false beliefs. What makes lying special amongst deceptive practices is that it is *linguistic* in nature – lies happen only in language. But not all deception is linguistic, and Team Avatar often uses non-linguistic deception to its advantage. The earliest example occurs in "The King of Omashu," where Aang dresses up as an elderly man in an attempt to sneak past the guards into the Earth Kingdom city of Omashu. In this same episode, King Bumi deceives Aang into believing that he is a frail old man, by dressing up in baggy robes and walking with a hunched back. Fellow earthbender Toph employs a similar form of deception in "The Blind Bandit," when she feigns being a helpless little girl, hiding her ability to earthbend from her parents and teacher. Throughout Book Three the members of Team Avatar disguise themselves as members of the Fire Nation colonies, in an attempt to avoid detection by the authorities. Even Momo gets in on the fun in my personal favorite example of non-linguistic deception in the series. In "Imprisoned," Aang attempts to deceive guards into believing that Katara is an earthbender by using air vents to lift a large rock, but instead the guards initially believe that Momo is an earthbending lemur.

In each of these cases, someone is left with a false belief. The Omashu guards believe that Aang is an old man, Aang believes that Bumi is weak and thus the optimal opponent in a duel, and the Fire Nation citizens believe that Aang and his "parents" are Fire Nation colonists. What is important in distinguishing lying from deception in general is that, in each of these cases, the false beliefs were caused not by linguistic utterances, but by non-linguistic elements, such as disguises.

With this lesson in hand, we have learned something important about lying: lying is linguistic in nature. Many of our examples of non-linguistic deception are accompanied by lies as well. For example, Aang tells the Omashu guards that his name is "Bonzu Pippinpaddleopsicopolis the Third." In this case, Aang *says* something false, which causes the guards to have a false belief.

But while lying is the most common form of linguistic deception, it is not the only form. When Aang tells the guard a false name, he is saying something in particular that is false: namely that his name is Bonzu Pippinpaddleopsicopolis the Third. But consider the events in "The Runaway," where Aang, Toph, and Sokka run several scams in order to earn money. In one such scam Toph is invited to play a game where she guesses which bowl a pebble is underneath. She proceeds to hustle the dealer by stating "How could I possibly play? I'm blind!"

In this case, Toph is misleading the dealer by implying – but not outright saying – that she will be helpless at the game. Strictly speaking, what Toph said is true – she is in fact blind. She *misled* the dealer, but she did not lie. So we must make a distinction between lying and merely misleading. We do so by focusing on what is (explicitly) said – the liar says something false.

With this in mind, perhaps we could define lying in the following way:

Lying$_1$: A person lies if and only if they say something false which causes someone to have a false belief.

This definition would count Aang's statement to the guards as a lie, and would *not* count his silly disguise as a lie, nor Toph's statement to the dealer. This seems right in all three cases, but there are other cases which reveal the flaws in this definition.

Brainwashed Beliefs: Why Falsity Is Not Enough

Lying$_1$ claims that a person lies when they say something false which causes someone to have a false belief. To see the issue with this definition, let's consider a case from "Lake Laogai." In this episode Team Avatar once again meet Jet, the former freedom fighter and now refugee. In a previous episode Jet was captured by the Dai Li, who brainwashed him into having a number of false beliefs. When Team Avatar confronts Jet for the first time, he tells them that he has put his gang behind him and started a new life. While Katara is hesitant to believe him after his previous betrayal, Toph declares that she knows he is not lying. Toph explains that when people lie there's a physical reaction which she can sense with her earthbending, but Jet has no such reaction, and so she declares that he must be telling the truth.

Later in that episode Team Avatar and Jet run into Longshot and Smellerbee, two members of Jet's gang. They excitedly rush toward him and ask how he escaped from the Dai Li, much to the shock of the others. Jet quickly claims that he has no idea what they're talking about, and Toph, very confused, declares that they are both telling the truth.

Sokka quickly deduces the problem: Toph assumed that her earthbending technique is a truth detector, when in fact it is a *lie* detector. What Jet had previously said was false – he did not abandon his gang and he was in fact captured, and so when Team Avatar believed him they came to believe something false. With the definition of Lying$_1$, this would count as a lie. But Sokka is right – it is not enough to say something false, one must also *believe* it to be false. Jet believes what he is saying is true, and thus cannot be lying, even though Lying$_1$ would count his statements as lies.

To fix this issue we can slightly alter our definition of lying in the following way:

Lying$_2$: A person lies if and only if they say something they believe to be false which causes someone to have a false belief.

According to Lying$_2$, Jet's statements do not count as lies, but our earlier examples still do.

The Great Divide Between True and False Beliefs

Unfortunately, Lying$_2$ won't do either. To see the issue with Lying$_2$, let's return to Aang's lie in "The Great Divide." In this case, Aang says something he believes to be false, and the people of the feuding tribes are led to have false beliefs about the origin of their conflict. But imagine that (apart from his initial statement about having been there), Aang was somehow coincidentally correct about the origins of their feud. According to Lying$_2$, Aang's story would no longer count as a lie, because his audience would not end up with a false belief, but a true one.

As another example, consider the interaction between Sokka and the knowledge spirit Wan Shi Tong in "The Library." Wan Shi Tong declares that humans are not welcome in his library because they only bother learning things in an attempt to destroy other humans. Sokka, knowing full well that their trip to the library is motivated by a search for knowledge which would allow them to destroy the Fire Nation army, declares that they are not interested in destruction but in knowledge for knowledge's sake. Sokka clearly lies to the spirit owl, and Wan Shi Tong knows this, declaring that "If you're going to lie to an all-knowing spirit being, you should at least put some effort into it." Sokka's lie is unsuccessful (although the spirit allows them to enter the library anyway).

In both cases, the intended audience does not end up with a false belief – either by coincidence or because they simply did not believe the lie. Thus, at least according to Lying$_2$, neither statement counts as a lie. We can fix this problem by proposing yet another definition:

> Lying$_3$: A person lies if and only if they say something they believe to be false with an intent to deceive.

Aang believes his story to be false, and he tells it in an attempt to deceive his audience into stopping fighting. Thus, according to Lying$_3$ his statement counts as a lie. Similarly, despite Wan Shi Tong clearly seeing through Sokka's lie, it still counts as a lie according to Lying$_3$, because Sokka believed it to be false and said it in an attempt to deceive the all-knowing spirit being. Finally, all the previous lies discussed still count as lies according to Lying$_3$, and Jet's brainwashed statements are still ruled out as lies.

Sharp Outfits and Fortunes Told:
Metaphors, Bullshit, and Lies

Before we move on to Ba Sing Se and its bald-faced lies, it is worth stopping for a moment to consider two other difficult cases. First, consider Azula's strained attempt at flirting in "The Beach." In this episode Azula attempts to flirt with Chan by complimenting his outfit, saying "That's a sharp outfit, Chan. Careful, you could puncture the hull of an *Empire* class Fire Nation battleship, leaving thousands to drown at sea . . . because . . . it's so sharp!" Now clearly Azula does not believe that Chan's outfit can literally puncture the hull of a battleship, she is speaking metaphorically. Further, let us imagine that she does not actually think that Chan's outfit is sharp (in the stylistic sense), but is merely pretending in order to start a flirty conversation. In this case Azula has said something she believes to be false (that Chan's shirt is capable of puncturing a battleship) with an attempt to deceive Chan into believing she likes his outfit, and, by extension, him.

While Azula may have lied insofar as she attempts to deceive Chan about her opinion of his outfit, it seems strange or unnecessary to think that she lied because she said something she believed to be false. That is: using metaphorical speech, or related forms of speech like irony or hyperbole, shouldn't count as lying. To avoid such cases, we can move to a slightly adjusted definition of lying:

> Lying$_4$: A person lies if and only if they say something they believe to be false with an intent to deceive, and they are not speaking hyperbolically, ironically, or metaphorically.

Before moving on, it will be helpful to distinguish lying from another related phenomenon: bullshit. In his influential book *On Bullshit*, contemporary philosopher Harry Frankfurt notes that bullshit, like lying, is aimed at persuading the audience.[5] But, unlike lying, where the liar is attempting to deceive the audience into believing something false, the bullshitter aims simply at persuading the audience. The bullshitter does not care, and might not even know, whether what he says is true or false – he is speaking without a care for the truth.

While bullshit may be common in everyday life, examples in *ATLA* are harder to find. For one possible example, consider the proclamations of Aunt Wu in "The Fortuneteller." While Aunt Wu is renowned for being able to see the future, she seems to lack actual magic ability apart from a singular insight into Aang's eventual battle against Fire Lord Ozai. Apart from this one prophecy, she tells the villagers unremarkable fortunes, including predictions of the weather, that they will have safe travels, and that they will find love. Fortunetelling is bullshitting if the fortuneteller cannot see the future but merely seeks to influence their audience in a certain way.

Bald-faced Lies in Ba Sing Se

Crucial to our definition of Lying$_4$ is the idea that lying requires an intention to deceive. However, some cases call this requirement into question, most notably what contemporary philosopher Roy Sorensen calls "bald-faced lies."[6] Bald-faced lies are lies where the liar has no intention of deceiving their audience. Before we turn to the examples of bald-faced lies found in Ba Sing Se, let's first consider a curious example from "Day of the Black Sun, Part 2: The Eclipse." Aang, Toph, and Sokka demand information from Azula, with Toph noting that she will be able to tell whether Azula is lying or not. Azula, ever confident, claims that she is a pretty good liar and then proclaims "I am a 400-foot-tall purple platypus bear with pink horns and silver wings." Despite the absurdity of this statement, she gives off no physical reaction and Toph is forced to admit that Azula is, in fact, a pretty good liar.

What's curious about this statement is that it is so absurd that Aang, Toph, and Sokka couldn't possibly believe it. That is, while it is something Azula believes to be false, and it is not hyperbolic, ironic, or metaphorical, it seems difficult to say that Azula said it with an intent to deceive. Nonetheless, Azula treats it as an example of lying, as does her audience.[7]

In his article discussing the term, Sorensen introduces the idea of bald-faced lies by giving examples of various statements which citizens of oppressive and totalitarian states are forced to make. This brings us, and our heroes, to Ba Sing Se, the titular "City of Walls and Secrets." As they explore the city, accompanied by their ever-present steward Joo Dee, in an attempt to find information about Appa and the war effort, Team Avatar consistently finds themselves stonewalled.

They begin by going to a pet shop in search of information about Appa. When Aang asks the shopkeeper where someone could purchase a stolen animal, the man begins to answer but, upon looking at Joo Dee's intense, smiling gaze flatly notes "That would be illegal." It is clear the man knows more than he can say.

Next, the team visits the university and talks to a student. They ask him which professor would know about the war with the Fire Nation, and again after a quick glance at Joo Dee he blurts out "I don't know, I'm not a political science student" and hurries off. Again, we are left with the impression the student knows more but cannot speak openly.

Frustrated at having wasted the day and received no information, the team is escorted home by Joo Dee. They immediately go across the way to the neighbor's house to seek out information without Joo Dee's presence, and their neighbor Pong tells them that the Dai Li forbids people to mention the war in public.

Later on, their suspicions are confirmed by Long Feng, the head of the Dai Li, who tells them that "it is the strict policy of Ba Sing Se that the war not be mentioned within the walls." As Long Feng explains, the Dai Li has determined that if the people knew about the war or were able to discuss it publicly, the city would be thrown into chaos. Thus, the Dai Li have adopted the mantra "There is no war in Ba Sing Se," in an attempt to keep the city "peaceful and orderly."

The state-mandated lies of the Dai Li are perfect examples of bald-faced lies, undisguised lies which lack an intent to deceive. The pet-shop owner must declare that he knows nothing of the black market and the student must state he is ignorant of the war. These two men, and many other citizens of Ba Sing Se, know the truth, but they are not allowed to say it openly. They are not attempting to deceive Team Avatar or one another; they are merely publicly stating what they must in order to survive.

Returning to our definition of lying, these statements would not count as lies, because the speakers are not attempting to deceive. Whether bald-faced lies should count as lies or are misnomers is a difficult conceptual and philosophical question.[8] Rather than solving that issue here, we can introduce one final definition of lying which allows for bald-faced lies, for those who wish to count these statements as lies.

In order to do this, we must first follow contemporary philosopher Thomas L. Carson in introducing a concept of warranting.[9] When someone warrants the truth of their statements, they are giving you reason to believe what they are saying is true. We generally warrant the truth of our statements, but there are important exceptions, like when we make obvious jokes or tell fictional stories.

We can further expand this idea by thinking not only of warranting individual statements, but of warranting contexts – situations in which what we say is taken to be warranted. A classic example of a warranting context is a trial, for example, Aang and Kyoshi's trial in "Avatar Day." By taking the stand during a trial you guarantee that everything you say during the trial is true, or put otherwise, you warrant the truth of all your statements. The purpose of a trial is to determine the truth of a situation and assess guilt, and thus all statements made must be warranted, and so trials are a paradigm example of warranting contexts.

Trials are not the only example of warranting contexts. We generally assume that public speech – speech made to other people in public spaces – is a warranting context as well. When you ask someone on the street for directions you assume what they say is true, without questioning it. That is: we expect that strangers are telling the truth – that they are speaking in a warranting context.[10]

With these concepts in hand, we can formulate one final definition of lying:

> Lying$_5$: A person lies if and only if they say something which they believe to be false in a warranting context, and they are not speaking hyperbolically, ironically, or metaphorically.

According to Lying$_5$, the state-mandated falsehoods of Ba Sing Se count as lies, although peculiar ones as they are bald-faced lies that all citizens know to be false (the same goes for Azula's claim about being a platypus bear). Thus, if we want to count bald-faced lies as lies, we will need to adopt Lying$_5$; if we do not wish to accept bald-faced lies as lies, we should adopt Lying$_4$.

Trust and Truth

To conclude our journey, let's consider the insidious nature of bald-faced lies. Our communities are built on trust, including trust that we can rely on one another to tell the truth when communicating. Bald-faced lies are the norm within totalitarian states. These lies undermine the trust which serves as the foundation of our communities, and thus split us further apart. In addition, the more falsehoods there are, the harder it becomes to recognize and believe the truth. In communities in which lying is expected, the truth fails to have meaning. And for those of us who seek the truth, that is an unsettling thought indeed. Because we do not want to end up living in a real-world equivalent of Ba Sing Se, we must value truth and refuse to allow bald-faced lies to become the norm.

Notes

1. In fact, the first lie of the series occurs at the end of the very first episode, "The Boy in the Iceberg," when Aang tells Katara that he doesn't know who the Avatar is or what happened to them.
2. In a list summarizing the top ten reasons why *ATLA* fans consider "The Great Divide" the worst episode of the series, Juliana Failde puts "Aang lied" as the number one reason; see her "Avatar: The Last Airbender – Why Fans Agree The Great Divide Is the Worst Episode in the Series," *CBR*, August 27, 2020, at https://www.cbr.com/avatar-the-last-airbender-worst-episode.
3. In what follows I largely follow and am indebted to Jennifer Saul's discussion of various definitions of lying in her book, *Lying, Misleading, and What Is Said: An Exploration in Philosophy of Language and in Ethics* (Oxford: Oxford University Press, 2012), 1–20.
4. For a brief overview of the ethics of lying, see Thomas L. Carson, "Lying and Ethics," in Jörg Meibauer ed., *The Oxford Handbook of Lying* (Oxford: Oxford University Press, 2019), 469–483.
5. Harry Frankfurt, *On Bullshit* (Princeton, NJ: Princeton University Press, 2005).
6. Roy Sorensen, "Bald-faced Lies! Lying without the Intent to Deceive," *Pacific Philosophical Quarterly* 88 (2007), 251–264.
7. Speakers can be wrong about whether they are lying or not, given that we are treating "lying" as a technical term with several possible definitions and related concepts. So while it is worth taking into account how the speaker and audience view a statement, their views are not definitive of whether this statement is a lie, properly understood.
8. For a good overview of this issue, see Saul, 8–12.
9. Thomas L. Carson, "The Definition of Lying," *Noûs* 40 (2006), 284–306.
10. It may help to understand warranting contexts by contrasting them with non-warranting contexts. For example, consider the practice of telling scary stories by the campfire (as Sokka does in "The Puppetmaster"). The audience does not generally regard the stories as having actually happened as told; the purpose of the scary story is not a history lesson but to be entertained.

15

The Rocky Terrain of Disability Gain in *Avatar: The Last Airbender*

Is Toph a Supercrip Stereotype or a Disability Pride Icon?

Joseph A. Stramondo

The hashtag #RepresentationMatters is widely used among disability activists on social media because disabled people are often simply ignored in popular culture. Several disabled characters inhabit the *ATLA* universe, but Toph Beifong is the most prominent. Unlike Teo with his wheelchair/ hang glider, Toph is a major character who plays an essential role in the victory over the Fire Nation's imperialism. A rarity in media, Toph's character has as much depth as any member of Team Avatar.

Could Toph Beifong be understood as what disability studies scholars call, pejoratively, the Supercrip narrative? That is, is Toph an *exceptional* disabled person who overcomes the disadvantages of disability with special talent and will-power? Alternatively, is her story perhaps better understood as an instance of disability pride? That is, does Toph show that disability isn't always a bad thing, but can be something positive that is worthy of being celebrated? These questions are salient because portrayals in pop culture have direct bearing on a group's identity and, hence, moral agency. For disabled people, stories about *why* they are disadvantaged are of particular importance because these narratives can either justify that disadvantage or challenge it. We will see that Toph Beifong's extraordinary earthbending and metalbending abilities, derived from her blindness, are not an example of a harmful Supercrip narrative, but an illustration of disability pride.

Avatar: The Last Airbender and Philosophy: Wisdom from Aang to Zuko, First Edition.
Edited by Helen De Cruz and Johan De Smedt.
© 2023 John Wiley & Sons, Inc. Published 2023 by John Wiley & Sons, Inc.

How and Why #RepresentationMatters

The feminist philosopher Hilde Lindemann's book *Damaged Identity, Narrative Repair* argues that narratives are the basis of identity, which, in turn, impacts agency, one's ability to act freely.[1] Put more plainly, the stories we tell in part determine who we are and what we can do.

Lindemann argues that narratives form identities from both the first-person and third-person perspective. Stories structure who we take ourselves to be: our self-concept consists of stories we tell ourselves and others about what we value most in our lives. However, these first-person stories are constrained by the stories others tell about who we are from their perspective, "other people weave the things about us that matter most to *them* into stories that also constitute our identities."[2]

Our identity is found where these first-person and third-person stories meet. Toph greatly values her earthbending capabilities and, when we meet her first in "The Blind Bandit," she identifies as an earthbending tournament champion. However, she can only do this because others also identify her as such. By contrast, regardless of whether Sokka values earthbending, he cannot identify as an earthbending tournament champion because no one else shares this story.

While identity formation relies on several kinds of stories, Lindemann highlights how master narratives are of special importance. These are "the stories found lying about in our culture that serve as summaries of socially shared understandings . . . consisting of stock plots and readily recognizable character types." They are indispensable for constructing identities from both the first and third person. They provide the raw materials for constructing identities in a way that is intelligible in a shared culture.[3] Uncle Iroh might describe himself as a "tranquil, wise, and eccentric teacher." This is a common master narrative that fits a variety of both fictional and real people. It is recognizable in Master Yoda, Socrates, and Benjamin Franklin. If this master narrative of "tranquil, wise, and eccentric teacher" was also available in the *ATLA* universe, such a self-description would be easily understood by Iroh and those he encounters. It could be an important thread in the tapestry of his identity that makes it intelligible.

While master narratives can construct comprehensible identities, Lindemann argues they can also *damage* identities by constricting agency. First, a master narrative can produce a deprivation of opportunity, when someone's opportunities are diminished because an oppressive master narrative describes their group as unworthy of holding a certain identity. As an example, Lindemann discusses lesbian couples who are denied the right to become parents because of oppressive master narratives about who "good parents" are. Second, infiltrated consciousness is when a person adopts a damaging master narrative about themselves, giving them a distorted view of who they are and which roles or activities they should take up.[4]

For Iroh, a damaging master narrative might be that of the "desexualized elderly person." This is the widely embraced story of the older person who does not desire or is not capable of sexual intimacy and romantic love. While many of the younger characters in the series have love interests of varied intensity, there is rarely any hint that Iroh values sexual or romantic relationships in his own life. This may be because Iroh is experiencing a deprivation of opportunity in which few of those he encounters view him as a sexual being. Or, perhaps, Iroh has internalized the norms of the "desexualized elderly person" narrative and does not see himself as the sort of person who should typically express himself sexually because of infiltrated consciousness.

Disability Pain and Disability Gain: Models of Disability and Well-being

While "disability" is a heterogeneous category spanning blindness, deafness, paralysis, dyslexia, dwarfism, and more, disabled people are often subject to similar stigmas and often report similar experiences of ableism, irrespective of diagnoses. Thus, it makes sense to think of disabled people in terms of a social group with an identity. Many master narratives that frame and damage disability group identity tell a story about how or why disabled people suffer.

One pervasive example is the master narrative of the "Disabled Person Better Off Dead" (BOD) that presumes disability is an experience of such severe suffering that many disabled people would be better off dead. Audiences look on sympathetically as spinal cord injured protagonists in movies such as *Million Dollar Baby*, *Gattaca*, and *Me Before You* seek out their own death.[5] A large part of the plot of *Million Dollar Baby* focuses on Hillary Swank's character wanting to end her life after she becomes paralyzed in a boxing accident, which the audience is supposed to uncritically accept is a fate worse than death.

The "Irrationally and Infectiously Happy Disabled Person" (IIH) is a master narrative that contrasts with BOD, but which is also damaging to disabled people. A paradigmatic example would be Tiny Tim from Charles Dickens's *A Christmas Carol*. At one point, Tiny Tim's father relates, "He told me, coming home, that he hoped the people saw him in the church, because he was a cripple, and it might be pleasant to them to remember upon Christmas Day who made lame beggars walk and blind men see."[6] Likewise, Artie Abrams in the TV show *Glee* is portrayed as someone who is always ready to befriend everyone from his wheelchair. Like BOD, IIH uncritically assumes that disability entails intractable and deep suffering. Unlike the BOD, the IIH proposes that disabled people should not seek out death, but be irrationally happy in the face of suffering, so they can serve the interests of non-disabled people, giving them comfort amidst the presence of such suffering in the world.

Both BOD and IIH assume that disability inevitably entails suffering, which is what contemporary philosopher Ron Amundson refers to as the "Standard View of Disability."[7] Amundson argues this standard view rests upon what disability studies scholars call the medical model of disability, which assumes that the disadvantages and harms of disability directly result from defects in the individual bodies and minds of disabled people. As such, the medical model supposedly explains why the standard view is true and why disabled people inevitably suffer. In contrast, the social model of disability offers an alternative explanation of the harms of disability that challenges the standard view. The social model holds that these disadvantages and harms result from socially constructed barriers. A classic example of the contrast between these models is how the medical model explains the disadvantage experienced by a wheelchair user in terms of spinal cord damage that prevents their climbing steps. Rather than focusing on the disability per se, the social model explains this same disadvantage as a result of the way society constructs architecture with stairs rather than ramps.[8]

Since the standard view is so prevalent, it isn't surprising that most people have also adopted the medical model of disability as an explanation for why disability inevitably reduces well-being. BOD tells the tragic story of the cripple whose suffering is intrinsic to their existence so that the only relief is death itself, and IIH says that the happiness of a disabled person is irrational, if useful, because suffering is baked right into their bodies and mind and any denial of that is delusional.

Clearly, BOD and IIH both damage disabled people's identities by constraining their agency. If it is widely believed that disabled people are inevitably suffering so that they are better off dead or serving as comfort for non-disabled people, other people are not going to grant them equal access to the goods of life. If they themselves adopt these identities, they might not even desire such access.

Toph's character doesn't fit either of these oppressive master narratives. She is definitely not irrationally happy. Often, she is grumpy and surly, but viewers are not led to think her better off dead. BOD and IIH aren't the only master narratives constructing disability identity. There are – at least – two other narratives that challenge the Standard View of disability by advancing the concept of *Disability Gain*.

Disability gain is the idea that, contrary to the assumptions of the Standard View, disability can sometimes increase a person's well-being by preventing a harm or producing a benefit. Some instances of disability gain are incidental: a disabled person might avoid being drafted during war time or might get to cut the line at a Disney theme park. However, other instances of disability gain seem more intrinsic to the experience. Contemporary philosopher Teresa Blankmeyer Burke writes about Deaf gain in a way that underscores examples that are less incidental and more intrinsic to disability itself. She describes sharpening her focus on philosophical thinking by shutting off her hearing aids while reading and writing to avoid auditory distraction. Likewise, she illustrates that Deaf parenting requires direct communication that focuses attention to lip reading or American Sign Language, so children can't just wave you off as they scroll social media or play a video game.[9] As we can see, disability gain does not presume that disability inevitably reduces well-being because of the sorts of bodies disabled people have. Disability gain rejects both the standard view and the medical model. While one does not have to accept the idea of disability gain to adopt the social model, they are surely compatible.

Two alternative narratives highlight disability gain and are arguably expressed by Toph's character: the master narrative of the Supercrip and the master narrative of the Proud Disabled Person. Both reject the inevitability of disabled people suffering solely from their disability and, so, both can potentially interpret how Toph's storyline contributes to the social meaning of disability.

The Master Narrative of the Supercrip: Overcoming Disability with Talent and Pluck

The master narrative of the Supercrip (SC) says that, while disability sometimes reduces a person's well-being, it need not be so, since some disabled people, by virtue of their compensatory talents and willpower, can overcome the difficulties of disability. These are the supercrips. SC depicts some people as admirable for flourishing despite their disability because they are exceptional. Thus, it seems to reject the standard view that disability always decreases well-being and the medical model that explains the harms of disability as caused by some intrinsic defect. Yet, while the SC rejects the standard view and medical model, it remains a damaging identity.

Disability studies scholar Sami Schalk argues that we should not refer to just any disabled person who achieves something of significance as a supercrip, but only those cases constructed by specific narrative mechanisms: "superlative language, scientific examination of the body and mind, comparison to a non-disabled norm . . . the suppression of negative emotions and emphasis on personal attributes . . . the depoliticization of disability through a focus on individuality."[10] For Schalk, these specific narratives render someone a supercrip because supposedly exceptional individual merit obscures the social conditions that they – and others like them – live in. From this characterization, we can see how SC can be damaging to a person's identity. In particular, its features imply that the disadvantages of disability can and should be overcome through individual virtue. Thus, those disabled people *not* living extraordinary lives are personally to blame for lacking such virtue and continuing to suffer.

SC implicitly rejects the medical model of disability since a supercrip does not suffer inevitably, but can flourish with enough grit. This does not mean the SC endorses the social model. Rather, SC is premised on something more like the moral model of disability, which disability rights activist Deborah Kaplan explains "regards disability as the result of sin."[11] On a narrow interpretation of the moral model, disability is framed as a divine punishment. However, there is a secularized version of the moral model that holds that the *harms* of disability – if not the disability itself – are the result of personal failings. If, "the only disability is a bad attitude" as the memes and T-shirts proclaim, then disabled people must have brought their suffering upon themselves with their laziness or lack of virtue. These disabled people must be suffering because they lack the celebrated talent and moral will of a Supercrip.

Undoubtedly SC is damaging to the group identity of disabled people. Take Toscar, a poor, poorly educated young man of color who had his legs amputated after a traumatic accident. Toscar could very well wind up being warehoused in a nursing home, barely surviving on government benefits in public housing, or unhoused and panhandling. When trying to understand who Toscar is, and what his disabled identity means, we might contrast him with a more well-known double amputee named Oscar. Oscar is white and from a socially connected, well-off family. He had plenty of support learning to walk with prosthetics after his legs were amputated just below the knees before his first birthday. Later, Oscar has every opportunity to excel in athletics and, at the age of 16, takes up running to rehabilitate a knee injury he got from playing rugby. After less than a year, Oscar uses his carbon fiber Flex-foot Cheetah prosthetic "blades" to win a gold medal in sprinting at the Paralympics.[12]

The upshot of our story is that Oscar Pistorius, the most famous of all supercrips, had many socially constructed advantages that led to his success, while Toscar's suffering is the result of systemic oppression, not moral failing. Yet, under SC this fact remains obscure. Toscar's lack of opportunity will go unrecognized. His consciousness may be infiltrated by the SC, so that he believes he is unworthy of basic human flourishing because he has not achieved superhuman success. SC denies the systemic (dis)advantages in Toscar and Oscar's lives, and claims that their divergent life courses are caused by their own behavior.

Toph Beifong certainly achieves greatness through her talent and determination, but it doesn't necessarily follow that her story arc is an SC. Schalk doesn't specify what is necessary or sufficient for giving a character supercrip status. I would argue that Toph's storyline doesn't have enough features to be an SC.

Toph is sometimes described in "superlative language," but this may be expected for anyone who becomes a master bender at a young age, regardless of disability status. Likewise, Toph is inevitably subject to "comparison to a non-disabled norm," especially when we first meet her earthbending competitively ("The Blind Bandit"). But, of course her competitors were non-disabled since, unlike Oscar Pistorius, Toph would not have access to the Paralympics. Toph doesn't undergo any straightforwardly "scientific examination of the body and mind," although one could interpret her discussion of learning earthbending from badgermoles as a kind of proto-scientific analysis of her abilities ("The Firebending Masters"). Since Toph is often gruff, she does not exhibit "the suppression of negative emotions." As a bender, there is some "emphasis on personal attributes." After all, not just anyone can shape a natural element to their will. But, this focus on an individual's special talent isn't any greater for Toph than it is for the non-disabled benders in the show, such as Aang. While there isn't anything like a politicized disability rights movement in *ATLA*, it would be wrong to view her story as "the depoliticization of disability through a focus on individuality," given her strong resistance to her ableist, overprotective parents.

The Proud Disabled Person as Counterstory

In addition to exploring how identities are damaged and agency constrained by oppressive master narratives such as BOD, IIH, and SC, Lindemann suggests that damaged identities can be repaired and agency expanded by what she calls counterstories, "which root out the master narratives in the tissue of stories that constitute an oppressive identity and replace them with stories that depict the person as morally worthy."[13] The story of Toph Beifong is an example of one such counterstory that I will call the master narrative of the Proud Disabled Person (PDP).

In her influential book *The Minority Body*, contemporary philosopher Elizabeth Barnes argues against what she terms the bad difference view – which is similar enough to the standard view that I will use it interchangeably. She maintains that disability is a mere difference, so, all things considered, it does not necessarily reduce well-being, even if it sometimes makes life more difficult. She argues that the disability pride movement's main function is to help disabled people make sense of their own experiences of disability being a mere difference.[14]

Specifically, Barnes discusses how the Bad Difference view has caused disabled people to suffer what contemporary philosopher Miranda Fricker calls hermeneutical injustice. This occurs when dominant assumptions about a group make it difficult for members of that group to understand their own experience. Barnes argues that hermeneutical injustice appears when disabled people try but fail to make sense of their experience of flourishing with a disability because it is so commonly assumed that disability consigns a person to a horrific, tragic fate.[15]

Barnes suggests disability pride resists this disadvantage in understanding, because it gives people "permission to celebrate" their disability "that dominant norms tell you that you should be ashamed of or apologetic about."[16] For Barnes, disability pride is not just about helping disabled people *feel* better about being disabled. Rather, it also can "affect what we can know" about being disabled. The effect of disability pride on people's self-knowledge is driven by their "demanding that norms and stereotypes about them be better informed by their own experiences."[17] It opens up the conceptual space needed for disabled people to understand their disability as something other than stereotypical tragedy.

The disability pride movement is not just composed of parades and hashtags, but also of stories. Disabled people can begin to celebrate their status as disabled when they have access to the right kind of counterstory. PDP has three main features: (i) it portrays disability as sometimes a gain rather than as pure tragedy; (ii) it portrays disabled characters as fully developed and nuanced, rather than relying on stereotype; (iii) it involves disabled characters as central drivers of a plot and not merely present to teach a moral lesson to non-disabled characters.

Toph Beifong is, I think, a good example of PDP. First, her storyline shows disability gain. Sure, sometimes being disabled makes Toph's life more difficult, but recall how her blindness facilitates her mastery of earthbending. If she had been sighted, Toph would have learned earthbending from a human teacher with her parents' support, rather than from the badgermoles, the original earthbenders. In such a scenario, she likely would have failed to realize her full potential. Relatedly, perhaps Toph's blindness caused her to be more fully immersed in earthbending, thus increasing her skill. Her primary connection to the world is through her ability to "sense" her environment through the dirt and rocks around her. Unlike a sighted waterbender, firebender, or airbender who uses their skill at various points when needed, Toph is always engaged in bending as a means to navigate her everyday life. We can imagine that such a complete immersion in earthbending would make her even more adept at it and should be considered a disability gain.

Toph also exhibits PDP's second feature: she is fully realized and nuanced. Many disabled characters in TV, film, and literature are mere regurgitations of disability stereotypes, lacking complexity or depth. Pop culture has many stereotypes, including disabled villains like Doctor Strangelove or Captain Hook. The writers of *ATLA* avoid playing into any of these stereotypes by portraying Toph being a fully realized character with a complex set of personality traits, emotions, and motivations. One example is Toph's approach to training Aang, or rather her flexibility in approach. After frustration mounts as Aang tries and fails to do the simplest of earthbending tasks, Toph subtly but importantly shifts her pedagogy. Instead of showing tough love with sarcastic quips about him lacking the steadfast disposition needed to earthbend, she compliments his ability to confront a saber-tooth moose lion, exclaiming "Earthbend, Twinkle Toes. You just stood your ground against a crazy beast. And even more impressive, you stood your ground against me. You've got the stuff" ("Bitter Work").

Third, Toph is one of the main drivers of the plot, not just a teacher of moral lessons to the "real" non-disabled protagonist, who is actually moving things along. Clearly, Toph is not present in *ATLA* only to teach a special lesson to Team Avatar, but is a fully integrated partner who plays a key role in bringing about the events depicted.

Ultimately, Toph is a great example of PDP. She gives disabled viewers "permission" to celebrate their own experiences of disability by serving as a pertinent counterstory to some of the damaging master narratives we have discussed.

Notes

1. Hilde Lindemann Nelson, *Damaged Identity, Narrative Repair* (Ithaca, NY: Cornell University Press, 2001).
2. Lindemann Nelson, 71.
3. Lindemann Nelson, 6.
4. Lindemann Nelson, vii, 21.
5. Joseph A. Stramondo, "How Disability Activism Advances Disability Bioethics," *Ethical Theory and Moral Practice* 25 (2022), 335–349.
6. Charles Dickens, *A Christmas Carol* (Philadelphia, PA: J.B. Lippincott Company, 1915), 83.
7. Ronald Amundson, "Disability, Ideology, and Quality of Life: A Bias in Biomedical Ethics," in David Wasserman, Jerome Bickenbach, and Robert Wachbroit eds., *Quality of Life and Human Difference: Genetic Testing, Health Care, and Disability* (New York: Cambridge University Press, 2005), 103.
8. Michael Oliver, *The Politics of Disablement* (Basingstoke: Macmillan, 1990).
9. Teresa Blankmeyer Burke, "Armchairs and Stares: On the Privation of Deafness," in H-Dirksen L. Bauman and Joseph J. Murray eds., *Deaf Gain: Raising the Stakes for Human Diversity* (Minneapolis: University of Minnesota Press, 2014), 3–22.
10. Sami Schalk, "Reevaluating the Supercrip," *Journal of Literary and Cultural Disability Studies* 10 (2016), 77–78.
11. Deborah Kaplan, "The Definition of Disability: Perspective of the Disability Community," *Journal of Health Care Law and Policy* 3 (2000), 352–364.

12. Biography.com editors, "Oscar Pistorius Biography," *Biography.com,* March 26, 2021, at https://www.biography.com/athlete/oscar-pistorius.
13. Lindemann Nelson, 150.
14. Elizabeth Barnes, *The Minority Body: A Theory of Disability* (New York: Oxford University Press, 2016).
15. Barnes, 169–172.
16. Barnes, 182.
17. Barnes, 183–184.

The Earth King, Ignorance, and Responsibility

Saba Fatima

In the "Tales of Ba Sing Se" there is a beautiful depiction of the friendship between Katara and Toph, where they treat themselves to a girls' day out at the Fancy Lady Day Spa. Afterwards, they walk the delightfully manicured paths of the city. The walk is ruined by three older girls who make fun of Toph's makeup, but after dealing expertly with these bullies, the two friends continue their walk. The urban landscape is simply breathtaking, and the city looks clean and peaceful. Everything seems to have its place and function; it seems that one can truly absorb the joys of life there. Ah! What a life it would be to live in Ba Sing Se.

But this seemingly peaceful city is completely removed from the realities of the ongoing conquest. The world is engulfed in a 100-year war, a war in which the Fire Nation has committed a genocide of the Air Nomads and effectively gained control over the Southern Water Tribes and most of the Earth Kingdom. The only bastions left against the Fire Nation are the Northern Water Tribe and, of course, Ba Sing Se, since the city of Omashu has recently fallen. Given this chaotic state of affairs, the serene atmosphere in Ba Sing Se seems surreal. In fact, the Avatar team (Aang, Katara, Sokka, Toph, and Momo) can sense something is wrong as soon as they enter the city.

Toph, an earthbender from a noble and rich family, already seems jaded to the grand spectacle and calls the city "a bunch of walls and rules" ("City of Walls and Secrets"). When the Avatar team first arrive, they are greeted by Joo Dee, their host, who insists that there is no war in Ba Sing Se and that everyone is safe there. If the Avatar and his friends were any other dignitaries and did not have an urgent message to deliver to the King, they might have been quite impressed with how calm and beautiful everything was. But because they are on a mission – one to inform the King of a viable plan to attack the Fire Nation during the upcoming solar eclipse – they uncover exactly how unsafe and vulnerable Ba Sing Se really is. As fans

Avatar: The Last Airbender and Philosophy: Wisdom from Aang to Zuko, First Edition.
Edited by Helen De Cruz and Johan De Smedt.
© 2023 John Wiley & Sons, Inc. Published 2023 by John Wiley & Sons, Inc.

know, the city eventually falls to the invading Fire Nation armies. So who is responsible for the downfall of the city?

This chapter will make the case that the Earth King of Ba Sing Se, King Kuei, willfully maintained ignorance of the true state of his kingdom so that he could enjoy the privileges that came with his position, while remaining derelict in his duty to his people. The King maintains this ignorance at the expense of his people, both by condoning certain urban designs and by resisting knowledge that upsets his lifestyle.

Walls: Creating Order and . . . Barriers

When the Avatar team first arrive at Ba Sing Se in "City of Walls and Secrets," Joo Dee tells them that the city has many walls and each wall serves a purpose, but we know there is more to the walls than their utility. After all, one of the ways that governments suppress political expression is through urban space planning; city designs can either give visibility to or cloak social, political, and economic issues.[1] While riding a train, team Avatar get a glimpse of the city from above: it looks magnificent with its long, winding, circular walls, each wall dividing one part of the city from the next. The tallest and widest wall, the Outer Wall, protects the city from outside and contains farmlands. The rest of the walls form rings within the city that divide people by their station in society. The lower ring houses artisans and craftsmen, people who keep the city running. In today's world, they might be termed essential workers and be paid a low wage. This lower ring is also the space where war refugees and other people displaced by the war reside. The middle ring contains the financial district, shops, restaurants, the Town Hall, and the homes of the middle class. The uppermost ring contains the political elite, such as military leaders, dignitaries, and of course the King's palace. It is within this ring that the Avatar team is lodged.

This sort of city planning all but ensures segregation between the socioeconomic classes and prevents any organization of community-based resistance. The walls maintain order, but they also shield the people in the middle and upper rings from the harsh reality of the lives of the people in the lower ring. Even Zuko, the Fire Nation prince, who is seeking refuge in Ba Sing Se's lower ring remarks that "This city is a prison. I don't want to make a life here" ("City of Walls and Secrets"). Zuko, who grew up as a prince and now is living as a refugee, comprehends the depth of disparity between the elite and the poor. For him, the city is far from serene and welcoming. It is constricting and overpopulated, and providing little access to the amenities we see at the beginning of "Tales of Ba Sing Se." But a person doesn't need to live in the lower ring to realize that the city is structured in a way that marginalizes essential workers, the poor, and the refugees, and that it keeps these people out of sight for the elite.

The way that the city is built allows the King and other members of the elite to be willfully shielded from the actual state of affairs of the war outside the outer walls and the poverty within the lower ring. The walls promote artificial social homogeneity and prevent cross-economic and cultural socialization. Sarah Schindler, a contemporary legal scholar, writes that man-made physical structures are often built in ways to block off access to certain regions for poor people and people of color.[2] Examples include an absence of sidewalks and crosswalks, low-hanging bridges that block access to public transport, and actual walls and physical blockades that restrict movement from predominantly Black neighborhoods to predominantly white neighborhoods. Schindler illuminates how elite classes live detached from lower and middle classes by design. Barriers are often made to appear as the natural order of things – for instance, missing sidewalks – and/or "aesthetically pleasing" design features of a physical space – such as the winding walls of Ba Sing Se, or the "attractive" covered bridges in the US that are too low for public transport to pass through. But they are anything but natural. These elements that may seem beautiful to the privileged are actually imprisoning for the vulnerable.

One could argue that often there is no malicious intent behind these design features and that it is quite possible that the primary purpose of lower ring wall was not to shield the Earth Kings from the realities of war and poverty. However, it is not intent that is important here, but rather the impact of retaining this urban planning. The walls allow the elite to live their lives in luxury without ever seeing the refugees and the poor.

Katara voices this very concern as she takes the monorail to the uppermost ring of the city, when she remarks: "Why do they have all these poor people blocked off in one part of the city?" Aang responds, "This is why I never came here before. I always heard it was so different from the way the monks taught us to live." Here, Aang is presumably referring to the way that Air Nomad monks generally lived a life of simplicity. For example, in "The Guru," Guru Pathik teaches that we live in world of illusion of separation, and that we are actually all one. Thus, the airbenders would not condone the segregation of the city dwellers. The Earth King purposely lives in an environment that allows him to stay oblivious to everything around him and live comfortably in affluence. The walls are built in a way to maintain his privilege through stratification between people who hold varying degrees of privilege. Furthermore, the refugees in the lower ring cannot revolt because that could mean expulsion back into the war zone. And those who are brave enough to protest are detained and brainwashed by the secret police, the Dai Li. For example, after Jet was arrested for creating a ruckus about Iroh and Zuko being firebenders, he was sent to the Dai Li base underneath Lake Laogai and consequently brainwashed into believing that there is no war in Ba Sing Se ("City of Walls and Secrets").

In "The Earth King" we see that in order for team Avatar to convince him of the war outside the walls, the King has to take the monorail to the edge of the outer walls. At this point, we learn that the King has never stepped foot in a train, been outside of his palace, or even walked among his people. The Earth King has maintained a life that is completely isolated from the everyday people he rules.

Must Resist Knowing Any Different

In "The Earth King," the Avatar team is finally able to break into the palace to tell the King about the devasting war with the Fire Nation. But understandably, he does not believe the kids right away, until they show him the remains of a drill that the Fire Nation used to attempt breaking the outer wall of Ba Sing Se. At that moment, he says: "I can't believe I never knew." While we, as the audience, breathe a sigh of relief, we may also feel bewildered at the King's statement. The philosophical concept of "epistemic ignorance" provides an excellent explanation of what allowed the King to remain unknowing about the war, even in the face of overwhelming evidence. Generally, when we think of ignorance, we think of absence of knowledge, something that can be rectified by simply learning more about the facts of the matter. For example, if someone was asked to name the capital of Nepal and they did not know it, we might say that this person simply does not know this particular fact and that they can rectify this ignorance by looking it up (it is Kathmandu). But there is more to epistemic ignorance than an absence of rectifiable knowledge. Epistemology is the study of figuring out how one knows something. So *epistemic ignorance* is the study of how or why we do not know certain things. Contemporary philosophers, such as Charles Mills, Miranda Fricker, and José Medina, have argued that we do not know certain facts about the world we live in by design.[3] Purposely remaining ignorant of certain facts helps the King of Ba Sing Se maintain his privilege.

Consider this scenario: suppose Ted, an older white cis man runs a successful talk show. During his run as the late-night host, he makes numerous misogynist comments to his guests – particularly to the women on his show – and his daily monologue contains sexist quips. Now suppose some feminists explain to him how his remarks uphold patriarchy in our society. In this example, it would be in Ted's interest to remain ignorant of feminist worldviews because acknowledging feminist insights might mean losing some or much of the privilege that comes from being an older white cis male who generates his wealth making these tired jokes. In fact, to keep up his ignorance, Ted may even insist that he cannot be sexist because he hires women all the time. What epistemic ignorance teaches us is that Ted willfully refuses to understand feminist perspectives. While he may genuinely believe that his jokes are mere jokes and that he is simply bantering with his guests, he actually displays willful ignorance by resisting knowing anything that would upend his affluent life by being accountable for the harm caused by his ignorance. But, at the same time, Ted can effortlessly recall plenty of evidence that would confirm the "knowledge" that he is not sexist.

Earth King Kuei is like Ted. Not only does he live in a way that physically shields him from actually knowing his people, he also does not care enough to know the affairs of his kingdom. In our scenario, the feminists are the Avatar team, who tell the King that his kingdom is in danger, but he finds the claim ridiculous. He clings to Long Feng (the Grand Secretariat, who is the head of the Dai Li) as a means of disproving the Avatar's assertions ("The Earth King"). Kuei expresses no genuine interest in his duties and spends most of his time entertaining his pet bear, Bosco, who enjoys the best of foods and even has a party thrown in his honor ("City of Walls and Secrets"). In fact, the King is so taken by his pet that the only reason he is even willing to hear the Avatar's message about the war is that Bosco has shown an interest in the Avatar. Throughout Book Two, we realize that it is not simply that the king is ignorant of the things going on in his magnificent city. Rather, even when he is shown evidence he cannot deny – much like the feminists who explain to Ted why his sexist "banter" is harmful to women – Kuei does not recognize the danger his city is in. Even when he sees the remnants of the Fire Nation drill on the outer walls, he chooses to delegate all that he can so that he can maintain his affluent lifestyle ("The Earth King").

Philosopher Shannon Sullivan explains that people who are in power or who carry certain privileges (such as being able-bodied, male, white, etc.) have their sense of knowledge shaped by ignorance.[4] This knowledge/ ignorance is constructed in our heads via what we are taught – such as the lie that Ba Sing Se is serene and secure – *and* what we are not taught – such as no information about the 100-year war raging outside the city. Knowledge and ignorance are thus intertwined to form what we consider "knowledge." The Dai Li, the secret police of Ba Sing Se, are even more extreme in their attempt to maintain ignorance as they brainwash anyone who resists into "knowing" that there is no war in Ba Sing Se – as was the case with Joo Dee in "City of Walls and Secrets" and in "Lake Laogai." In this sense, there is a collective denial of the war, especially within the middle and upper rings. And this collective denial is relatively easy to maintain as the ignorance is actively fostered by the state.[5] There are many examples of this in our day-to-day life as well. For example, in our school systems, we are taught *a* particular version of history, generally one that has the approval of the state. In fact, some nation-states actively ban teaching the history of minorities in their country. In the case of Ba Sing Se, this knowledge/ignorance is just more actively maintained by brainwashing anyone who directs too much attention toward the war. And this actively produced knowledge/ignorance ("there is no war in Ba Sing Se") helps maintain the knowledge/ignorance of the Earth King. Because he is so powerful and lives a life of leisure, he has no need to work to undo that ignorance. For Kuei, the facade of peace is maintained via a violent police state and through class segregation. More importantly, he maintains his epistemic state quite willfully because it is to his benefit.

The Buck Stops Here

Initially, when one watches Book Two, one may think that the "real" evil character is Grand Secretariat Long Feng, who seems to be the mastermind behind the "foolish" King. He makes a concerted effort to keep the King out of the day-to-day affairs of Ba Sing Se. For example, during the party for Bosco, Long Feng throws a wrench in team Avatar's plan to alert the Earth King about the war with the Fire Nation. Instead, he pulls Aang and his friends aside into a private meeting to intimidate them. We learn from this meeting that the King is merely a figurehead and Long Feng is not only the Grand Secretariat but also the head of the secret police, the Dai Li. He then explicitly threatens Aang and his friends and lets them know that any attempt to inform the King of the true events will result in expulsion from the city, which would make their search for Appa more difficult. Furthermore, the Dai Li, under the leadership of Long Feng, brainwash anyone who mentions the war or attempts to raise awareness about the plight of the refugees.

Given this, it is easy to villainize Long Feng and consider the King a "mere" fool. This desire to place blame on an all-nefarious character plays into an archetype where there is supposedly a more evil, sinister person behind the person who appears to wield the power. This desire to villainize secondary players in politics leads to a failure to demand accountability of those in power. It lets us pretend that the King is one of the good guys.

But the truth is that the Earth King *does* wield power. It is true that Kuei became a ruler at a very young age, but he had many years to reform and make himself a king worthy of his people. Instead, he buried himself in his pleasures and did everything he could to maintain his physical and epistemic distance from the state of affairs of the Earth Nation. Even when Long Feng is finally exposed – no credit to the King here – for betraying the political interest of the Earth Kingdom, the King still does not step up to his responsibilities, but rather delegates the real work of planning to the Council of Five. After learning of such a massive betrayal, the Earth King yet again places his trust in who he erroneously believes to be Kyoshi Warriors ("The Earth King"). He fails to realize that they are actually the Fire Nation Princess and her friends in disguise. He not only accidently reveals to them the plans of invasion of the Fire Nation, he also eventually flees the city, leaving Azula in control of Ba Sing Se.

So, although the King is portrayed as childlike, absorbed in himself, and incapable of making decisions without the direction of others, he *is* an adult with a great deal of privilege. Simply because we cannot attach a malicious intent to him, does not absolve him of his responsibilities as a ruler. In fact, it is precisely the privileges attached to being a rich king that compel the audience to give him the benefit of the doubt. A similar level of charity in judgment – for example, viewing someone as having childlike innocence – would not be afforded to a common soldier or a peasant from the lower ring who had committed a crime. The King actively causes a lot of harm to the Earth Kingdom and the world at large. The greatest villainy then lies not in Long Feng's conniving, but in the King's success in maintaining his power and privilege through urban barriers and willful ignorance.

Ultimately, we have to pay attention to architectural and epistemic barriers that keep the elite, including the King, secluded from the lower and middle classes, from poverty, from dissent, and shielded from a 100-year war that threatens the city. The King's willful ignorance about the state of affairs in his kingdom requires accountability. If such abuse of power and privilege is not held accountable, no real change can occur. For in the end, the King remains the same self-absorbed monarch and the walls that divide fellow humans by class remain intact; even the Dai Li survive the war.

Notes

1. Jeffrey Hou and Sabine Knierbein, "Shrinking Democracy and Urban Resistance: Toward an Emancipatory Politics of Public Space," in Jeffrey Hou and Sabine Knierbein eds., *City Unsilenced: Urban Resistance and Public Space in the Age of Shrinking Democracy* (New York: Routledge, 2017), 3–15.
2. Sarah Schindler, "Architectural Exclusion: Discrimination and Segregation Through Physical Design of the Built Environment," *The Yale Law Journal* 124 (2015), 1934–2024.
3. Charles Mills, "White Ignorance," in Shannon Sullivan and Nancy Tuana eds., *Race and Epistemologies of Ignorance* (Albany, NY: SUNY Press, 2007), 13–38; Miranda Fricker, *Epistemic Injustice: Power and the Ethics of Knowing* (Oxford: Oxford University Press, 2007); José Medina, *The Epistemology of Resistance: Gender and Racial Oppression, Epistemic Injustice, and Resistant Imaginations* (Oxford: Oxford University Press, 2013).
4. Shannon Sullivan, "White Ignorance and Colonial Oppression: or, Why I Know So Little of Puerto Rico," in Shannon Sullivan and Nancy Tuana eds., *Race and Epistemologies of Ignorance* (Albany: SUNY Press, 2007), 153–172.
5. For more on this, see Chapter 14: "There Is No Truth in Ba Sing Se."

17

The Middle Way and the Many Faces of Earth

Thomas Arnold

How one-sided are earth, earthbending, and earth-related society in *ATLA*? Seemingly very, but actually not at all. As we'll see, the show slowly reveals that there is more to earth than initially meets the eye. In gently leading us beyond one-sided appearances and in showing us how false alternatives can be left behind in favor of better options, *ATLA* turns out to be a deeply philosophical work of art.

Earth Is Earth Is Earth Is Earth?

Even more so than with the other elements, earth, earthbending, and earth-related society initially appear to be fairly one-dimensional: earth is rough, earthbenders are tough (not to say "Toph"), they exhibit a firm will and a brute strength, and the society of the Earth Kingdom is rigid – like rock. To rephrase Gertrude Stein's famous line: Earth is earth is earth is earth. (Incidentally, "Stein" means "rock" in German and "Gertrude" derives from the Germanic word for "strength.")

The typical earthbender is stoic and not very philosophical or spiritual.[1] Yet, this is not the whole truth, as Uncle Iroh points out in the episode "Bitter Work." When teaching Prince Zuko the basic meanings of the different elements, Iroh characterizes earth as the element of "substance" and adds "the people of the Earth Kingdom are diverse and strong. They are persistent and enduring." Strength, persistence, and endurance all fit the cliché of earthiness, but diversity does not. However, if we follow Iroh's hint, Earth reveals its many faces.

As *ATLA* illustrates, toughness and hardness can be accompanied by great sensitivity, rigidity by openness, roughness by love. Thus, the show sets up a one-sided stereotype which over time dissolves into a balanced, at

Avatar: The Last Airbender and Philosophy: Wisdom from Aang to Zuko, First Edition.
Edited by Helen De Cruz and Johan De Smedt.
© 2023 John Wiley & Sons, Inc. Published 2023 by John Wiley & Sons, Inc.

times even ambivalent picture of everything earth-related; earth beyond stoniness, so to speak.

King Bumi rules Omashu, which is introduced as an ordered and well-organized city, with mighty walls and tough guards who kick out the cabbage merchant due to some rotten cabbages in his load ("My cabbages!") and demand respect for the elderly – so far, so earthy. In a flashback however, the young not-yet-king Bumi asks Aang to look around and admonishes him, "Instead of seeing what they want you to see, you gotta open your brain to the possibilities" ("The King of Omashu"). On the one hand, Bumi is the head of a strict hierarchy, but on the other, he is so very open-minded and fun-loving as to be unpredictable. He appears to be weak and old, but turns out to be old and very strong indeed. He seems mad and indeed remains a little crazy on a second, third, or even fourth look, but he is also highly rational, for example, when he initially refrains from fighting the Fire Nation. Even the encounter with his pet, Flopsie, is steeped in this duality. Initially, Flopsie appears to be a small rabbit-like creature, then turns out to be a gigantic goat gorilla – which in turn first seems to be extremely wild, angry, and dangerous, but then reveals itself to be (mostly) playful and (mostly) harmless. At the conclusion of the episode, the fast-growing crystal (jennamite) which had appeared to threaten Katara's and Sokka's lives, is shown to be just rock candy. Earth is not quite earth, after all. Later in the series, this duality of appearance and substance takes on the much more sinister quality of subterfuge, propaganda, and brainwashing once Team Avatar gets to Ba Sing Se. Recall the slogan "There is no war in Ba Sing Se."[2]

Toph Beifong is introduced in the toughest, roughest possible setting, Earth Rumble 6, an earthbending tournament in which the audience is in danger of getting killed by flying rocks even before the event actually commences ("The Blind Bandit"). Toph goes on to quickly defeat "The Boulder" after he overcomes his conflicted feelings about fighting a little blind girl.[3] When the Aang Gaang visit her at home, she initially tries to uphold appearances in order to confirm her parents' image of her as a helpless young lady of high standing. Once she joins Team Avatar, she affirms her wild, "earthen" identity and reveals herself as a merciless, even slightly sadistic fighter, as well as an incredibly tough and hard teacher. Then again, she is also very sensitive – not just to movement, but to lying as well – and vulnerable, although she does not like people perceiving her in that way. In "The Tales from Ba Sing Se" we even see her enjoying a "girls' day out" with Katara, including a visit to the Fancy Lady Day Spa.

Importantly, in the comic-book *The Rift* we witness how Toph's Father, Lao Beifong, initially refuses to accept Toph as his daughter because she displays none of the behavior he wants her to adopt.[4] Once he accepts her powerful and wild side, they reconcile and she even acts as a representative and executive partner of Earthen Fire Industries, his business venture, thus incorporating both the shrewd business side of her family as well as her own nature.

Additionally, despite being a supposedly non-imaginative earthbender, Toph is also the most innovative bender in the series, as she invents a new bending discipline, metalbending. In fact, earthbending itself spawns the most sub-disciplines within the *Avatar* universe: metalbending, sandbending, glassbending (as witnessed in the novel *The Shadow of Kyoshi*[5]), and lavabending.

Earthbending is not quite what it seems. While it appears to be basically nothing more than throwing rocks about, which might be good for building stuff and conducting siege warfare, in the tale of "The Cave of Two Lovers" we learn that the original human use of earthbending was motivated by love and the need for secrecy. Oma and Shu, two lovers from feuding villages meet in secret. After learning earthbending from the badgermoles, they create a labyrinth under the Kolau Mountains between their villages which only they can navigate. Far from the blunt practicality of typical earthbending activities, the first earthbenders used their abilities for reasons of evasion and freedom from strife – motives not typically associated with earthbending!

Earth, earthbending, and earthbenders turn out to be much more complex and multi-faceted than they initially seem. Put a little more abstractly: their initial appearance does not represent their whole substance. The ethical import is clear: don't judge a book by its cover. Rather than trust one-sided appearances, we ought to sound out the hidden depths, otherwise we might miss something essential, the crystal inside the geode, so to speak.

So far, we have progressed from one-sidedness to (at least) two-sidedness, from cliché to reality, from the definite to the ambiguous, even from appearance to substance. We can also see duality, ambiguity, or two-sidedness outside of the Earth element. In "The Avatar and the Firelord," both Iroh and Aang independently voice the idea of a duality in the story of Sozin and Roku, and interpret it as a reason for hope, and the condition of possibility to escape the current conflict. At the end of this episode, once the entanglement of the former Fire Lord and the former Avatar has become apparent, Aang draws the conclusion, "If anything, their story proves anyone's capable of great good and great evil." At the same time, Iroh tells Zuko, "Born in you, along with all this strife, is the power to restore balance to the world." Understanding and recognizing the two conflicting sides within himself and the chance this ambivalence or duality offers, appears to be a turning point in Zuko's redemption. Let us now progress from two-sidedness to three-sidedness and explore how earth, earthbending, and earthbenders exemplify the idea of "the middle way."

Neither/Nor

ATLA is full of conflicts. These range from inner struggles to quarrelling within the team, from the fight between two tribes[6] to the Great War. Most of these conflicts are framed as a seemingly exhaustive alternative: to be friend or foe, to be in or out, to win or lose, to kill or be killed. The parties involved equally see themselves as polar opposites: good vs. evil, strong vs. weak, beautiful vs. ugly, and – ultimately – us vs. them. Prominent examples are Aang's fight against Fire Lord Ozai and the Avatar's scruples about killing another person, and Zuko's quest to regain his honor and Uncle Iroh's intervention.[7] In all these cases, the protagonists are faced with two extremes.

ATLA (and the Avatar) deals with these conflicts by rejecting false alternatives, both explicitly and implicitly. More often than not, some third option is discovered, a way out – a middle way – and the conflict is resolved or dissolved rather than simply solved. (A mere solution accepts and perpetuates the premise of a conflict, whereas a resolution or dissolution rejects the initial framework as conceptually flawed to begin with.) Instead of choosing one of two sides, the whole presupposition of irreconcilable and contradictory sides is put into question in the series. The Avatar, after all, is the great bridge between worlds (not just between those of spirits and humans), but also between different sides. Thus, he fights evil, but he does not give in to its logic: he does not strive to kill or win, just to end conflicts. Aang's or Ozai's deaths would be solutions to the conflict as Ozai conceives of it, but neither death would resolve the conflict.

Rather than killing Ozai or letting himself be killed, Aang takes Ozai's power of bending. With the help of the Lion Turtle, he finds an option that allows him to stop the Fire Lord while retaining his Air Nomad principles. The framework of "kill or be killed" is dissolved, invalidated through Aang's feat of energybending. Likewise, Prince Zuko ultimately rejects the dichotomizing worldview and self-image his father had forced on him, thus winning friends and self-esteem, as well as the throne, until finally proclaiming "a new era of love and peace" ("Sozin's Comet, Part 4: Avatar Aang").

The phrase "a middle way" refers to the idea that some alternatives are false. In the *Dhammacakkappavattana Sutta*, considered to be the first sermon of the Buddha, he recommends the "middle way" between the extremes of seeking happiness in sensual pleasures on the one hand and self-mortification on the other.[8] Rather than choosing one of them or compromising between the extremes, the Buddha plainly refuses (these) extremes as our only options. He simply rejects the alternative "seek pleasure or seek pain" and offers the middle way as a life in which we seek neither pleasure nor pain, but understanding, care, and finally cessation of striving and strife.[9]

In Western philosophy, the terms "false alternative," "false dilemma," and "false dichotomy" refer to an informal fallacy which revolves around exactly such an illegitimate restriction of options. "You are either with us or against us" is a clear example – it is false because a person or group could be undecided or uninvolved. Philosophy (especially logic) provides the tools to uncover such fallacious reasoning and problematic assumptions.

As *ATLA* is full of such false alternatives and their resolution or dissolution, the show functions as practical philosophy (be it Western, Native American, or Asian), teaching us to question alternatives and seek a middle way.

Earth's Many Ways

To see how *ATLA* does this beyond the major conflicts already mentioned, let's take a closer look at our examples from Earth. As it turns out, not only do they teach us to see two-sidedness, ambiguity, or duality, they also reveal and incorporate the tenets of the middle way, that is, the rejection of false alternatives.

King Bumi is very much one to think outside the box, up to the point of leaving boxes altogether – as he himself acknowledges by omission. In response to Katara's question to Aang, "So, this crazy king is your old friend Bumi?," the king only says "Who you calling old? Ok, I'm old" ("The King of Omashu"). Bumi forces Aang to think differently from the way he normally would, as none of the tasks Bumi assigns to him are at all straightforward. For Aang's confrontation with Fire Lord Ozai, Bumi advises Aang to "think like a mad genius" ("The King of Omashu"). In this case, madness and being crazy represent the middle. Luckily, Bumi's hope is fulfilled and Aang finds an extra option to end the final confrontation, the "crazy" idea of neither killing nor being killed, realized through his "mad," newly acquired skill of energybending.

Bumi explicitly discards another important alternative in "Return to Omashu." When describing the ideal earthbending teacher to Aang, Bumi explains the idea of "neutral jing." "Neutral jing" refers to a stance beyond attacking and retreating – a third option to direct your energy. This third option eschews both offense and defense; it is neither one nor the other. Thus, the alternative between fight and flight is rejected, in favor of listening and waiting, or simply doing nothing for the time being – which is precisely the idea behind Bumi's reluctance to initially defend himself and his city against the attack of the Fire Nation. As we find out in the course of their dialogue, there are many more jings ("technically, there are 85"), some of which Momo might or might not have mastered, depending on whether we trust King Bumi in his assessment of the winged lemur's abilities.

Another bad case of either/or thinking underpins how Toph's parents see the world, namely as exhaustively divided into capable, "normal" people and helpless disabled ones – a false alternative Toph undermines, as she is both blind *and* powerful. Arguably, her parents are also sexist, trying to force her to live like a "proper" girl as opposed to an earthbending fighter. Toph fights these false alternatives by finding a middle way, being both a girl and a fierce fighter, just like the Kyoshi warriors.

Lastly, in "The Cave of Two Lovers" Katara reads the story of the two lovers engraved on their tombstones. Through her we witness how they undermine the feud of their villages by falling in love – this can be seen as a first rejection of the false alternative "one village or the other, us or them." When Shu is killed, Oma is stricken with grief and unleashes a "terrible display of her earthbending power. She could have destroyed them all," Katara tells us. This would have constituted another way to reject the false alternative by simply negating both sides and demolishing both villages. However, in doing so, Oma would have remained within the logic of war and opposition itself, positing herself as over against the villages, perpetuating the violence, "but instead she declared the war over. Both villages helped her build a new city where they would live together in peace." This is the true and lasting rejection of the false dilemma, because now the whole framework of the war is gone and the question "us or them" becomes meaningless as both become part of something greater, the city of Omashu, a monument to love and loss. This way, neither side wins nor loses, because winning and losing are both tied to a conflict that is now dissolved.

An honorable mention for finding a middle way goes to the comic-book *The Promise*, in which the decolonialization of Yu Dao becomes a hot topic, bringing the Earth Kingdom and the Fire Nation to the brink of war, and Aang close to killing Zuko.[10] The false alternative we are faced with here is embedded in the question of whether the city of Yu Dao belongs exclusively either to the Fire Nation or the Earth Kingdom. It takes almost the whole book for the protagonists to understand that these options are not exhaustive, but in the end, the question is answered by a resounding "both" as well as "neither."

What Can We Learn?

Earthbenders embody the idea that we do not have to accept a worldview based on polar opposites. Instead, as these characters in *ATLA* show, we can reject such false alternatives and pick a third (fourth, fifth) way: we may very well also choose neither or both. The suggestion to look for more options, rather than to accept what is handed to us, is one of the core ethical as well as conceptual ideas of the show, exemplified in part by the many faces, facets, and ways of earth. Obviously, similar cases can be made for the other elements and other characters. A parallel two-step from one-sidedness to ambiguity and from polar opposites to the middle way is presented by the sun warriors in "The Fire-Bending Masters." In this episode, the chieftain explains to Aang that "Fire is life, not just destruction." Fire is not identical with any of its appearances. It is substantially beautiful and horrible; it can bring warmth and pain; it is one thing as well as another. But the sun warriors' teachings also stress a middle way, in that fire should be neither too small, nor too big. (And might we speculate that the right jing for fire is not so much a positive, attacking jing, but a dancing jing?)

Following the show's logic, what can we learn? First, questioning one-sided accounts often rewards us with substantial, rich complexity; almost nothing simply is what it is, and no one is simply who they appear to be. Bumi is not just the old head of a strict hierarchy, Toph is neither just tough nor just a little helpless girl, and earthbending is not just (for) throwing rocks about.

Second, we learn that not every pair of alternatives is exhaustive and that conflicts often rest on false dilemmas. Such conflicts could easily be resolved or dissolved by dismantling their faulty underlying assumptions. We do not have to choose between positive or negative jing. We do not have to split the world into girls and fighters, helpless disabled people and powerful able-bodied people. And we do not have to choose sides in a conflict. Instead, we can (sometimes) reject and end the conflict itself.

These ideas are fundamental to logic as well as ethics. One-sided thinking is superficial and reductive; it leads to over-simplification when engaging with other people and doing research. Thinking only in polar opposites leads us to take any nuanced difference as fundamental disagreement, any critical opposition as indiscriminate enmity, enabling tribalism and populism. Thinking only in polar opposites forces us to accept ideologies foreign to our own thinking on pain of being ostracized. Rescinding such thinking allows us to develop a nuanced perspective. It fosters peaceful coexistence and productive dispute, that is to say, plurality. Showing (rather than preaching) this logic and its beneficial effects to both kids and adults is, to my mind, the most profound philosophical achievement of *ATLA*.

Notes

1. See Chapter 3: "The Personalities of Martial Arts in *Avatar: The Last Airbender*."
2. For more on the capital city of the Earth Kingdom, see Chapter 14: "There Is No Truth in Ba Sing Se."
3. For more on Toph and her disability, see Chapter 15: "The Rocky Terrain of Disability Gain in *Avatar: The Last Airbender*."
4. Gene Luen Yang, *The Rift* (Milwaukie: Dark Horse Comics, 2015).
5. F.C. Yee and Michael Dante DiMartino, *The Shadow of Kyoshi* (New York: Amulet Books, 2020).
6. See "The Great Divide," Book One, Episode 11, in which two Earth Kingdom tribes, the Gan Jin and the Zhang quarrel. Interestingly, Aang solves the old conflict by convincing both tribes that their grudge rests on conflicting, but equally wrong stories about the same event. While this initially looks like a great parable about one-sidedness, lack of communication and distortion of facts through history, it (also) turns out to be a lesson in the power of fiction, as Aang simply made the "original," "true" story up on the spot.

7. For more on Aang's dilemma, see Chapter 26: "Ahimsa and Aang's Dilemma."

8. *Samyutta Nikaya* 56.11, in Bhikkhu Bodhi, *The Connected Discourses of the Buddha* (Boston: Wisdom Publications, 2000).

9. For close connections between Buddhism and *ATLA*, see Chapter 25: "A Buddhist Perspective on Energy Bending, Strength, and the Power of Aang's Spirit" and Chapter 27: "The Avatar Meets the Karmapa."

10. Gene Luen Yang, *The Promise* (Milwaukie: Dark Horse Comics, 2013).

PART IV
FIRE

18

The Battle Within

Confucianism and Legalism in the Nation, the Family, and the Soul

Kody W. Cooper

Confucianism and Legalism are two schools of Chinese philosophy. This chapter will explore contrasts between Confucian and Legalist visions of the nation, the family, and the soul through Zuko's journey. We'll uncover the tension between the legacies of his two great-grandfathers, Sozin and Roku, and see that the battle within Zuko and the royal family is at root a philosophical struggle between these two differing philosophical visions. Finally, we'll see that Zuko's battle within reflects something true about human nature that the Legalists and the Confucians partly grasped, and which one twentieth-century villain-turned-hero, Aleksandr Solzhenitsyn, helps clarify.

The Fire Lord's Legalist Philosophy

The Chinese Legalists were a school of thinkers and officials who were influential in the Qin dynasty (221–206 BCE). One of the most prominent Legalists, Han Fei (c. 280–233 BCE) was skeptical about the goodness of human nature. He adopted the axiom from his teacher Xunzi that "human nature is evil."[1] Hence, the Legalists believed that people are born bad and therefore need strict parental and legal rule with terrifying sanctions for their breach, as Toph once mused about citizens in the Fire Nation ("The Avatar and the Firelord").

After Zuko spoke out against a cynical military stratagem to sacrifice a division of new recruits, the Fire Lord accused him of filial disrespect. Ozai sentenced Zuko to duel him in an *agni kai*. Prostrated before his father, Zuko refused to fight, apologized, and asked for mercy: "I meant you no disrespect. I am your loyal son." Ozai replied in Legalist fashion by

Avatar: The Last Airbender and Philosophy: Wisdom from Aang to Zuko, First Edition.
Edited by Helen De Cruz and Johan De Smedt.
© 2023 John Wiley & Sons, Inc. Published 2023 by John Wiley & Sons, Inc.

inflicting the severe punishment of burning his son's face: "You will learn respect. And suffering will be your teacher" ("The Storm").

Ozai shared this view with his father Azulon, the previous Fire Lord: to show mercy would result in disorder and chaos. Several years before, when Ozai's brother Iroh lost his son Lu Ten and his bloodline ended, Ozai beseeched Azulon to revoke Iroh's birthright: "I am your humble servant here to serve you and our nation. Use me." Azulon reacted with fury: "You dare suggest I betray Iroh, my firstborn!? Directly after the demise of his only beloved son? I think Iroh has suffered enough. But you? Your punishment has scarcely begun!" ("Zuko Alone") Azulon then commanded a severe penalty: Ozai would have to kill his own son Zuko so that he could understand the pain Iroh had suffered. Azulon did not command this cruelty for cruelty's sake. Rather, Legalism required a horrifying penalty to prevent the chaotic cycle of palace intrigue and insurrection that Ozai's plan might spawn. Azulon's sanction doubled as severe parental discipline toward the overly ambitious second son.

The Legalist understanding of parental rule was apparent in other families like the Beifongs. Unbeknownst to her parents, Toph was not a frail, helpless little girl but was actually an incredible earthbender who became the champion of Earth Rumble 6, an earthbending tournament. Her father Lao witnessed Toph's talent with his own eyes when she single-handedly defeated Xin Fu, the Boulder, and several other powerful Earthbenders ("The Blind Bandit").

So why did Lao then announce that Toph would have to be severely punished, by being prevented from competitive earthbending, and be guarded 24 hours a day? Not because she was helpless, but because Toph had disobeyed his parental rule. This required a strict punishment or chaos would ensue. As Han Fei put it, "Indeed, the strictly kept household sees no fierce servants, but a compassionate mother has spoilt children. From this I know that authority and position are able to suppress violence, but that virtue and favor are not sufficient to stop disorder."[2]

Both parents and sovereigns ought to severely punish sanction transgressions: "Humaneness may make one shed tears and be reluctant to apply penalties, but law makes it clear that such penalties must be applied."[3]

This Legalist philosophy informed and was propagated through the public-school system of the Fire Nation. Aang, posing as a Fire Nation colonial named Kuzon, learned from his Fire Nation music teacher that "young people must have rigid discipline and order." After Aang got in a schoolyard fight he had to bring his "parents" to a conference with the headmaster. The headmaster threatened to send Aang to reform school, namely, the coal mines. Sokka, posing as Kuzon's father Wang Fire, knew what the headmaster wanted to hear when he bellowed at Kuzon: "Young man, as soon as we get home, you're going to get the punishment of a lifetime" ("The Headband").

Censure and Legalist Education

The Legalists advocated the governing method of censure, which means "inspection and punishment."[4] Legalists insisted that measures should be in place that clearly delineate a hierarchical relationship between the ruler, his ministers, and the people. As the *Shiji* details, if "the relative duties between superior and inferior are made clear, then none in the empire whether worthy or unworthy, will dare do otherwise than exert his strength and fulfill his duties in devotion to the ruler."[5] This perfectly encapsulates Fire Nation political philosophy under Fire Lord Ozai. As Aang learned while posing as Kuzon, all children began each school day by saluting a picture of the Fire Lord and reciting the Fire Nation Oath:

> My life I give to my country. With my hands I fight for Fire Lord Ozai and our forefathers before him. With my mind I seek ways to better my country. And with my feet may the march of civilization continue. ("The Headband")

Citizens of the Legalist nation were thus taught to see themselves as virtuous. As Fire Lord Sozin, who instigated the war, told Avatar Roku: "Our nation is enjoying an unprecedented time of peace and wealth . . . We should share this prosperity with the rest of the world" ("The Avatar and the Fire Lord"). And Zuko recalls that "Growing up, we were taught that the Fire Nation was the greatest civilization in history, and somehow, the war was our way of sharing our greatness with the rest of the world" ("The Day of Black Sun, Part 2: The Eclipse").

Hence, education in Legalism is subordinated to the purposes of statecraft and empire. Team Avatar discovered this at Wan Shi Tong's Library, which sought to cultivate and protect knowledge for its own sake. The kids sought to find useful information that could help defeat the Fire Lord, only to discover firebenders had invaded the Library and burned the section with all the books about the Fire Nation ("The Library"). This isn't surprising once one understands the underlying Legalist philosophy of the Fire Nation. As Legalist philosopher Li Si advised the emperor: the ruler ought to employ severe measures to solidify his power, and that includes burning all books that could threaten his sovereignty.

The Phoenix King

All of this was ordered to maintain and extend the authority of the Fire Lord. Eventually, Ozai declared that the Fire Nation should burn down the Earth Kingdom and transform the world to a state in which he would be "ruler of everything" ("Sozin's Comet, Part I: The Phoenix King"). In his quest for world domination, he styled himself as the Phoenix King, and demanded that all in his presence bow down to him, as to a god-king.

This is a Legalist conception of the person of the sovereign. As Han Fei explained: "Nothing is more valuable than the royal person, more honourable than the throne, more powerful than the authority of the sovereign, and more august than the position of the ruler."[6]

Doubtless, Zuko received schooling informed by Legalism to form him as his father's heir. Yet, this education was tempered by his mother Ursa's Confucian emphasis on kindness and compassion. While he didn't realize it at the time, after his mother's exile, Zuko's banishment would be the "best thing" Ozai could have done for his son because it put him "on the right path" to receive a Confucian education from his uncle ("Sozin's Comet, Part 4: Avatar Aang").

Zuko's Confucian Schooling

Scarred and banished, Zuko began a quest to capture the Avatar. Accompanied by his Confucian uncle Iroh, Zuko slowly learned an alternative to Legalist philosophy.[7] Iroh taught that humaneness (*ren*), mercy toward others, self-restraint, education, and learning did *not* lead to disorder, that is, to one's inner life and external relationships becoming something akin to an overturned cart of cabbages.

Iroh's education of Zuko combined exhortation with example. While they were fugitives in the Earth Kingdom, Zuko complained that they were royalty and that the people of the Earth Kingdom should give them whatever they wanted. Iroh taught Zuko that "there is a simple honor in poverty" and that begging for sustenance was more honorable than resorting to theft and violence. Iroh was willing to beg and even dance and sing in a debasing way to survive. When his uncle suspected Zuko was stealing food and money, he insisted that Zuko should develop the habits of thought and action that would give him "inner strength" and be a bulwark against surrendering to his "lowest instincts" ("Avatar Day").

Iroh thus channeled the teachings of Kong Fuzi, also known as Confucius (551–479 BCE). As Confucius taught:

> Wealth and honor are what people desire, but one should not abide in them if it cannot be done in accordance with the Way. Poverty and lowliness are what people dislike, but one should not avoid them if it cannot be done in accordance with the Way.[8]

In other words, Zuko could not acquire genuine honor without *ren*. And indeed, after he betrayed Iroh and helped Azula defeat Aang in the catacombs of Ba Sing Se, he experienced the dissatisfaction of ersatz honor.

Formerly the greatest general in the Fire Nation, Iroh lost his imperial and violent drive to conquer when his son Lu Ten died in battle. Instead, he devoted himself to *ren* for, as Confucius taught, "The humane find peace in humaneness."[9] With this inner peace comes the capacity to establish order in the world. To take one of many examples, when an apparent cutthroat tried to rob him in Ba Sing Se, Iroh made it clear that he could easily have dispatched him with violence. Instead, he spoke kindly to and listened to the man, and made him a cup of tea. Iroh was wise enough to see that the man wasn't the "criminal type." What he found was that the man had experienced a deep pain and hurt that could be assuaged through friendship and encouragement. "So you really think I could be a good masseur . . . This is so great! No one has ever believed in me!" ("Tales of Ba Sing Se")[10]

Confucius once explained *ren* in conversation with a student:

> The Master said, "It is loving people." He asked about wisdom. The Master said, "It is knowing people." When Fan Chi did not understand, the Master said, "Raise the upright, put them over the crooked, and you should be able to cause the crooked to become upright."[11]

Zuko's education had left him crooked. Iroh practiced *ren* toward Zuko and imparted wisdom, patiently enduring his anger, bitterness, and verbal abuse. Iroh sometimes communicated those lessons through the principle of *wuwei* (associated with, but not exclusive to Daoism), as when he did not protest when Zuko desired to part ways with him. *Wuwei* is similar to what King Bumi called "neutral jing": doing nothing, but listening and waiting ("Return to Omashu"). Several times, Iroh patiently waited until the time was right to impart the lessons Zuko needed to hear, for example, when he remained silent in prison until it was the right time to reveal Zuko's great-grandparentage.

During his travels in the Earth Kingdom, Zuko met various people who also had been burned by the Fire Nation and lost family in the war. This helped him to get educated about Confucian principles. As the Confucian philosopher Mencius explained: "The mind's feeling of pity and compassion is the beginning of humaneness (*ren*)."[12] In contrast with the Legalists, Mencius emphasized the natural or innate tendencies in human nature toward benevolence: "one who lacks a mind that feels pity and compassion would not be human."[13] Hence, on the Confucian view, Zuko's realization that the mission outlined by the Fire Nation Oath was "an amazing lie" was an unfolding of his innate goodness, arrived at by the right sort of education ("The Day of Black Sun, Part 2: The Eclipse"). In short, under Iroh's tutelage, Zuko came to believe in Confucian principles, including the idea that true honor cannot be achieved unless sought in accord with *ren*.

Confucianism Confronts Legalism

The struggle between Legalism and Confucianism in the drama of the Fire Nation came to the fore when Zuko confronted Ozai in the name of *ren*. Zuko decried his burning and banishment as cruel. Ozai replied that Zuko had "learned nothing" and that "your uncle has gotten to you," and threatened him with the death penalty. Zuko maintained that actually he had "learned everything" and proclaimed that Iroh was his "real father" ("The Day of Black Sun, Part 2: The Eclipse"). Hence, in accordance with Confucianism, Iroh *had* taught Zuko a form of familial piety. He loved Zuko as his son. And Zuko resolved to live by the Confucian axiom to observe the "intentions" and "actions" of his true father, Iroh.[14]

Sozin did not accept a balance of powers in which each nation enjoyed its freedom and distinctive way of life. This constituted a threat to the global order that could only be forestalled by the spread of Legalism under the imperialist banner of the Fire Nation. But Zuko insisted the Fire Nation should shed its Legalist imperialist ambitions and instead coexist with the other nations in a new Confucian-inspired era of peace and kindness. Zuko had learned that his legacy was not only informed by Sozin's philosophy, but also by Avatar Roku's, which he chose to embrace.

Confucianism and Family

Zuko's Confucian path is further evident in that, after his disavowal of the royal family, he chose a new family: Team Avatar. The Aang Gaang embodied the Confucian values of benevolence and honorable piety in family life, which derived in large part from the Confucian family values of Sokka and Katara, the legacy of their parents.[15]

Katara's deep love for her mother Kya was a defining feature of her character, and Kya's self-sacrifice for her children was an essential precondition of the genesis of Team Avatar. Sokka's and Katara's filial piety for their father, the Chieftain of the Southern Water Tribe Hakoda, was reciprocated with deep and abiding parental affection. Katara lamented that her father left her and Sokka at the South Pole when he went off to war: "I know that the world needs him, but doesn't he know how much that we need him, too? How could he just leave us behind? . . . I was so sad and angry and hurt." Katara vented her feelings, but respectfully: "I understand why you left. I really do. And I know why you had to go. So why do I still feel this way?" As Confucius taught: "In serving his parents, a son may remonstrate with them, but gently."[16]

The contrast between Hakoda and Ozai could not be starker. Ozai was willing to kill Zuko to get the throne while Hakoda was willing to sacrifice his own life to protect his home and children. In contrast with the fractured, mistrustful, and scheming royal family, Kya and Hakoda had sown in Sokka and Katara the Confucian familial bonds that had the capacity to expand and adopt new members.

After discovering Gyatso and the other Air nomads had been killed by Sozin's troops, Aang lost his temper and went into the Avatar state. It was at that moment he realized he really had been orphaned, and he only calmed down when he was adopted into a new family. As Katara explained to him: "You still have a family. Sokka and I. We are your family now" ("The Southern Air Temple").

Eventually, Team Avatar adopted another member, Toph, who relished her rebellion against her biological parents. While Katara showed that girls could be warriors, she also embraced the feminine virtues of care, which are praised in Confucianism. She patched up clothing, shopped for the group, expressed compassion for each of her new family members, and healed them when they were hurt. While her mothering was annoying at times, the group came to appreciate how Katara fulfilled this role.

Sokka explained that he could not remember his mother Kya's face. When he tried to think of her, it was Katara's face he saw. Even Toph, who chafed at her parents' Legalist rule and the familial order Katara tried to maintain, praised Katara as compassionate, kind, and caring, "more than my own mom." Katara's maternal love eventually convinced Toph into feeling ashamed at having run away, and she requested Katara's assistance in writing a letter home. The Confucian value of piety practiced in the Avatar family seemed to tame the "wild child" a bit ("The Runaway"). While Zuko's adoption was in some ways rockier than Toph's, he also came to be accepted as a full member of the family.

Zuko's Legacy

Zuko struggled to choose between Confucian and Legalist visions. These two legacies were at war in his own soul, inasmuch as he was the great grandchild of both Roku and Sozin and had been schooled in both philosophies. In Iroh's view, this boiled down to a "battle within":

> Evil and good are always at war inside you, Zuko. It is your nature, your legacy. But there is a bright side. What happened generations ago can be resolved now, by you. Because of your legacy, you alone can cleanse the sins of our family and the Fire Nation. Born in you, along with all the strife is the power to restore balance to the world. ("The Avatar and the Firelord")

Zuko's *agni kai* with Azula was a culminating clash between the rival philosophies. Azula adopted a Legalist understanding of human nature wholesale. She looked at people as fundamentally self-interested and therefore untrustworthy. "Trust is for fools, fear is the only reliable way" ("Sozin's Comet Part 3: Into the Inferno"). She thus used the threat of horrible sanctions against those around her to achieve her ends, including her supposed best friends Mai and Ty Lee.

Meanwhile, Zuko embraced the bitter but ultimately fruitful work of forging the bonds of trust and love in his adoptive family. Zuko practiced *ren* through humility and various self-sacrificial acts to help the Aang

Gaang on their mission. His Confucian love and friendship with Katara turned out to be his salvation, as Katara's help was essential to defeating Azula and cleansing the royal family and nation of their sins.

Every Soul Experiences the Battle Within

In conclusion, it is fitting to ask: why does Zuko's story resonate so powerfully with us? Unfortunately, we can't ask Sokka's instincts for the answer, so I'll offer my own hunch.

The Legalists emphasized natural tendencies toward evil. While some Confucians such as Xunzi agreed with this, Confucians like Mencius were truer to the Master's teachings in emphasizing natural tendencies toward good. Zuko's story suggests that both schools point to something true in human nature, that human beings have the natural capacity for both good and evil, and that it is all too human to be deceived by evil masquerading as good.

We can see evidence for this in our world when we compare Zuko's story to that of a twentieth-century villain who believed he was a hero as a communist youth, was imprisoned in the *gulag*, came to see that his country had adopted an evil ideology (Stalinism), and heroically chose to oppose, expose, and help bring down the regime.[17] As Aleksandr Solzhenitsyn narrates his archetypal story:

> Looking back, I saw that for my whole conscious life I had not understood either myself or my strivings. What had seemed for so long to be beneficial now turned out in actuality to be fatal, and I had been striving to go in the opposite direction to that which was truly necessary to me. But just as the waves of the sea knock the inexperienced swimmer off his feet and keep tossing him back onto the shore, so also was I painfully tossed back on dry land by the blows of misfortune. And it was only because of this that I was able to travel the path which I had always really wanted to travel.
>
> It was granted me to carry away from my prison years on my bent back, which nearly broke beneath its load, this essential experience: *how* a human being becomes evil and *how* good. In the intoxication of youthful successes I had felt myself to be infallible, and I was therefore cruel. In the surfeit of power I was a murderer and an oppressor. In my most evil moments I was convinced that I was doing good, and I was well supplied with systematic arguments. And it was only when I lay there rotting on prison straw that I sensed within myself the first stirrings of good. Gradually it was disclosed to me that the line separating good and evil passes not through states, nor between classes, nor between political parties either – but right through every human heart – and through all human hearts. This line shifts. Inside us it oscillates with the years. And even within the hearts overwhelmed with evil, one small bridgehead of good is retained. And even in the best of all hearts, there remains . . . an un-uprooted small corner of evil.[18]

If Solzhenitsyn is right, then Zuko's story resonates with us precisely because every soul experiences the battle within. And each of us must choose whether we will be the hero or the villain in our own stories.

Notes

1. *Sources of East Asian Tradition*, ed. William Theodore de Bary, vol. 1 (New York: Columbia University Press, 2008), 102. Xunzi was later seen as a heterodox Confucian.
2. *Han Feizi*, book 19, chapter 50, at http://www.xinfajia.net/9213.html.
3. *Sources of Chinese Tradition*, compiled by Wm. Theodore de Bary and Irene Bloom, 2nd ed., vol. 1 (New York: Columbia University Press, 1999), 199–203. Chapter 49 at http://afe.easia.columbia.edu/ps/cup/hanfei_five_vermin.pdf.
4. *Sources of East Asian Tradition*, 118, n.3.
5. *Sources of East Asian Tradition*, 118.
6. *Chinese Philosophy in Classical Times*, ed. and trans. E.R. Hughes (London: J.M. Dent, 1954), 254.
7. For an alternative view on Iroh, see Chapter 20: "Uncle Iroh, from Fool to Sage – or Sage All Along?"
8. "Selections from the Confucian Analects: On Humaneness," in *Sources of Chinese Tradition*, comp. Wm. Theodore de Bary and Irene Bloom, 2nd ed., vol. 1 (New York: Columbia University Press, 1999), 48–50, 52, 56, 59, 61–62, at http://afe.easia.columbia.edu/ps/cup/confucius_humaneness.pdf.
9. "Selections from the Confucian Analects: On Humaneness," at http://afe.easia.columbia.edu/ps/cup/confucius_humaneness.pdf.
10. See also Chapter 22: "Compassion and Moral Responsibility in *Avatar: The Last Airbender*."
11. "Selections from the Confucian Analects: On Humaneness," at http://afe.easia.columbia.edu/ps/cup/confucius_humaneness.pdf.
12. "Selections from the Mencius: On Human Nature," in *Sources of Chinese Tradition*, comp. Wm. Theodore de Bary and Irene Bloom, 2nd ed., vol. 1 (New York: Columbia University Press, 1999), 129, at http://afe.easia.columbia.edu/ps/cup/mencius_human_nature.pdf.
13. "Selections from the Mencius: On Human Nature."
14. Confucius, *Analects* 1.11.
15. For a different take, see Chapter 12: "Spirits, Visions, and Dreams."
16. Confucius, *Analects* 4.18.
17. The *gulag* is the "prison camp system that arose in the Soviet Union after 1929." For that definition and a discussion see David Hosford, Pamela Kachurin, and Thomas Lamont, "GULAG: Soviet Prison Camps and Their Legacy," at https://gulaghistory.org/nps/downloads/gulag-curriculum.pdf.
18. *The Solzhenitsyn Reader: New and Essential Writings 1947–2005*, ed. Edward E. Erickson Jr. and Daniel J. Mahoney (Wilmington, DE: ISI Books, 2006), 265–266.

19

Not Giving Up on Zuko
Relational Identity and the Stories We Tell

Barrett Emerick and Audrey Yap

When we first meet Zuko, we know he's the bad guy. He's got a big scar on his face, he's a prince of the Fire Nation, and he's trying to capture the Avatar. The audience isn't alone in thinking they know who Zuko is. His father (Fire Lord Ozai) and sister (Azula) think him weak, disrespectful, and undeserving of the crown. Aang, Katara, Toph, and Sokka spend a lot of the series thinking (with good reason!) that he's their enemy. But by the end of the series it's clear that Zuko's changed. He's neither a saint nor a monster, just a person who makes a lot of mistakes, hurts people he loves, but ultimately chooses to go in a new way.

You might think that this change in Zuko's character means that people were wrong about him at first, but we're going to argue that it's more complicated than that. On our account, Zuko is all of the things people think he is: disappointing family member, nemesis and villain, ally and hero. This chapter is about the role that others play in who we are as people. Because of other people, we can genuinely have several different identities that aren't necessarily compatible with each other. Ultimately, as we'll see, sometimes redemption and the choice to go in a new way is only made possible by others.

Personhood as a Social Practice

Someone's identity – who they are as an individual – is formed of what philosopher Hilde Lindemann called a "connective tissue of narratives," all woven together around important values, relationships, projects, and experiences.[1] Let's say you identify as a painter. Being a painter is a big deal for you – it's what we'll call an identity-defining project. You're probably also much more than a painter – you might also be an athlete, a sister, a friend,

Avatar: The Last Airbender and Philosophy: Wisdom from Aang to Zuko, First Edition.
Edited by Helen De Cruz and Johan De Smedt.
© 2023 John Wiley & Sons, Inc. Published 2023 by John Wiley & Sons, Inc.

and someone who loves dogs; and each of those things contributes to the tapestry of your identity. Each plays an important role in making you, you. We are all of us telling stories with our lives; who and what we are is made up in part by the narratives we construct through our living.

We're not the only ones who get to contribute those narratives. Others play a crucial role in how we are able to tell our stories and whether we are even able to do so. Lindemann argues that a major part of what it is to be a person is to be in relation to others. If we were completely isolated from all others and couldn't have any kinds of social connections with them, we might still be human but we wouldn't count as *persons* in this technical sense.[2] What that means is that *being* a person is a social *practice*; it is active and dynamic, changing over time.

Lindemann argues that others help to "hold" us in our personhood. Holding someone in personhood involves treating them as if they are playing a particular role in the human drama. Specifically, this plays out via the *expression* of our inner lives, followed by the *recognition* and *response* of others as we perform our parts. Persons also then need to have the capacity to express (in one way or another) their inner lives, which they do through bodily engagement with the world and others. But expression alone isn't enough; that expression also needs recognition and uptake by others. That's why we're not the only ones who get to contribute to the narratives that make up our identity. We have the first-person stories we tell about ourselves, but the third-person stories that other people tell about us also shape who we get to be in crucial ways.[3]

What we're arguing is that the recognition and response of others in some-one's life can influence not only material aspects of their futures, but also who they might become. That's true not just for someone's identity-defining pro-jects like becoming a painter, but for their ethical characters as well.

Zuko's Stories

That's why it's such a big deal when Aang decides to trust Zuko, with Toph's support ("The Western Air Temple"). Aang has as much reason as anyone to distrust Zuko or to decide that he is irredeemably villainous, always someone to be feared and fought. And yet, when Zuko claims that he's changed, Aang hears him out. He doesn't accept Zuko's change of heart uncritically, but he is open to believing that what Zuko says is true. Zuko has an inner life that he expresses, is recognized by Aang, and to which Aang then responds more and more over time. Aang thereby opens up a possible future for Zuko in which Zuko can demonstrate that he is trust-worthy in small, everyday moments around camp and by being Aang's teacher, as well as in big moments when he risks his life to save others. Zuko then becomes the person he aspires to be, growing into that identity and changing not just his ways but who he is as a person.

As we imagine monsters and robots, they're both determined or programmed to be and act a certain way, and there's no overriding that programming. Persons aren't like that. Aang recognizes that treating Zuko like a person means recognizing that he has agency and the capacity to do things differently in the future. Zuko's upbringing in the Fire Nation might have set him up to act in particular kinds of ways, but that's different from saying he's irrevocably *programmed* to act like that. By treating him as a person, Aang and his friends help to create space for Zuko to write a new chapter in his life's story, different from the one his father and sister imagine for him. The world would be better if more of us treated others the way the Aang Gaang treats Zuko.

That doesn't necessarily mean that Zuko wouldn't be able to do so if Aang didn't treat him that way. As we said, Zuko has agency; he is capable of choosing how to act and is responsible for his choices. But, if Lindemann is right that persons are like actors performing their identities, there are very strong incentives to stay on script and penalties for going off script. So, if everyone holds you in an identity and consequently expects a certain type of performance from you, it can be very hard to do otherwise. On the other hand, when others recognize and respond to your efforts to perform a new identity, that can make it easier to do so.

Sometimes, just having one person believe in you in that way can be enough. Often, however, we need more, such as the support of, and the ability to find our place in, a larger moral community. Sokka is slower to believe that Zuko had changed his ways than Aang. Katara, having previously been betrayed by Zuko, is the slowest of all. Zuko's ability to live into that identity is affected by how much recognition his efforts secure, and how others respond in light of that recognition. As in Katara's case, recognition and response can often be sensitive to past histories. It's understandable that she is reluctant to trust Zuko again, given their shared past, though she does not reject him outright. In contrast, when Zuko saves the Earth Kingdom villagers from the soldiers who are extorting them, they reject him as soon as they find out that he's Prince Zuko and not just any wanderer ("Zuko Alone"). Although as viewers, we can tell that he has a story of himself from his childhood, of a boy who's trying to do his best to live up to his demanding father's expectations, that can't be who he is to the villagers. Their third-person story of him, and their responses to him, are fundamentally shaped by their relationship to the Fire Nation. Who he is to them isn't just shaped by his actions in the moment, but also by the weight of history and oppression. Although it is painful for Zuko, their reaction is understandable given the legacy of violence he inherits as the prince of the Fire Nation; it makes sense that the villagers would refuse to trust him even though he had worked to protect them.

What Zuko's rejection by the Earth Kingdom villagers illustrates is that stereotypes, positive or negative, might skew and distort what type of recognition people get. Sometimes this can have damaging or devastating impacts on who they become. In a racist society, for instance, a Black person's actions are often interpreted as threatening or violent, where something as simple as being in a public space is treated as suspicious. Such skewed recognition can and has led to police violence, the breakdown of community, mass incarceration, and murder. In a carceral society, even people who have served their full sentence will often only be recognized by others as offenders, and will have a harder time securing things like housing and employment after release from prison.

Personhood and Redemption

Society could be structured so we can be more like Aang. Our social systems could treat people more like agents – as persons and not as things – who are capable of changing their ways and growing to become more than who they once were. This doesn't mean that people who've done wrong won't still have to do a lot of hard work to make up for it, or that we should just trust people unconditionally as soon as they ask for it. Aang is right to be wary and turn him away when Zuko first appears at their camp ("The Western Air Temple"). Until that moment their shared history involved Zuko trying to injure or capture Aang and his friends. And Zuko's first apology doesn't go well either; he's clumsy and anxious for them to accept it – and to accept him – and he expects too much from them. When he apologizes for the second time in that episode he does a better job: he names particular ways he acted wrongly, accepts responsibility for having done so, and expresses his commitment both to acting differently in the future and to making up for those past wrongs. He acknowledges that his life has been hard but doesn't offer that as an excuse for his actions – just as an explanation. And, he helps to add context to his actions by explaining that he was taught to believe that regaining his honor was the most important thing he could do, and that the only way to do that was to please his father by capturing the Avatar. Part of what it means for him to change his ways and to be on the road to becoming a new person is understanding that his honor is something that cannot be given to him by someone else. Instead it is something he must earn by acting rightly and playing his part to end the war. He needs the Aang Gaang to recognize his efforts and allow him the opportunity to do so.

Empathy is often crucial to this whole process. When Zuko apologizes to Toph for accidentally burning her feet, he acknowledges that firebending is dangerous, that fire is unpredictable, and that he should have been more careful ("The Western Air Temple"). Aang had made a similar mistake with Katara when trying to learn to firebend ("The Deserter"). That point of connection opens up space for him to recognize Zuko's apology as a genuine effort to accept responsibility, to make up for his actions, and as a desire to go in a new way. In short, Aang recognizes that Zuko, like the rest of us, is a fallible being who doesn't have to spend the rest of his life making the same mistakes.

This story shows that it's not bad that other people get to influence who we are, especially not when they're people who love us and can *hold us in personhood* even when we can't do it ourselves. This kind of practice is fairly common when those we love grow older and no longer behave in familiar ways. Loved ones might become angry or upset at our presence, forget who we are, and perhaps even try to physically harm us. A gentle and loving parent might develop a progressive disease affecting their cognitive capacities. This may result in them mistaking their child for a stranger, perhaps leading them to strike out and harm a person they once nurtured and protected.[4] But that child might still hold them in their personhood, continuing to weave their identity-constituting stories as a kind and loving person.

By the end of Book Three, Zuko is no longer the bad guy of the story but a valued member of the team, eventually even standing up to his sister and moving into the path of a lightning bolt that was about to strike Katara ("Sozin's Comet, Part 3: Into the Inferno"). Zuko's redemption is enabled by those in his moral community holding him in personhood. Specifically, his friends and uncle hold him in an identity in which he *is* a good person, deserving of care, friendship, and love, who can work to make things right and play a part in ending the war.

As powerful as their efforts to hold him in his new identity are, though, Zuko's redemption arc wouldn't be possible without Uncle Iroh. In fact, it might not have even begun. It's clear throughout the series that Iroh cares deeply for and believes in Zuko, even saying in Book One that he sees him as his own son ("The Siege of the North, Part I"). In Book Two, Iroh challenges Zuko for unquestioningly accepting the destiny that his father had chosen for him, rather than a destiny that he would choose for himself. "It's time for you to look inward and start asking yourself the big questions," Iroh says at Lake Laogai: "Who are you, and what do you want?" Though Zuko doesn't have a clear answer at the time, he takes a big step and frees Appa from captivity. He then falls ill in the grip of what Iroh calls a spiritual metamorphosis, before emerging as the prince he was meant to be ("Lake Laogai"). Those changes don't happen right away, though. At the end of Book Two, Zuko chooses his sister over his uncle and thereby rejects a potential new path ("The Crossroads of Destiny").

Early in Book Three, Iroh is held captive by the Fire Nation and refuses to speak to his nephew, seemingly angry with Zuko for acting wrongly; in doing, so he demonstrates his belief that Zuko is capable of being better ("The Headband"). This might seem surprising; we often think of anger and blame as forms of hostility, an indication that a relationship is ruptured, or that the blamed person is irredeemably bad. But implicit in moral anger itself is the recognition that the person does not have to be held in that past identity. We don't become angry with a lightning bolt when it starts a fire – at least not like we would with an arsonist. After all, the lightning bolt isn't a person; we might be angry that the fire caused damage and harm, but it doesn't make sense to blame the lightning bolt or hold it responsible. The arsonist, however, is a person who acted wrongly. When we become angry with them, we recognize them as an agent who made a choice – and that means they *could* make a different choice in the future. That's part of why Zuko's eventual apology to Iroh (and Iroh's interrupting it with a strong hug) is so moving. Iroh had challenged Zuko to be better and when Zuko lived up to that challenge, figuring out for himself what it meant within the confines of his life's narrative to be a good person, Iroh accepted him back immediately, welcoming both the change and the new person who sat before him ("Sozin's Comet, Part 2: The Old Masters").

Opening Up Possibilities

Wouldn't things be better if there were more people like Iroh and Aang? In saying that, we don't mean to paper over the fact that this is often very difficult in practice. We also don't mean to suggest that everyone should always forgive those who wrong them. Indeed, some of the time people who have been wronged should hold on to anger if they need to do so, and others shouldn't pressure them to forgive. Moreover, not all relationships should be sustained, nor should reconciliation always be everyone's goal. In many cases, it's best overall for the victim to leave their relationship with the wrongdoer in ruins. So, in arguing for more Irohs and Aangs in the world, we aren't saying that victims should be the ones to carry that weight. Instead, we think a better solution would be to have a *moral community* that opens up space for wrongdoers and potential wrongdoers (which is to say everyone) to go in a new way. Lindemann's account of personhood is grounded in the idea that we are fundamentally social beings, always becoming who we are via relationships with others. The work of holding each other in their identities thus falls on *many* people and social institutions. In the absence of this moral community, there can be a lot of luck in the process. Only some of us have Irohs in our life (whose belief in our goodness is a crucial part of what makes us become good), or Aangs who give us the space to change. Zuko is lucky in that he has both. It may seem unjust that who a particular person can become is so strongly affected by others in their life. If so, we suggest that we should work to arrange society so as to provide a wider array of possibilities to everyone.

But Zuko is lucky in other ways too. After all, he's a prince of the most powerful nation in the world and has all kinds of advantages that others don't have. So we might wonder: what's the difference between Zuko and other privileged young men – "golden boys" who get more than their share of second chances? After all, there's no shortage of people who mourn the damaged life prospects of young men facing the consequences of their own bad actions.[5] For example, Brock Turner was a student at Stanford University who was convicted of sexually assaulting a woman in 2015. His father described the emotional toll of the guilty verdict on his son as "a steep price to pay for 20 minutes of action."[6] Unlike Turner's father, we (and probably Iroh too) don't think that emotional toll is excessive; it's totally appropriate for Turner to feel profound guilt and remorse for his reprehensible actions – just as Zuko does. But Turner's father also made those remarks within a carceral context that we oppose – one that assumes that punishing someone and holding them responsible are the same thing. The focus for us isn't on punishing wrongdoers – it's on creating a world where fewer wrongs are committed, where those who are wronged are cared for, and where wrongdoers work to repair their wrongs. So, Turner's moral community should absolutely hold him responsible for his actions – *including feeling anger and distrust toward him,* and expect him to work to make up for them – and that means treating him like a person who can do so.[7] The specific contours of such reparative work have to be determined within a particular context and moral community, responding to the particular needs of all those involved and especially the wronged person. None of what we have argued for here is about letting anyone off the hook for their wrongful actions. Quite the opposite: if we write someone off as a lost cause, as a thoroughgoing villain or an irredeemable monster, we let them off too easily. The hard work of moral growth and living up to the potential entailed by our agency is often only possible in circumstances where others recognize that we are capable of doing so.

Here's what's illuminating about the way Iroh treats Zuko: he doesn't deny that he's done wrong or has hurt others. He doesn't make excuses for his behavior, or try to paint a rosy picture of his character, but maintains a space for his nephew to become a different person, in which Ozai's and Azula's stories aren't the definitive ones for his life. Iroh isn't in denial, but instead holds Zuko in his personhood by treating him consistently, even stubbornly, as though he can do good things, even as he recognizes when Zuko fails. When Iroh and Zuko reunite at the White Lotus encampment, Iroh tells his nephew that he was not angry, but rather afraid that Zuko had lost his way – something that Zuko admits as well ("Sozin's Comet, Part 2: The Old Masters"). Iroh holding Zuko in his personhood is instructive and morally important. It lets us imagine how different things might be if the parents of golden boys didn't excuse them or deny their wrongdoing, but rather recognized the harms their loved one caused, *and* expected them to do better moving forward.

Notes

1. Hilde Lindemann, *Damaged Identities, Narrative Repair* (Ithaca, NY: Cornell University Press, 2001), 72.

2. This consequence of the view might sound terrible, but it actually explains some of the harm of practices like solitary confinement that deprive people of any meaningful social interaction for major portions of their lives. Those kinds of practices might keep people's bodies alive, but they don't allow them the ability to be persons, since they don't allow them to be in meaningful relation to others.

3. Hilde Lindemann, *Holding and Letting Go: The Social Practice of Personal Identities* (New York: Oxford University Press, 2014), 16.

4. Lindmann tells a story like this about a woman and her mother with Alzheimer's (2014, 154–155).

5. This is what Kate Manne calls "himpathy," or having an excess of sympathy for relatively privileged men. Kate Manne, *Down Girl: The Logic of Misogyny* (New York: Oxford University Press, 2017).

6. Victor Xu, "The Full Letter Read by Brock Turner's Father at His Sentencing Hearing," *The Stanford Daily*, June 8, 2016, at https://www.stanforddaily.com/2016/06/08/the-full-letter-read-by-brock-turners-father-at-his-sentencing-hearing.

7. By contrast, we don't think his father treated him as a person in that way.

20

Uncle Iroh, From Fool to Sage – Or Sage All Along?

Eric Schwitzgebel and David Schwitzgebel

Book Three of *ATLA* portrays Uncle Iroh as wise and peace-loving, in the mold of a Daoist sage. However, in Book One, Iroh doesn't always appear sage-like. Instead, he can come across as lazy, incompetent, and unconcerned about the fate of the world.

Consider Iroh's very first appearance in *ATLA*, in "The Boy in the Iceberg," after Prince Zuko sees a giant beam of light across the sky, signaling the release of the Avatar from an iceberg:

ZUKO: Finally! Uncle, do you realize what this means?
IROH: [playing a game with tiles] I won't get to finish my game?
ZUKO: It means my search is about to come to an end. [Iroh sighs with apparent lack of interest and places a tile on the table.] That light came from an incredibly powerful source! It has to be him!
IROH: Or it's just the celestial lights. We've been down this road before, Prince Zuko. I don't want you to get too excited over nothing.

On the surface, Iroh's reaction appears thoughtless, self-absorbed, and undiscerning. He seems more concerned about his game than about the search for the Avatar, and he fails to distinguish a profound supernatural occurrence from ordinary celestial lights. Several other early scenes are similar. Iroh appears inept, distractible, lazy, and disengaged, very different from the energetic, focused, competent, and concerned Iroh of Book Three.

We will argue that Iroh's Book One foolishness is a pose, and Iroh's character does not fundamentally change. In Book One, he is wisely following strategies suggested by the ancient Chinese Daoist philosopher Zhuangzi (fourth century BCE) for dealing with incompetent leaders. His seeming foolishness in Book One is in fact a sagacious strategy for minimizing the harm that Prince Zuko would otherwise inflict on himself and others – a gentle touch that more effectively helps Prince Zuko find wisdom than would be possible with a more confrontational approach.

Avatar: The Last Airbender and Philosophy: Wisdom from Aang to Zuko, First Edition.
Edited by Helen De Cruz and Johan De Smedt.

We will also present empirical evidence that – contrary to our expectations before collecting that evidence – Iroh's wisdom-through-foolishness is evident to most viewers unfamiliar with the series, even on their first viewing. Viewers can immediately sense that his superficial foolishness has a deeper purpose, even if that purpose is not immediately apparent.

Iroh as a Zhuangzian Wise Fool

Like Iroh, Zhuangzi mixes jokes and misdirection with wisdom, so it's not always clear how seriously we are to take him. Zhuangzi presents several obviously fictional dialogues, including one between the philosopher Confucius (fifth century BCE) and his favorite disciple, Yan Hui. Yan Hui asks Confucius' political advice:

> I have heard that the lord of Wei is young and willful. He trifles with his state and does not acknowledge his mistakes. He is so careless with people's lives that the dead fill the state like falling leaves in a swamp. The people have nowhere to turn. I have heard you, my teacher, say, "Leave the well-governed state and go to the chaotic one. There are plenty of sick people at the doctor's door." I want to use what I have learned to think of a way the state may be saved.[1]

Zuko, like the lord of Wei in Yan Hui's telling, is a young, willful prince, leading his companions into danger, unwilling to acknowledge his mistakes. Even more so, the Fire Nation is led into peril and chaos by Fire Lord Ozai and Princess Azula. If ever a nation needed wise redirection by someone as practiced in conventional virtue as Confucius and his leading disciples, it would be the Fire Nation.

Zhuangzi's "Confucius," however, gives a very un-Confucian reply: "Sheesh! You're just going to get yourself hurt." Through several pages of text, Yan Hui proposes various ways of dealing with misguided leaders, such as being "upright but dispassionate, energetic but not divisive" and being "inwardly straight and outwardly bending, having integrity but conforming to my superiors," but Zhuangzi's Confucius rejects all of Yan Hui's ideas. None of these conventional Confucian approaches will have any positive effect, he says. Yan Hui will just be seen as a plague and a scold, or he will provoke unproductive counterarguments, or he'll be pressured into agreeing with the leader's plans. At best, his advice will simply be ignored.[2] Imagine a well-meaning conventional ethicist trying to persuade Zuko (in Book One), much less Ozai or Azula, to embrace peace, devoting themselves to improving the lives of ordinary people! It wouldn't go well.

So what should Yan Hui do, according to Zhuangzi's Confucius? He should "Fast his mind." He should be "empty" and unmoved by fame or accomplishment. "If you're getting through, sing. If not, stop. No schools. No prescriptions. Dwell in unity and lodge in what cannot be helped, and you're almost there."[3] Advising another worried politician a few pages later, Zhuangzi's Confucius says:

> Let yourself be carried along by things so that the mind wanders freely. Hand it all over to the unavoidable so as to nourish what is central within you. That is the most you can do. What need is there to deliberately seek any reward? The best thing is just to fulfill what's mandated to you, your fate – how could there be any difficulty in that?[4]

Zhuangzi's advice through his fictional Confucius is cryptic – intentionally so, we think, in order to frustrate attempts to rigidify it into fixed doctrines. Nevertheless, we will rigidify it here, into two broadly Zhuangzian or Daoist policies for dealing with misguided rulers:

1. Do not attempt to pressure a misguided ruler into doing what is morally right. You'll only be seen as noxious or be ignored. Instead, go along with what can't be helped. "Sing" – that is, express your opinions and ideas – only when the ruler is ready to listen.
2. Empty your mind of theories and doctrines, as well as desires for fame, reward, or accomplishment. These are unproductive sources of distortion, wrangling, and strife.

Zhuangzi advocates this two-pronged approach to dealing with misguided rulers, but he doesn't explicitly explain why this approach might work.

Here *ATLA* can help us understand Zhuangzi. We can see how Iroh, by embodying these policies (especially in Book One), helps to redirect Zuko onto a better path. We thus gain a feel for Zhuangzian political action at work. Iroh doesn't resist Zuko's unwise plans, except in indirect, non-threatening ways. He suggests that Zuko relax and enjoy some tea ("The Boy in the Iceberg," "Bato of the Water Tribe"), and at one point, he redirects their ship to a trading town in search of a gaming tile ("The Waterbending Scroll"). At another point, he allows himself to relax in a hot spring, delaying the departure of their ship ("Winter Solstice, Part 1: The Spirit World"). Despite these suggestions and redirections, he does not outright reject Zuko's quest to capture the Avatar and even helps in that quest. He does not make himself noxious to Zuko by arguing against Zuko's plans, or by parading his sagely virtue, or by advancing moral or political doctrines. Indeed, he actively undercuts whatever tendency Zuko or others might have to see him as wise (and thus noxious or threatening, judgmental or demanding) by playing the fool – forgetful, unobservant, lazy, and excessively interested in tea and the tile game Pai Sho. In this way, Iroh keeps himself by Zuko's side, modeling peaceful humaneness and unconcern about fame, reward, wealth, or honor. He remains available to help guide Zuko in the right direction, when Zuko is ready.

A related theme in Zhuangzi is "the use of uselessness." For example, Zhuangzi celebrates the yak – big as a cloud but lacking any skill regarded as useful in ancient China and thus not forced into labor – and ancient, gnarled trees – no good for fruit or timber and thus left in peace to live out their years.[5] Zhuangzi's trees and yak are glorious life forms, for whom existence is enough, without further purpose. Uncle Iroh, though not wholly useless (especially in battle) and though he can devote himself to aims beyond himself (in caring for Zuko and later helping Aang restore balance to the world), possesses some of that Zhuangzian love of the useless: tea, Pai Sho, small plants and animals which need no further justification for their existence. Through his love of the useless and his simple appreciation of existence, Uncle Iroh unthreateningly models another path for Zuko, one of joyful harmony with the world.

We can distill Iroh's love of uselessness into a third piece of Zhuangzian political advice:

3.   Don't permit yourself to become too useful. If the ruler judges you useful, you might be "cut down" like a high-quality tree, becoming a tool at the ruler's disposal. Be useful only to the extent required to avoid being noxious.

Iroh is an expert firebender with years of military experience who could surely be a valuable asset in capturing and dispatching the Avatar if he focused on it. However, Zuko rarely recruits Iroh's aid beyond the minimum. Through conspicuous napping, laziness, and distractibility, Iroh encourages Zuko and others to view him as a mostly harmless, and not particularly valuable, traveling companion.

By following Zhuangzi's first piece of advice (don't attempt to pressure a misguided ruler), the Daoist can stay close to a misguided leader in an unthreatening and even foolish-seeming way without provoking resistance, counterargument, or shame. By following Zhuangzi's second piece of advice (empty your mind of doctrines and striving), the Daoist models an alternative path, which the misguided leader might eventually in their own time appreciate – perhaps more quickly than would be possible through disputation, doctrine, intellectual engagement, or high-minded sagely posturing. By following Zhuangzi's third piece of advice (embrace uselessness), the Daoist can avoid becoming a disposable tool for the ruler's schemes. This is Iroh's Zhuangzian approach to the transformation of Zuko.

Throughout Book One and the beginning of Book Two, we observe only three exceptions to Iroh's Zhuangzian approach. All are informative. First, in multiple episodes Iroh is stern and directive with Zuko when instructing him in firebending. We see that Iroh is capable of opinionated command; he is not lazy and easygoing in all things. But elementary firebending appears to require no spiritual insight, so there need be no threatening moral instruction or questioning of Zuko's projects and values.

Second, Iroh gives Zuko one stern piece of advice that Zuko rejects, seemingly thus violating Policy 1. In "The Storm," Iroh warns of an approaching storm. When Zuko refuses to acknowledge the risk, Iroh urges Zuko to consider the safety of the crew. Zuko responds "The safety of the crew doesn't matter!" and continues toward the storm. When they encounter the storm and the crew complain, Iroh attempts to defuse the situation by suggesting noodles. Zuko is again offended, saying he doesn't need help keeping order on his ship. However, at the climax of the episode, when the storm is raging and the Avatar is finally in sight, Zuko chooses to let the Avatar go so that the ship can steer to safety. The viewer is invited to suppose that in making that decision Zuko is reflecting on Iroh's earlier words. Iroh's advice – though at first seemingly ignored and irritating to Zuko, and thus un-Zhuangzian – was well placed after all.

Third, consider Iroh's and Zuko's split in the fifth episode of Book Two, "Avatar Day," which was set up in the first episode of Book Two, "The Avatar State." Azula has tricked Zuko into thinking that their father Ozai wants him back. In an un-Zhuangzian moment, Iroh directly, though mildly, challenges Zuko's judgment: "If Ozai wants you back, well, I think it may not be for the reasons you imagine . . . in our family, things are not always what they seem." This prompts Zuko's angry retort: "I think you are exactly what you seem! A lazy, mistrustful, shallow old man who's always been jealous of his brother!"

The immediate cause of their split seems trivial. They have survived briefly together as impoverished refugees when Zuko suddenly presents Iroh with delicious food and a fancy teapot. Iroh enjoys the food but asks where it came from, and he opines that tea is just as delicious in cheap tin as in fancy porcelain. Zuko refuses to reveal how he acquired the goods. Iroh is remarkably gentle in response, saying only that poverty is nothing to be ashamed of and noting that their troubles are now so deep that even finding the Avatar would not resolve them. When Zuko replies that there-fore there is no hope, Iroh answers:

> You must never give in to despair. Allow yourself to slip down that road and you surrender to your lowest instincts. In the darkest times, hope is something you give yourself. That is the meaning of inner strength.

A bit of sagely advice, kindly delivered? This is the next we see of Zuko and Iroh:

ZUKO: Uncle . . . I thought a lot about what you said.
IROH: You did? Good, good.
ZUKO: It's helped me realize something. We no longer have anything to gain by traveling together. I need to find my own way.

Zuko's and Iroh's falling out reinforces *ATLA*'s Zhuangzian message. As soon as Iroh deviates from the first of the three Zhuangzian policies – as soon as he challenges Zuko's morality and starts offering sagely advice, however gently – Zuko reacts badly, rejecting both the advice and Iroh himself.

Zuko and Iroh of course later reunite and Zuko eventually transforms himself under the influence of Iroh, with Iroh becoming more willing to advise Zuko and dispense explicit wisdom, in proportion to Zuko's readiness for that advice and wisdom. Apart from his un-Zhuangzian moments in the first part of Book Two, Iroh "sings" only when he is getting through, just as Zhuangzi's fictional Confucius advises. Otherwise, Iroh acts by joke, misdirection, and a clownishly unthreatening modeling of peaceful humaneness and unconcern.

Viewers Appreciate That Iroh Is Wise from the Beginning

Iroh's wisdom in Book One is hidden beneath a veneer of foolishness. We thought that ordinary, first-time viewers might tend to agree with Zuko's angry assessment of Iroh as lazy and shallow. Viewers who are more knowledgeable, we thought, would be more likely to see the wise motives behind Iroh's facade. We decided to test this empirically by recruiting online participants to view three scenes, and then rate Iroh's wisdom.

Our approach fits within the general framework of "experimental aesthetics." A central aesthetic property of a work of art is how people respond psychologically to it. Those responses can be measured empirically, and in measuring them, we gain understanding of the underlying mechanisms by which we are affected by a work of art. If Iroh is perceived differently by viewers unfamiliar with the series than he is by knowledgeable viewers, then the experience of *ATLA* changes with repeated viewing: In the first view, people read Iroh's actions as foolish and lazy; in the second view, they appreciate the wisdom behind them. If, in contrast, Iroh is perceived as similarly wise by unfamiliar and knowledgeable viewers, then *ATLA* operates differently: It portrays Iroh in such a manner that ordinary viewers can discern from the beginning that a deeper wisdom drives his apparent foolishness.

We recruited 200 participants from Prolific, an online source of research participants commonly used in psychological research. All participants were US residents aged 18 to 25, since we wanted an approximately equal mix of participants who knew and who did not know *ATLA* and we speculated that most older adults would be unfamiliar with the series. We asked participants to indicate their familiarity with *ATLA* on a 1–7 scale from "not at all familiar" to "very familiar." We also asked six multiple-choice knowledge questions about the series (for example, "What was the anticipated effect of Sozin's Comet?"). In accordance with our preregistration at https://aspredicted.org/a4kj6.pdf, participants were classified as "knowledgeable" if their self-rated knowledge was four or higher and if they answered four or more of the six knowledge questions correctly.[6]

Somewhat to our surprise, the majority of respondents – 63% – were knowledgeable by these criteria, and almost none were completely unfamiliar with the series: 95% correctly answered the first (easiest) knowledge question, identifying Aang as the name of the main character. Perhaps this was because our online recruitment language explicitly mentioned *Avatar: The Last Airbender*. It is thus possible that we disproportionately recruited *Avatar* fans or those with at least a passing knowledge of the series.

Participants viewed three short clips (about 60–90 seconds) featuring Iroh and another three short clips featuring Katara, in random order, with half of the participants seeing all the Iroh clips first and the other half seeing all the Katara clips first. The Iroh clips were scenes from Book One in which Iroh is superficially foolish and that we described above: the opening scene described at the beginning of this chapter, the scene in which Iroh falls asleep in a hot spring instead of boarding Zuko's ship at the appointed time, and the scene in which Iroh "wastes time" redirecting Zuko's ship in search of a Pai Sho piece. The Katara clips were similar in length; they were clips from Book One, featuring some of her relatively wiser moments.

After each scene, participants rated the character's (Iroh's or Katara's) actions on six seven-point scales: from lazy to hard-working, kind to unkind, foolish to clever, peaceful to angry, helpful to unhelpful, and, most crucially for our analysis, wise to unwise. After watching all three scenes for each character, participants were asked to provide a qualitative (open-ended, written) description of whether the character seemed to be wise or unwise in the three scenes.

As expected, participants rated Katara as wise in the selected scenes, with a mean response of 1.85 on our 1 (wise) to 7 (unwise) scale, with no statistically detectable difference between the unfamiliar (1.95) and knowledgeable (1.80) groups.[7] (Note that wisdom here is indicated by a relatively low number on the scale.) However, contrary to our expectations, we also found no statistically significant difference between unfamiliar and knowledgeable participants' ratings of Iroh's wisdom. Overall, participants rated him as somewhat wise in these scenes: 3.04 on the 1–7 scale (3.08 among unfamiliar participants, 3.02 among knowledgeable participants).[8] (Although Katara was rated as overall wiser than Iroh, this is likely because we picked scenes of Katara displaying wisdom and Iroh displaying superficial foolishness. Different scene choices would presumably have produced different average judgments.)

For example, 81% of unfamiliar participants rated Iroh as wise (3 or less on the 7-point scale) in the scene described at the beginning of this chapter, where Iroh superficially appears to be more concerned about his tile game than about the supernatural sign of the Avatar. (Virtually the same percentage of knowledgeable participants describe him as wise in this scene: 83%.) The unfamiliar participants' written responses suggest that they tend to see Iroh's calm attitude as wise, and several unfamiliar participants appear already to discern that his superficial foolishness hides a deeper wisdom. For example, one writes:

> I actually believe that though he appears to be childish and foolish that he is probably very wise. He comes off as having been through a lot and understanding how life works out. I think he hides his intelligence.

And another writes:

> I am not familiar with the character, but from a brief glance he seems to be somewhat foolish and unwise. For some reason however, it seems like he might be putting on a facade and acting this way on purpose for some alter-ier [sic] motive, which would mean that he actually is very wise. I do not have any evidence for this though, it's just a feeling.

Although not all unfamiliar participants were this insightful into Iroh's character, the similarity in mean scores between the unfamiliar and knowledgeable participants speaks against our hypothesis that knowledgeable participants would view Iroh as overall wiser in these scenes. Nor did unfamiliar participants detectably differ from knowledgeable participants in their ratings of how lazy, kind, foolish, peaceful, or helpful Iroh or Katara are.[9]

Although these data tended to disconfirm our hypothesis, we wondered whether it was because the "unfamiliar" participants in this study were not completely unfamiliar with the series. Recall that 95% correctly identified the main character's name as Aang. Many, perhaps, had already seen a few episodes or already knew about Iroh from other sources. Perhaps knowledge of *ATLA* is a cultural touchstone for this age group, similar to *Star Wars* for the older generation, so that few respondents were truly unfamiliar with the series?

To address this possibility, we recruited 80 additional participants, ages 40–99 (mean age 51), using more general recruitment language that did not mention *ATLA*. In sharp contrast with our first recruitment group, few of the participants – 7% – were "knowledgeable" by our standards, and only 28% identified "Aang" as the main character in a multiple-choice knowledge question.

Overall, the unfamiliar participants in this older group gave Iroh a mean wisdom rating of 3.00, not significantly different from the mean of 3.08 for the unfamiliar younger participants.[10] ("Hyper-unfamiliar" participants who failed even to recognize "Aang" as the name of the main character similarly gave a mean Iroh wisdom rating of 2.89 [not statistically significantly different from the mean rating of the other participants].) Qualitatively, their answers were also similar to those of the younger participants, emphasizing Iroh's calmness as his source of wisdom. As with the younger participants, some explicitly guessed that Iroh's superficial foolishness was strategic. For example:

> I'm not familiar with these characters, but I think Iroh is (wisely) trying to stop his nephew from going down "the path of evil." He knows that playing the bumbling fool is the best way to give his nephew time to realize that he's on a dangerous path.

And

> He comes off a as [sic] very foolish and lazy old man. But i [sic] have a feeling he is probably a lot wiser than these scenes show.

We conclude that ordinary viewers – at least viewers in the United States who can be accessed through Prolific[11] – can see Iroh's foolish wisdom from the start, contrary to our initial hypothesis. Future research could potentially explore what tropes and cues are responsible for giving viewers such an early signal of Iroh's wisdom.

A Zhuangzian Sage All Along

In Book One, Iroh behaves in ways that are superficially foolish, despite acting in obviously wise ways beginning around the middle of Book Two. There are three possible aesthetic interpretations. One is that Iroh begins the series unwise and learns wisdom along the way. Another is that Iroh is acting wise, but in a subtle way that is not visible to most viewers until later in the series, only becoming evident on a second watch. A third is that, even from the beginning, it is evident to most viewers that Iroh's seeming foolishness conceals a deeper wisdom. On a combination of interpretive and empirical grounds, the third interpretation is the best supported.

To understand Iroh's wisdom, it is useful to look to the ancient Daoist philosopher Zhuangzi, specifically his advice for dealing with incompetent rulers by following peacefully along with them, unthreateningly modeling disregard for fame and accomplishment while not being too useful for their ends. Since Zhuangzi provides no concrete examples of how this is supposed to work, we can look to Iroh's character as an illustration of the Zhuangzian approach to political advising. In this way, *Avatar: The Last Airbender* – and the beloved Uncle Iroh – can help us better understand Zhuangzi in particular and the Daoist tradition in general.[12]

Notes

1. "Zhuangzi," trans. Paul Kjellberg, in P.J. Ivanhoe and B.W. Van Norden eds., *Readings in Classical Chinese Philosophy,* 2nd ed. (Indianapolis: Hackett, 2005), 226–227. Except where indicated, all references to Zhuangzi are to Kjellberg's translation, with a few minor changes. In interpreting Zhuangzi, we treat only the "Inner Chapters" as canonical.
2. Ibid., 227–228.
3. Ibid., 228–229.
4. For this passage we use Ziporyn's translation, which we find clearer than Kjellberg's, from *Zhuangzi: The Essential Writings,* trans. Brook Ziporyn (Indianapolis: Hackett, 2009), 29.
5. E.g., "Zhuangzi" (2005), 213.
6. Full methodological details, raw data, and supplementary analyses are available in the online appendix at https://osf.io/t375r/ and https://github.com/dschwitz-PSL/Avatar-Schwitzgebel-Repository.
7. Pooled $SD = 0.79$, $t(192) = 1.35$, $p = .18$.
8. Pooled $SD = 1.23$, $t(192) = -0.35$, $p = .73$.
9. The largest difference was on Iroh's kindness: $M_{unfamiliar} = 2.66$, $M_{knowledgeable} = 2.27$, pooled $SD = 1.07$, $t(192) = 2.49$, Bonferroni corrected $p = .13$ (10 comparisons).
10. Pooled $SD = 1.15$, $t(139) = -0.43$, $p = .67$.
11. As always, it's somewhat speculative how well any research will generalize beyond the actual pool of participants who are recruited. But we think that the conclusion is of broader interest if we go for the bolder claim that viewers in general will recognize Iroh's wisdom. Of course, viewers from a far different culture might not know what to make of Iroh, or of the tropes on which the series relies.
12. For helpful discussion, thanks to Jeremy Pober, the editors of this collection, and commenters on social media posts on Facebook, Twitter, and *The Splintered Mind* blog.

21

Being Bad at Being Good
Zuko's Transformation and Residual Practical Identities

Justin F. White

Partway through Book Three of *Avatar: The Last Airbender*, as Zuko seeks to leave behind the dominant ideals of the Fire Nation and join Team Avatar, he finds himself doing things that betray those aspirations. After accidentally burning Toph, he cries in frustration, "Why am I so bad at being good?" ("The Western Air Temple") When we meet Zuko in Book One, his purpose is clear. He single-mindedly pursues the Avatar as a way to restore his "honor" and regain his place in his family and nation. Over time and under his uncle Iroh's influence, however, Zuko starts experiencing inner turmoil about who he has become and about his growing dissatisfaction with current ideals of the Fire Nation. But even his eventual resolution to change is only the beginning of a journey marked by backsliding. Why does he have such difficulty in changing?

Aspiration, Transformation, and Practical Identity

Zuko's plight illuminates the process of aspiration, including common challenges to the aspirant. As contemporary philosopher Agnes Callard understands it, aspiration typically involves a "deep change in how one sees and feels and thinks."[1] And this deep change is often intertwined with a change in what contemporary philosopher Christine Korsgaard calls practical identity, a "description under which you value yourself, . . . under which you find your life to be worth living and your actions to be worth undertaking."[2] But as Zuko shows, practical identities are complex, sometimes unwieldy, and changes in explicit self-conceptions can take work, time, and perhaps some luck to bring about the deep change one aspires to. Even after he explicitly disavows his past actions, Zuko finds

Avatar: The Last Airbender and Philosophy: Wisdom from Aang to Zuko, First Edition.
Edited by Helen De Cruz and Johan De Smedt.
© 2023 John Wiley & Sons, Inc. Published 2023 by John Wiley & Sons, Inc.

himself reverting to past behaviors, doing things that (on some level) he wishes he would not. These actions frustrate him – "Why am I so bad at being good?" – but they are not mere lapses in judgment. They come naturally and express an identity that Zuko had long embraced and cultivated but is now trying to leave behind.

The arc of Zuko's transformation illustrates the interplay between two dimensions of practical identity. On the one hand, as Korsgaard's account emphasizes, our explicit self-conceptions and values matter. They guide our actions and shape how we see the world. But Zuko's struggles suggest that such self-conceptions and aspirations are only part of the story. According to the philosopher Martin Heidegger's (1889–1976) notion of being-in-the-world, our practical identity depends more on our existential engagement with the world than on our explicit self-conceptions.[3] And these different dimensions of practical identity do not always align. As Heidegger scholar William Blattner writes, "Some of the most challenging conflicts in our lives arise when who we are existentially engaged in being stands in tension with who we think of ourselves as being."[4] Zuko is frustrated because, despite consciously trying to change, his being-in-the-world conflicts with his Korsgaardian practical identity. His world is still shaped (residually) by an identity he wants to shed.

The way Zuko's world and actions continue to be shaped by an identity he is trying to leave behind highlights a key difficulty of transformation. Zuko's desire to prove his worth to his father and his rage have so thoroughly permeated his being-in-the-world that they are second nature. They shape his orientation toward the world and fuel his firebending. For better or worse, his spontaneous actions do not always fall in step with his conscious commitments. The same skills and dispositions Zuko previously cultivated as central to his identity now lead to unwanted actions and keep him from aspired-to actions. To become good in the way he wants, Zuko must not only cultivate the dispositions that will allow his aspired-to identity to become part and parcel of his being-in-the-world, but he must clear out or modify the residual influence of his past identity and its dispositions and values.

Family, Shame, and Honor (Book One)

In "The Boy in the Iceberg" we meet Zuko as a dishonored prince living in exile. Fueled by rage, insecurity, and a need to prove his worth to his father (Fire Lord Ozai), he seeks the Avatar in order to restore his "honor" and re-establish his place in his family and the Fire Nation. Zuko believes that capturing the Avatar will change his father's estimation of him as a failure and disgrace to the Fire Nation.[5]

The scar Zuko carries from his father's attack during their one-sided duel serves as a reminder that Zuko's upbringing and family dynamic are, to put it gently, complicated. With a caring but eventually absent mother, a competitive dynamic with a violent and volatile sister, and a father who sees him as inadequate and inferior to his sister and who ultimately attacks him, Zuko grew up trying and failing to live up to his father's expectations. But striving to live up to those expectations came to define Zuko's self-conception: "I've always had to struggle and fight and that's made me strong. It's made me who I am" ("The Siege of the North, Part 2"). It's unlikely that Zuko has read Korsgaard's *Sources of Normativity*, but the way he connects his self-conception ("I've always had to struggle and fight") to his identity ("made me who I am") might make you wonder. Zuko identifies as a fighter who overcomes obstacles, no matter what, and this self-understanding shapes how he seeks the Avatar.

However, even when this self-understanding dominates Zuko's outlook, there are limits to what he will do to capture the Avatar. In "The Storm" he initially ignores Iroh's advice and decides to head into a dangerous storm, even if it puts himself and his crew at risk. When Zuko says, "The safety of the crew doesn't matter. Finding the Avatar is more important than any individual's safety," he sounds a lot like his father who was ready to sacrifice military recruits. In the end, however, Zuko moves the ship to safety despite seeing the Avatar fly away. This could seem like a small change in plan, a minor setback to Zuko's pursuit, but choosing to preserve the lives of others distinguishes him from his father and sister and lays the groundwork for more significant future change.

At the end of Book One, Admiral Zhao tells Zuko, "You should have chosen to accept your failure, your disgrace" ("The Siege of the North, Part 2"). But given his self-conception as a fighter who overcomes struggle, Zuko is uninterested in resignedly accepting his perceived failure and disgrace. His path forward, however, is less clear, partly because conflict is brewing between different dimensions of his identity. On the one hand, Zuko sees and explicitly values himself as a fighter whose strength came through struggle, and his current struggle is to prove his strength to his father by capturing the Avatar. We will call this his reflective (Korsgaardian) practical identity. But on the other hand, Zuko sees the world in ways that conflict with that explicitly embraced self-conception. In Heidegger's phenomenological account, the self-understandings that attune us to the world are best indicated by how we see and engage with the world, by our being-in-the-world. Although explicit self-conceptions typically shape our existential engagement (our being-in-the-world), Zuko shows how they can come apart. Since capturing the Avatar is his explicit and nearly all-consuming goal, moving the ship to safety shows a (small) tension between his explicit self-conception and his being-in-the-world. While he says the crew's safety doesn't matter when compared to capturing the Avatar, his actions suggest he sees things differently.

"It's time for you to decide": Inheriting, Finding, and Choosing Destiny (Book Two)

In "The Avatar State" Zuko reflects on his situation: "Three years ago I was banished. I lost it all. I want it back. I want the Avatar. I want my honor, my throne. I want my father not to think I'm worthless." From Zuko's perspective, his father's approval is still largely paramount. Those explicit desires form his explicit self-understanding and significantly affect his being-in-the-world, so he is deeply affected when Azula condescendingly calls him a failure and an embarrassment to their father, and declares him an official enemy to the Fire Nation.

At this point, any cracks in Zuko's allegiance to his father are small. He sees the world through the lens of an honor which depends on capturing the Avatar: "There is no honor for me without the Avatar" ("Avatar Day"). When Iroh cautions that capturing the Avatar may not resolve his situation, Zuko replies, "Then there is no hope." As Zuko sees it, capturing the Avatar is the only way to restore his honor and (re)gain his father's love. Soon after this exchange, he leaves Iroh and goes his own way.

But Zuko's own way is a work in progress, a working out of (apparently) conflicting values and ways of being. In flashbacks ("Zuko Alone"), we learn that Azula called Iroh weak when he returned from the war after his son was killed. We also see Zuko's kind mother tell a younger Zuko, "Never forget who you are." We don't know exactly what his mother has in mind, but we've already seen Zuko care about others in ways that his father and sister do not.[6] We again see Zuko care when he helps an Earth Kingdom family get their son back after he had been taken by soldiers. When he saves the boy and reveals that he is a Fire Nation prince, however, the family turns on him, and he again sets out on his own.

Soon after, Zuko reunites with Iroh and starts to actively change, albeit intermittently. Iroh believes "people can change their lives if they want." He adds, "I believe in second chances" ("The Serpent's Pass"). Having changed his own life, Iroh wants to help Zuko change his. During this time, Zuko goes on a date with Jin, a girl from Ba Sing Se. Because things go well, she is surprised when he rejects her. When she asks what is wrong, he replies, "It's complicated." Zuko could be describing himself as he works through his complicated self and his orientation toward the world ("Tales of Ba Sing Se").

While in Ba Sing Se, Zuko finds a flyer that Aang had made in order to find Appa, rekindling his desire to find the Avatar. Iroh encourages him to let the Avatar go, but Zuko says, "I want my destiny." Iroh replies, "What that means is up to you," pushing Zuko to take responsibility for his destiny and to not passively inherit the expectations of others ("Lake Laogai"). When Zuko later finds Appa, Iroh urges him to move on.

"I know my own destiny, Uncle."
"Is it your own destiny, or is it a destiny someone else has tried to force on you . . . It's time for you to look inward and begin asking yourself the big questions. Who are you? And what do *you* want?" ("Lake Laogai")

Although Zuko says chasing the Avatar is his destiny, he also feels constrained by it. Of course, we can voluntarily set constraints on our ourselves in unproblematic ways. To be someone's lover or friend, for example, is to commit to act in certain ways and not in others. In the end, Zuko lets Appa go. But soon after, he says that he doesn't feel right, things go blurry, and he collapses ("The Earth King"). While Zuko is feverish and delirious, Iroh describes the sickness, "Your critical decision . . . was in such conflict with your image of yourself that you are now at war within your own mind and body . . . You are going through a metamorphosis, my nephew. It will not be a pleasant experience. But when you come out of it, you will be the beautiful prince you were always meant to be" ("The Earth King"). Like Zuko's mother's plea to not forget who he is, Iroh's description of the metamorphosis suggests Zuko was already more (at least potentially) than his father's expectations for him. And releasing Appa helped him realize that potential.

Zuko emerges from the fever a changed person, but the fragile transformation, including his confidence that he can make his own path, is soon tested. Azula lays a trap to capture Iroh, and Zuko is imprisoned after challenging Azula. While held captive with Katara, he describes his scar as the mark of a banished prince. He will never be free of the mark, he says, but he now realizes that he is free to determine his destiny ("The Crossroads of Destiny"). The awareness of his freedom doesn't resolve the internal conflict, however, as we see when he must choose between siding with Iroh or Azula (and the possibility of regaining his position in the royal family).

AZULA: You can still redeem yourself.
IROH: The kind of redemption she offers is not for you.
AZULA: At the end of this day, you will have your honor back. You will have father's love. You will have everything you want.
IROH: Zuko, I'm begging you. Look into your heart and see what it is you truly want. ("The Crossroads of Destiny")

The challenge Zuko faces is that his heart (or practical identity) is not univocal. As much as his mother and Iroh talk about not forgetting who he is, seeing what he truly wants, and becoming who he is meant to be, Zuko's practical identity is fractured, unsettled.

Book Two ends with Zuko's fragile transformation taking a step back. Unable to resist Azula's offer of "everything you want," he sides with her and attacks Aang. Zuko has changed – he sees himself differently and his allegiance to his father and the current iteration of the Fire Nation has weakened – but he still sees the world as affording ways to show he is not weak and to (re)gain his father's approval. His being-in-the-world is still shaped by rage and the desire to prove himself to his father. Iroh was right that letting Appa go was at odds with Zuko's explicit self-image, but the transformation Iroh predicted is far from complete. Becoming aware of his true desires is (at best) only part of the change he seeks. To become the "beautiful prince" he was meant to be, he must align his existential engagement with "what he truly wants." His aspired-to desires must become part and parcel of his being-in-the-world.

Being Bad at Being Good: Rethinking Honor and Destiny (Book Three)

When Zuko returns home, he (re)gains his place in the Fire Nation, his "honor," and his father's approval ("The Awakening"). He has everything he always wanted, has satisfied the desires that had guided him to that point, "but it's not at all what I thought it would be" ("The Headband"). Later, he admits "I should be happy now, but I'm not" ("The Beach"). As happiness eludes him, he experiences moral vertigo: "I'm confused. I'm not sure I know the difference between right and wrong anymore." He says "anymore," but he might be giving himself too much credit, or perhaps he has confused confidence with knowledge.[7] Although Zuko was previously confident in his path, his actions suggest less-than-ideal moral knowledge.

His distress grows when he attends a meeting of the war council and acts as the perfect prince (the son his father wanted) but feels that he isn't himself ("Nightmares and Daydreams"). Soon after, in front of a picture of his mother, he commits to set things right ("Day of the Black Sun, Part 1: The Invasion"). He confronts his father, tells him that he will not take orders from him anymore, and rejects the version of the Fire Nation his father has cultivated ("Day of the Black Sun, Part 2: The Eclipse").

The Fire Nation Zuko knows was shaped by his great-grandfather Sozin's war conquests. But when Zuko learns that Avatar Roku was also his great-grandfather, it allows him to rethink firebending and imagine a Fire Nation compatible with peace and kindness. This ultimately helps him break with Ozai's version. As Iroh predicted ("The Avatar and the Fire Lord"), the struggle between his great-grandfathers helps Zuko understand his inner struggle, the eventual resolution of which lays the groundwork for a different Fire Nation.

When Zuko offers to teach Aang to firebend, he describes himself as a changed person: "I've changed. And I, uh, I'm good now" ("The Western Air Temple"). He understands why Team Avatar wouldn't trust him because he has done some awful things. But, he says, "*I'm not that person anymore.*" The group rejects his offer, though Toph expresses some sympathy: "Considering his messed-up family and how he was raised, he could have turned out a lot worse."

When Toph later goes to visit Zuko, she startles him and he accidentally burns her feet. He cries out, "Why am I so bad at being good?" He is understandably frustrated with himself for injuring Toph immediately after claiming that he was good and wasn't "that person anymore." Toph's description of the incident is insightful. Asked if Zuko attacked her, she says, "Well, he did and he didn't. It was sort of an accident." It makes sense to say that Zuko attacked her – attacking an intruder fits Zuko's life to that point. But attacking a desired ally also conflicts with his new self-image, with who he wants to be. Zuko wants a deep change, a change in his being-in-the-world. However, this deep change of aspiration is difficult. Even if conscious aspirations about who we want to be (typically) figure into our being-in-the-world, such aspirations do not change our being-in-the-world as thoroughly or as quickly as we'd like. We can find ourselves, like Zuko, seeing and inhabiting the world in ways that stem from residual practical identities we are trying to shed.

The way Zuko says, "I'm good now" and "I'm not that person any-more," suggests that he thought that by standing up to his father and changing his explicit commitments, he had already achieved the desired change. He learns the hard way that who we are, including how good and bad we are, involves not only our conscious self-conceptions (and aspirations) but also our being-in-the-world more broadly. By rejecting his father and committing to join the Avatar, Zuko changes his reflective practical identity. But to be good at being good, to not be "that person anymore," Zuko must also change his practical perception, his bodily skills and dispositions – more generally, his being-in-the-world.

Zuko soon gets a chance at redemption when the assassin he had hired finds the temple and attacks Team Avatar. When Zuko tries to call off the hit, the assassin is undeterred, and Zuko is injured while trying to stop him. His actions change Team Avatar's opinion, and they accept him into their group.

When re-introducing himself, Zuko says,

> I've been through a lot in the past few years. And it's been hard. But I'm realizing that I had to go through all those things to learn the truth. I thought I had lost my honor and that somehow my father could return it to me. But I know now that no one can give you your honor. It's something you earn for yourself by choosing to do what's right. All I want now is to play my part in ending this war, and I know my destiny is to help you restore balance to the world.

The two dimensions of Zuko's practical identity are again aligning, now in a morally better place. However, joining the Avatar creates an unexpected problem. When he starts to teach Aang firebending, Zuko has trouble firebending himself ("The Firebending Masters"). He soon realizes that his firebending is weaker because, in joining Aang, he has lost his rage that had previously fueled it. Sensing that the current Fire Nation has distorted the original way of firebending, Zuko wants to become a different firebender, one whose bending has different motivations and is not fueled by rage. When he visits the Sun Warriors with Aang, his perspective on firebending changes. This new perspective provides the energy and direction necessary for his firebending to return, now no longer subject to his rage's volatility.

Becoming Good at Being Good

Through much of Books Two and Three, Zuko is negotiating the relationship between an evolving self-conception and a changing, but recalcitrant being-in-the-world. He starts with a conscious self-conception of a banished prince single-mindedly focused on capturing the Avatar in order to gain his father's acceptance and restore his "honor." Now he has teamed with the Avatar to overthrow his father and restore the honor of the Fire Nation. Changing his conscious practical identity was no small feat, but Zuko wants a deeper transformation. He wants to change his existential engagement, his being-in-the-world. That change involves overcoming some residual aspects of his prior way of being. But despite the obstacles they create, his earlier self-understanding and his being-in-the-world as a fighter who makes his own way also make possible the distinctive path he eventually takes.

Toward the end of this transition, he reflects on his confusion after gaining his father's acceptance: "I realized I'd lost myself getting there. I'd forgotten who I was" ("The Ember Island Players"). Zuko's journey to this point culminates when he sacrifices himself to save Katara from Azula's potentially fatal attack. Zuko is becoming good at being good: not just thinking of himself as changed or better, but seeing the world differently and responding accordingly. If Zuko's mother and Iroh are right, this was largely a matter of improved self-understanding, of Zuko remembering who he is. But improved self-understanding and better moral ideals are only part of the story. His transformation highlights common, if complicated, aspects of personal change. When we aspire, we commonly find ourselves being "bad at being good," desiring things we wish we didn't and doing things we wish we wouldn't. Zuko poignantly reminds us that becoming who we want to become – becoming good at being good – is often a struggle, during which we think of ourselves as we want to become and persist through setbacks, including the times when we find ourselves being bad at being good, guided by the very identities we want to leave behind.

Notes

1. Agnes Callard, *Aspiration: The Agency of Becoming* (Oxford: Oxford University Press, 2018), 2.

2. Christine Korsgaard, *Sources of Normativity* (Cambridge: Cambridge University Press, 1996), 101.

3. See Martin Heidegger, *Being and Time*, trans. John Macquarrie and Edward Robinson (New York: Harper Collins, 1962). In *Phenomenology of Perception*, Maurice Merleau-Ponty gives similar priority to our engaged bodily being-in-the-world; Maurice Merleau-Ponty, *Phenomenology of Perception*, trans. Donald Landes (New York: Routledge, 2013). In *Normativity and Phenomenology in Husserl and Heidegger* (Cambridge: Cambridge University Press, 2013), Steven Crowell develops a Heideggerian account of practical identity, which he thinks better accounts for the nature of practical identity than Korsgaard's account.

4. William Blattner, *Heidegger's Being and Time* (London: Continuum, 2006), 89.

5. We first hear Ozai's estimation of Zuko through Zhao ("The Southern Air Temple"), so maybe we should take it with a grain of salt. But it seems consistent with Ozai's character. He calls Zuko's refusal to duel with him "shameful" ("The Storm"), and he tells Azula that Zuko is a failure ("The Siege of the North, Part 2"). See also "The Waterbending Scroll."

6. Significantly, Zuko's father and sister call him weak when he expresses concern for others.

7. Zuko himself later recognizes as much when, after more fully changing, he says, "I'm good now. I mean, I thought I was good before but now I realize that I was bad" ("The Western Air Temple"). But before that realization, perhaps in a last-ditch effort to hold together or avoid facing his deteriorating moral framework, Zuko hires a hitman to kill Aang ("The Headband").

22

Compassion and Moral Responsibility in *Avatar: The Last Airbender*

"I was never angry; I was afraid that you had lost your way"

Robert H. Wallace

A lot of very bad things happen in *ATLA*. Katara and Sokka's mother dies in a Fire Nation raid. Zuko is physically and emotionally abused by his father. Jet commits acts of terrorism. Hama kidnaps and tortures civilians for revenge. The Fire Nation's war on the Earth Kingdom causes devastation; they even have labor camps. The Air Nomads are wiped out in a genocide. Aang discovers the skeleton of his guardian and mentor, Monk Gyatso. In stopping the Fire Nation and helping Aang restore balance to the world, Team Avatar must confront all these very bad things. Clearly, one major concern of the show is how we should best hold people *morally responsible* for the bad things they do to each other.

Consider an example that raises an ethical puzzle. Appa gets abducted in "The Desert," and Team Avatar later encounters the sandbending thieves in the desert. When Aang hears that they muzzled Appa, he becomes enraged. Entering the Avatar state, he demands to know where Appa is and starts destroying the sandbenders' skiffs. When the sandbenders try to apologize and make amends Aang only gets more destructive. In the end, Katara must calm him down, and he starts crying.

This is gut-wrenching stuff. On the one hand, Aang seems right in angrily blaming the sandbenders for abducting and muzzling Appa; someone deserves to get yelled at for hurting Appa! On the other hand, Aang does not accept an apology and his anger nearly gets the better of him. Aang is the Avatar, after all, and in his Avatar state, he is incredibly dangerous. Here, then, is an ethical puzzle: it seems both good and appropriate to get mad at people who do bad things. But anger can be toxic, self-destructive, and get out of control. What gives?

Avatar: The Last Airbender and Philosophy: Wisdom from Aang to Zuko, First Edition. Edited by Helen De Cruz and Johan De Smedt.

Anger, Blame, and Responsibility

Many contemporary philosophers believe that there is an important connection between holding someone responsible and being angry at them.
The British philosopher P.F. Strawson (1919–2006) argued that to blame
someone – to hold them responsible for a wrongdoing – is just to feel and
express certain kinds of moral anger toward them.[1] If you do a bad thing
to my friend, I might *resent* you for it and tell you off. This is an intuitively
compelling account of what blame consists in, and many contemporary
philosophers agree. On this kind of view, Aang is just holding the thieves
responsible for hurting Appa when he gets angry at them.

This intuitively compelling idea is bolstered by the connection between
responsibility and moral desert. We might think that the thieves *deserve* to
have some bad things happen to them. A natural outcome of being the
recipient of someone's moral anger is the pain of feeling guilty. Maybe we
think some people deserve that bad feeling – like the people who abducted
Appa – and so being worthy of blame is just to be worthy of the pain of
guilt.[2] Relatedly, we might think that the pain of guilt is the normal
pathway by which we show moral understanding. Feeling guilty about
something you did is a sign that you think it was wrong. Beyond this, we
might think that anger and blame are an especially important way to stand
up for ourselves in the face of injustice, as feminist and anti-racist philosophers have pointed out.[3] So, in these ways, it seems like anger can be good.
It helps us confront injustice and hold wrongdoers responsible.

On the other hand, there is surprising agreement among a diverse range
of philosophers who argue that anger is very bad.[4] Classical Buddhist
thought suggests that anger is one of the poisons in our nature, something
that gives rise to pain and suffering (and a false sense of what the world is
really like).[5] The Stoic philosophers thought something similar. The Roman
Stoic philosopher Seneca (4 BCE–65 CE), for instance, says that anger is
"hideous and wild . . . greedy for revenge . . . awkward at perceiving what
is true and just." Anger is just "the desire to repay suffering."[6] How could
the desire to make someone else suffer ever be good?

Beyond this, we tend to think highly of people who let go of angry
blame. As contemporary philosopher Glen Pettigrove has pointed out,
many of our moral heroes – "Socrates, Buddha, Jesus, Abraham Lincoln,
Mahatma Gandhi, Martin Luther King Jr., Nelson Mandela, and the Dalai
Lama" – exemplify *meekness*, a virtue historically characterized by
responding to ill-treatment in a calm and kindly fashion.[7] We often admire
those who *don't* get angry when they are wronged, but instead respond
with compassion, the awareness that other persons suffer and a desire to
alleviate that suffering.

Most of us can recognize this tension in our thinking about moral
responsibility and its connection with anger. We cannot hope to address
every aspect of this tension here. But *ATLA* has a lot to say about this

puzzling tension regarding how we think about angry blame and responsibility. Below, we'll see that the show highlights strategies for holding one another responsible *without* the bad effects of anger. These strategies often involve forgiveness and compassion. Although the strategies *ATLA* highlights do not solve the tension in our thinking about anger, they do help alleviate it by offering us examples of how to respond to wrongdoing without angry blame.

Katara and the Uses and Misuses of Angry Blame

Katara is an especially important character in *ATLA* when considering anger and responsibility. She has a lot of fiery blame to go around, and this is often portrayed as a good thing. For instance, in "The Waterbending Master" she uses her anger to confront the sexism of Master Pakku, who refused to train women waterbenders: "someone has to slap some sense into that guy!" Here, we see that angry blame has a point – it can be used to change the actions of other people, maybe by making them feel guilty and realize that they have done wrong. Consider Pakku's guilt upon becoming aware that Katara is the granddaughter of his once-fiancée Kanna. But Katara often encounters others who harbor destructive anger, and her story arc illustrates a way we might avoid letting our anger become destructive.

Recall Seneca's worry that anger is greedy for revenge, that it is just the desire to repay suffering. Why would that be the case? As contemporary philosopher Martha Nussbaum points out, a focus on a past wrong generates a desire to retaliate and diminish the wrongdoer.[8] And it is easy to see how this desire can get out of hand. Consider Katara's brief infatuation with Jet, the Earth Kingdom partisan and budding terrorist whom she ultimately rebuffs. Jet's anger at the Fire Nation is so intense that he is willing to murder innocent Earth Kingdom citizens, blaming them for collaborating with the enemy. They need to be "punished" ("Jet"). Or consider Katara's encounter with the bloodbending Hama ("The Puppetmaster"). Hama was kidnapped and imprisoned by the Fire Nation in their genocidal attempt to wipe out all waterbenders. To escape, Hama learns to waterbend the blood in other living creatures. She kidnaps and imprisons Fire Nation civilians to pay back what the Fire Nation did to her.

Katara knows that Jet and Hama are wrong to seek revenge on innocent civilians. Nonetheless, in "The Southern Raiders" Katara is offered the chance to go on a "field trip with Zuko" to find Yon Rha, the man who killed her mother, and she starts desiring revenge.

When Zuko joins Team Avatar, he seeks Katara's forgiveness and acceptance by offering to help her find the man who killed her mother, Kya. Zuko suggests that finding the murderer is about justice, but Aang recognizes that Katara's motivation is revenge. Katara agrees and suggests that's what Yon Rha deserves. Aang says that Katara sounds like Jet. He quotes the monks: "revenge is like a two-headed rat viper. While you watch your enemy go down, you're being poisoned yourself" – something that Buddhists and Stoics would heartily agree with. Aang eventually relents and agrees to let Zuko and Katara borrow Appa – working through this is something Katara needs to do herself – but he implores her to let her anger out, and then let it go. He hopes Katara can find compassion and forgiveness. She does, but not in in the way that Aang expects.

Katara bloodbends her way to finding Yon Rha. And she looks like she's going to kill him. She turns rain into ice spikes, pointing them at Yon Rha and stopping right before they pierce him. He begs for mercy and even *acknowledges* that Katara deserves revenge, offering Katara *his own mother's life* out of a twisted sense of "fairness." But Katara can't bring herself to kill the mother, or Yon Rha. Although she can't forgive, she forgoes revenge. Yon Rha isn't worth it.

Katara seems to have stayed angry. Yet her anger no longer generates a desire for revenge. Puzzlingly, Katara is willing to forgive Zuko after her encounter with Yon Rha. Why? Contemporary philosopher Lucy Allais has argued that forgiveness is like "wiping the slate clean" by refusing to take a person's bad actions as evidence about their character.[9] Holding someone responsible (and ceasing to blame them when you forgive them) is sometimes a matter of *who they are* and not simply about what they have done. Zuko's formerly villainous actions are not representative of his present character. He already feels guilty and has resolved to change. In comparing him with Yon Rha, Katara "wipes the slate clean" and forgives Zuko.

On the other hand, Yon Rha is presently cruel and pathetic. He even wanted to sacrifice his own mother to save himself because he finds her burdensome! Yon Rha appears incorrigible, and so Katara's blame is not worth it. Interestingly, then, the show suggests that the purpose of blame sometimes outstrips blameworthiness. Yon Rha deserves blame, but for Katara, *expressing* this blame is moot. Thus, even if she stays angry and cannot forgive, she does not need revenge.

So, *ATLA* suggests that angry blame can have its uses, but that we must learn how to let it go when it is no longer fitting or productive.

Iroh and Compassionate Responses to Wrongdoing

Next, let's think about Uncle Iroh. He is no stranger to anger and strong negative emotions. In "The Siege of the North, Part 2," he angrily confronts Admiral Zhao, who seeks to kill the moon spirit: "Whatever you do to that spirit, I will unleash on you tenfold. Let it go, now!" He is upset and exasperated with Zuko in "Lake Laogai" when he discovers that his nephew is the "Blue Spirit" trying to abscond with Appa from Lake Laogai: "You never think things through!" But Iroh often chooses not to respond to wrongdoers with anger. In fact, he often seems to forgo blame entirely in responding to wrongdoing.

After being betrayed by Zuko at the end of Book Two, Iroh does some curious things. At first, he refuses to speak to Zuko while he is imprisoned rather than show any outward anger. He later helps Zuko discover that his maternal grandfather was the previous Avatar, Avatar Roku. Finally, after escaping prison and reuniting with Zuko, he immediately forgives Zuko, or rather, he lets Zuko know he never blamed him at all – at least not in the sense of angry blame. He offers this tearbending remark: "I was never angry; I was afraid that you had lost your way." As Yap and Emerick argue in Chapter 19, Iroh consistently holds Zuko responsible for his wrongdoing, while giving Zuko space and support to become better.

Some contemporary philosophers have moved away from an anger-centric (or more generally emotional) way of understanding holding someone responsible. The contemporary philosopher T.M. Scanlon, for instance, thinks that to blame someone is to adopt whatever attitude is appropriate toward another person when they have impaired their relationship with you, perhaps by holding less-than-good attitudes toward you.[10] I can't think of a clearer example of manifesting a relationship-impairing attitude than betraying a loving parental figure so that they end up in prison as a traitor. Since Zuko has hurt his relationship with Iroh, perhaps Iroh's refusal to speak with Zuko is just an appropriate recognition of the damaged relationship.

But *ATLA* sometimes goes beyond this relational way of thinking about blame and responsibility. Recall that, according to Pettigrove, many of our moral heroes exemplify *meekness*, the character trait of not responding to ill-treatment with anger. Iroh has many virtues, and meekness is certainly one of them. Consider his encounter with Tycho, the would-be mugger in Ba Sing Se during "City of Walls and Secrets." Instead of being angry, he comments that the mugger has a weak stance, and corrects it! He asks *why* the mugger is doing this, and eventually, we get a hilarious jump cut to Iroh and Tycho sipping tea, with the former encouraging the latter to pursue his dreams of becoming a masseur.

On a relationship-based way of thinking about blame, we might say that everyone has a basic moral relationship with everyone else, including strangers. And if someone tries to mug you, it does seem like that person has attitudes that impair even that basic relationship. Iroh, however, does *not* respond to Tycho as if any relationship between them – even the basic moral relationship we have with strangers – has been damaged at all. Iroh responds to his aggressor by seeking understanding. And, with understanding in hand, he responds with compassion. Notice that Iroh is not engaging with the wrongdoing itself, but is instead concerned with the motivations behind the wrongdoing, the suffering that might drive someone to act wrongly toward others – for instance, poverty and fear of failing at a dream career. Instead of addressing the wrong, Iroh addresses the root causes behind it by responding with compassion.

You might think that Iroh is *forgiving* Tycho for mugging him, but this is a mistake. Forgiving is also a way of addressing the wrong. Commonsensically, we tend to think that there is a strong connection between compassion and understanding, and between understanding and forgiveness. You know the adage: to understand is to forgive. The idea here seems to be that a deeper understanding of why someone performs a wrong action tends to mitigate our anger toward them.[11] Consider how someone partway through watching *ATLA* for the first time would respond to the spoiler that Iroh gets mugged in Ba Sing Se: they would probably be upset at the mugger! But in context, Tycho is endearing. We forgive him, but not because Tycho apologizes or makes amends. Rather, Tycho becomes endearing because Iroh's first response is to perceive the wider context in which Tycho is not a threat. As contemporary philosopher Pamela Heironymi has suggested, in some important sense, to forgive someone is to recognize that they are no longer a threat to you.[12] What is so compelling about Iroh's interaction with Tycho is that he – literally and figuratively – disarms the threat before any further wrongdoing occurs. *ATLA* suggests, then, that sometimes the best way to respond to a wrongdoer is not to blame them at all.

Zuko, Self-blame, and Self-compassion

Zuko is a very angry character, but let's just focus on one compelling detail: much of his anger is *self-directed*. After he betrays Iroh and "defeats" Aang at the end of Book Two, Zuko visits Ember Island with Azula, Mai, and Ty Lee ("The Beach"). There, Zuko admits that "for so long now I thought if my dad accepted me, I'd be happy. I'm back home now. My dad talks to me. Ha! He even thinks I'm a hero. Everything should be perfect, right? I should be happy now, but I'm not! I'm angrier than ever and I don't know why!" After repeated prompts from the others about *who* or *what* he is angry about, Zuko finally snaps: "I'm angry at myself!"

Why is he angry at himself? Zuko says he doesn't know right from wrong anymore, but it is apparent that he feels guilty for betraying Iroh. He angrily blames himself for the wrong that he has done. And it seems like he is right to do so. That was a terrible thing to do! Many of us experience self-blame, which goes beyond just feeling guilty, but instead is characterized by actively expressing self-anger. It is possible that self-blame can be good in the same way that angry blame can be good: it might get us to really see that we've done wrong and motivate us to do better.

But there is something suspicious about blaming yourself, since you are both the person expressing and receiving anger. Imagine that Sokka teases Toph, and that Toph teases Sokka right back. Now imagine that Sokka gets upset at Toph for teasing him. It seems unfair for Sokka to get mad since he just teased Toph himself! In this scenario, Sokka is being a *hypocritical* blamer. He isn't entitled to be upset. As contemporary philosopher R. Jay Wallace might put it, Sokka is making an unfair exception for himself.[13] Notice that when Zuko blames himself, he is *also* being hypocritical. He blames someone (himself) for the bad things he himself has done!

Maybe Zuko's self-blame could be appropriate because his character changes over time; a redeemed Zuko, who would never do those bad things, could get mad at the past Zuko who did.[14] But is Zuko's self-blame the catalyst for his change in character? The show seems to suggest otherwise. Indeed, the show seems to suggest that his self-blame is *counterproductive* to this end. Zuko's inner moral conflict makes him physically sick in "The Earth King."

Zuko's successful redemption begins with the recognition of his own suffering. When he finally confronts his father Ozai in "The Day of the Black Sun Part 2: The Eclipse," he begins by acknowledging how *he himself was hurt*. He tells his father that it was "cruel" and "wrong" to challenge a 13-year-old to an Agni Kai. He notes the "incredible lie" told to everyone in the Fire Nation, that they were the greatest civilization on earth and that the war was their way of sharing greatness with the world. The lie was harmful to Zuko, and everybody else in the Fire Nation.

In recognizing how he has been hurt, Zuko seems to be exercising self-compassion. As contemporary philosopher Simon Keller and psychologist Felicia A. Hupert define it, self-compassion involves the judgment that you are in a bad condition, that it would be better if it could be alleviated, and that you can feel concern for yourself as if from an outside perspective as one-among-many.[15] Unlike self-blame, self-compassion is anti-hypocritical because you are extending to yourself the same grace you should extend to others.

It is important to note that Zuko is not excusing his wrongdoing in recognizing his own suffering. It is instead a means for him to understand and take ownership of the wrongs he has done. For instance, when he makes his appeal to join Team Avatar in "The Western Air Temple," he again begins by acknowledging that he's "been through a lot in the past few years, and it's been hard." But he notes that this hardship helped him realize the true nature of honor in choosing to do what's right. He then apologizes to Toph for accidentally burning her feet, saying that "fire can be dangerous and wild. So, as a firebender, I need to be more careful and control my bending, so I don't hurt people unintentionally." Upon hearing this, Aang realizes that Zuko understands how easy it is to hurt the people we love and accepts Zuko as his firebending teacher. Zuko's self-compassion, almost paradoxically, enhances his ability to hold himself responsible. Here, *ATLA* reminds us that being angry at ourselves sometimes prevents us from understanding our own suffering, which is often the root of our wrongdoing in the first place.

Sometimes We Can Let Go

Although we have focused on how *ATLA* models responsibility without anger, the show doesn't say straight out that we should stop angrily blaming one another. Angry blame plays an important role in some of its most important positive moments – Katara confronting Pakku and Iroh defending the moon spirit, for instance. But *ATLA* highlights that we can choose not to be angry with wrongdoers. Our nurturing community – the people who raise us and shape our formative years – seems to have a kind of duty to safely usher us into moral adulthood and to help us cope with what is genuinely puzzling in our ethical lives. Media for children and young adults have an important role to play here, even for adults. In this role, *ATLA* succeeds in many ways. Even though there is a tension between what is good about blame and what is bad about anger, *ATLA* shows us some strategies that might help us live with this tension. It offers the lesson that, sometimes, we can let go of expressing anger and act with compassion toward ourselves and others.

Notes

1. P.F. Strawson, "Freedom and Resentment," in Michael McKenna and Paul Russell eds., *Free Will and Reactive Attitudes: Perspectives on P.F. Strawson's "Freedom and Resentment"* (Burlington, VT: Ashgate, 1962), 19–36.
2. Andreas Brekke Carlsson, "Blameworthiness as Deserved Guilt," *The Journal of Ethics* 21 (2016), 89–115.
3. See for instance: Amia Srinivasan, "The Aptness of Anger," *The Journal of Political Philosophy* 26 (2018), 123–144; Audre Lorde, "The Uses of Anger: Women Responding to Racism," in *Sister Outsider* (Trumansburg, NY: Crossing Press, 1981), 124–133; Marilyn Frye, *The Politics of Reality: Essays in Feminist Theory* (Berkeley, CA: The Crossing Press, 1983).
4. This is a prominent theme in the work of philosophers who do not think anyone has free will – and so no one deserves blame or punishment. See for instance: Derk Pereboom, *Free Will, Agency, and Meaning in Life* (Oxford: Oxford University Press, 2014).
5. Owen Flanagan, *The Geography of Morals: Varieties of Moral Possibility* (New York: Oxford University Press, 2017). This book contains rich descriptions and explorations of this tradition of thought.
6. From Seneca's *De Ira*, as quoted in Flanagan, 169–170.
7. Glen Pettigrove, "Meekness and 'Moral' Anger," *Ethics* 122 (2012), 341–370.
8. Martha Nussbaum, *Anger and Forgiveness: Resentment, Generosity, and Justice* (Oxford: Oxford University Press, 2016). See chapter 2 of her book for more details.
9. Lucy Allais, "Wiping the Slate Clean: The Heart of Forgiveness," *Philosophy & Public Affairs* 36 (2008), 33–68.
10. T.M. Scanlon, *Moral Dimensions: Permissibility, Meaning, Blame* (Cambridge, MA: Belknap Press of Harvard University Press, 2008).

11. See Glen Pettigrove, "Understanding, Excusing, Forgiving," *Philosophy and Phenomenological Research* 74 (2007), 156–175.
12. Pamela Hieronymi, "Articulating an Uncompromising Forgiveness," *Philosophy and Phenomenological Research* 62 (2001), 529–555.
13. R. Jay Wallace, "Hypocrisy, Moral Address, and the Equal Standing of Persons," *Philosophy & Public Affairs* 38 (2010), 307–334.
14. For a very similar and more technical version of this idea, see Kyle G. Fritz and Daniel J. Miller, "Two Problems of Self-blame for Accounts of Moral Standing," *Ergo* (forthcoming).
15. Simon Keller and Felicia A. Huppert, "The Virtue of Self-compassion," *Ethical Theory and Moral Practice* 24 (2021), 443–458.

PART V
AIR

23

The Fire Nation and the United States

Genocide as the Foundation for Empire Building

Kerri J. Malloy

The building of empires is more than using military or economic might to impose the power of a stronger political entity over a weaker one. To dilute the severity of the actions taken to secure power over others, empires construct narratives that justify their use of force. The political entity that is conquered is erased and replaced by its destroyer and becomes a mere footnote in the origin story of the empire.[1] Appealing to the myth of ordering an unorderly world, an empire is explained as a necessity to ensure the future security of civilization. Empires are thus built through the intentional destruction of peoples who are deemed either a threat or an impediment to the progress of a so-called superior society. To achieve the dream of empire, genocide is common and goes without explanation in the history of nations. Genocide results from a complex process of intentions, ideologies, and actions that are put in motion to achieve an outcome that benefits the perpetrators. Indeed, genocide is part of the history of the United States and of the Fire Nation in *Avatar: The Last Airbender* that is typically unquestioned and underplayed.

Forging an Empire

For the Fire Nation, the drive to establish an empire was the dream of Fire Lord Sozin. Recognizing the peace and prosperity that the Fire Nation enjoyed and the benefits this could bring, he proposed that "We should share this prosperity with the rest of the world. In our hands is the most successful empire in our history. It's time we expanded it" ("The Avatar and the Fire Lord"). The results were catastrophic, undoing

Avatar: The Last Airbender and Philosophy: Wisdom from Aang to Zuko, First Edition.
Edited by Helen De Cruz and Johan De Smedt.
© 2023 John Wiley & Sons, Inc. Published 2023 by John Wiley & Sons, Inc.

the balance of the four nations achieved through their independence from and interdependence with each other. Sozin's vision for the future required the removal of the one obstacle that could keep his dream from becoming a reality, the Avatar. The death of Avatar Roku supplied the opportunity to ensure fulfillment of his dream. Knowing that the Avatar would be reborn an Air Nomad, Sozin ordered the genocide of the Air Nomads ("The Avatar and the Fire Lord"). As a result, the ambition of the Fire Nation to establish a global empire went unchecked for a century.

By contrast, the move to empire in the United States was not one individual's dream. It was the dream of an entire nation to fulfill manifest destiny – the nineteenth-century ideology that said it was ordained by God, and therefore inevitable, that the United States would expand its dominion over the land. In fact, the desire to obtain the lands held by Indigenous peoples was clear from the start. In 1783, George Washington unequivocally expressed the desires of the nation in a letter to James Duane (one of other founding fathers of the US), "there is nothing to be obtained by an Indian War but the soil they live on. . ."[2] Acquisition of land became the driving factor for the conquest of land and the genocide of Indigenous peoples. In 1845, Washington's sentiments were echoed by John O'Sullivan when he wrote in support of the annexation of Texas as "the fulfillment of our manifest destiny to overspread the continent allotted by Providence for the free development of our yearly multiplying millions."[3] The spirit of conquest imbued the history of the United States as it expanded its influence and territorial hold around the globe. The march toward empire was made over the corpses of the Indigenous peoples who called the coveted lands home since time immemorial.

ATLA's opening refers to "the old days, a time of peace when the Avatar kept the balance between the Water Tribes, Earth Kingdom, Fire Nation, and Air Nomads. But that all changed when the Fire Nation attacked." The Fire Nation's desire for empire disrupts the delicate balance of peace, and the only force that can restore equilibrium, the Avatar, has vanished. The resulting turmoil of that absence takes the form of a hundred-year war and a belief amongst some that the cycle of the Avatar's rebirth has been broken. The opening ends with a "hope that the Avatar will return to save the world" ("The Boy in the Iceberg"). In this series opening, the genocide of the Air Nomads remains unmentioned, an active erasure of a people in favor of the narrative of empire, even if seen in this unfavorable light. The absence of the Avatar upends the social order. The Fire Nation's decision to eliminate the Air Nomads is motivated by their fear of consequences from the possible actions by the Avatar. They thereby remove the one check on their unbridled ambitions. According to Thomas Hobbes (1588–1679) and John Locke (1632–1704), the removal of that fear as a constraint disrupts the social order. This allows for the intentional use of violence that destabilizes the world.[4] Erasure is not an exclusive tool of those who create worlds of fantasy. It is also the tool of those with real-world power.

As sociologist Heinrich Popitz (1925–2002) asserts, "The power of action is the power to do harm," to subject the victim to the desires of the perpetrator, including the purposeful removal from history.[5]

Fictitious revision of history is at play even in the ballads of patriotism sung in the United States. This includes the national anthem, which evokes "the land of the free and home of the brave," with no mention of the Indigenous populations that were the targets of warfare and genocide that the United States empire is built upon. In Samuel Francis Smith's "My Country 'Tis of Thee," a song sung by elementary school children and fraternal organizations, the Euro-American settlers are refashioned into the original inhabitants. Through the lyrics "Land where my fathers died" and "My native country," the existence of Indigenous peoples is blatantly ignored, while the atrocities of the past go unacknowledged and the Euro-Americans replace the Indigenous as the first peoples of the land. The logic of empire diminishes the past's violence by erasing it in the national narrative and history to secure its past and justify its present. Ignorance imbues the national psyche, which understands past atrocities as necessary and matter of fact for progress.

When Kanna "Gran Gran" talks about the destruction of the Air Nomads in her first encounter with Aang, she says, "No one has seen an Airbender in a hundred years. We thought they were extinct. Until my granddaughter and grandson found you" ("The Boy in the Iceberg"). She retells the narrative of the Fire Nation, casting the destruction of the Air Nomads as an "extinction" rather than a "genocide," thereby depicting their extermination as an unavoidable occurrence rather than an extraordinary crime. The isolation of the Southern Water Tribe from the rest of the world leaves them susceptible to, and inadvertent replicators of, the propaganda of the Fire Nation. The Fire Nation's extreme violence in creating an empire is thus portrayed as mundane and inevitable.

Genocide as Empire-building

The full extent of the Fire Nation's atrocities does not remain hidden for long, however. Aang's return to the Southern Air Temple reveals the horrors visited upon the Air Nomads. Katara attempts to temper Aang's expectations by explaining the brutality of the Fire Nation, but Aang dismisses her warnings out of hand: "Just because no one has seen an Airbender doesn't mean the Fire Nation killed them all. They probably escaped" ("The Southern Air Temple"). Their arrival at a deserted temple does not dampen Aang's hope of finding other Airbenders. Hope is replaced by rage when he finds the remains of his mentor Gyatso, surrounded by Fire Nation armaments. Aang's emotional response is reminiscent of that of people who learn about the atrocities committed by the United States in its efforts to fulfill the dream of manifest destiny. With a shock of realization, they recognize that the narrative embraced since childhood lacks historical accuracy. Thus, the comfort and security they have known since an early age are disrupted.

The United States' intentional extermination of diverse peoples is an inseparable part of the processes used to build its continental empire. Seen as a means to securing the land, destroying Indigenous peoples is understood as a necessity, rather than a tactic of empire building. Indeed, the displacement and violence against Indigenous people was seen as necessary to achieve the perceived manifest destiny of the US. For example, on November 29, 1864, a Cheyenne and Arapaho village along Sand Creek in the southeast of the Colorado Territory was attacked by US volunteers under the command of Colonel John M. Chivington. Women, children, and the elderly were massacred throughout the day by the volunteer force using howitzers to take out the villagers; when the carnage was over, the volunteers mutilated the corpses of the vanquished.[6] The imperial desires of the United States took the form of extreme violence resulting in a mass atrocity that stains the nation's history. Yet, it remains absent from most history textbooks, ensuring that a new generation of citizens will be ignorant of the tactics employed to pursue the United States' imperialist ambitions.

Appropriating History and Place

Adding insult to injury, the United States has appropriated the Indigenous populations that were the targets of extermination policies to further its goal of empire. The quintessential image of the Boston Tea Party has become a hallmark of the American Revolution. Revolutionaries disguised themselves as "Indians," making loud war whoops as they boarded the *Dartmouth*, the *Eleanor*, and the *Beaver* and tossed the cargo of tea into Boston Harbor.[7] European Americans, assuming the savage identity that they disdained, laid the foundations for their empire using the imagery of those who would become the victims of imperial progress.

The narrative that excludes reference to those who perished in the construction of empire is reinforced by the repurposing and use of sites and structures of the victims. These places are recommissioned into monuments for the empire builders. The possibility that Air Nomads had survived the Fire Nation's attack raises Aang's hope of reconnecting with them. Those hopes are short-lived, however. In the Northern Air Temple, Team Avatar encounters usurpers who have gone native – reimagined themselves as the Air Nomads – becoming Air Walkers, using gliders and other technologies to take to the heavens ("The Northern Air Temple").[8] Though the Air Walkers have mastered the skies, they are not Airbenders. They are refugees from the Earth Kingdom, displaced from their home by a flood and victims of the century-old war, who have appropriated the Air

Nomad's home and place in local lore. To avoid further victimization, the Air Walkers become collaborators, designing and building war machines for the Fire Nation ("The Northern Air Temple").

The appropriation of the Air Nomads' identity and home is reinforced by the destruction of their cultural heritage. The mural that depicts their history has been severely altered and disfigured by steam pipes and machinery, hallmarks of the progress made at the expense of the Air Nomads' annihilation. Seeing the vandalism, Aang musters the dispassionate response, "This is supposed to be the history of my people" ("The Northern Air Temple"). Aang finds solace in a temple section that hasn't been altered, but that is quickly shattered by a wrecking ball that tears through the wall, decapitating the statue of a monk. Aang responds with the anger and disgust that anyone who witnesses the destruction of their heritage would share: "Do you know what you did? You just destroyed something sacred for a stupid bath house!" ("The Northern Air Temple"). Sadly, destruction of the sacred is a tool used in constructing empires that separates people from the physical embodiments of their spiritual beliefs.

Removal of the sacred disrupts the integral relationship of Indigenous peoples and the land – the geography and environment that has influenced the development of their identity, worldview, language, and religion. This disruption makes them strangers in their lands. On February 26, 1860, a group of men made their way across the one-mile channel between the city of Eureka and the island of Tuluwat in Humboldt Bay, California. For the Wiyot, the island of Tuluwat is the physical and spiritual center of their world. Approximately 200 Wiyot elderly women and children were killed. Wiyot men had left the island to gather supplies to complete the world renewal ceremony, during which Wiyot pray, fast, sing, and dance for all inhabitants of the world. The sacredness of the island and the ceremony were desecrated by those who sought retribution for the infringement of Indigenous peoples on their ranch lands.[9] In destroying and desecrating the sacred sites of their victims, perpetrators of genocide actively work to erase and replace what they perceive as an obstacle to their empire building. In the United States these sites have become cities, national parks, and farm-lands. The descendants of the perpetrators view these places as monuments to progress and appropriate use of the land, hiding the horrors of the past in plain sight.

Silent Wounds

The adverse mental and psychosocial effects on nations and communities that have been affected by genocide are "silent wounds" that impact individuals and societies.[10] The knowledge of the genocide committed against the Air Nomads haunts Aang, inhibiting his ability to master the Avatar state. The grief he experiences over the loss of his people forms an emotional blockage that prevents him from fully realizing his powers as the Avatar. Guru Pathik guides Aang through the process of accepting his grief and helps him realize that the Air Nomads are still present within him ("The Guru"). Aang's success in confronting and working through the trauma associated with the loss of his people is presented simplistically. This is vastly different from the experiences and trauma of the Indigenous peoples in the United States. For Indigenous people, the trauma of the genocide has taken the form of high rates of alcoholism, drug abuse, depression, domestic violence, suicide, and self-disdain.[11] This trauma is not as easily addressed as opening a chakra. It requires individual and community healing. In what form and how that healing will take place remains a work in progress.

Built with violence obscured in their histories, empires take on a glorified persona that charts the nations' progress through fictional and historical accounts. Those on whose lands and bones the new order is built become minor footnotes in the larger narrative. The genocide of the Air Nomads is an essential component in the story of the Fire Nation's imperialism and the ability of the Avatar to thwart those ambitions. Yet, it is treated as a sidebar in the overall story of *ATLA*. For Aang, the resulting trauma of his people's loss affects his ability to move in and out of the Avatar state, thereby hindering his ability to return balance to the world.

In comparison, the United States embraced the idea of manifest destiny as a justification for the genocide of the original inhabitants of the continent. The process of genocide employed in the fulfillment of that destiny receives little attention in the telling of the nation's history, a continuation of the erasure and replacement process that was initiated with the first European footsteps on the continent's eastern shores. Unlike in the *ATLA* universe, restoration of a balance remains out of reach, as the country struggles with deep societal divisions due to its violent past. The foundations of the Fire Nation and the United States were built on unstable grounds, causing one to collapse and the other to wrestle with a reckoning on its origins.

Notes

1. Patrick Wolfe, "Settler Colonialism and the Elimination of the Native," *Journal of Genocide Research* 8 (2006), 387–400.
2. "George Washington to James Duane, September 7, 1781," in Francis Paul Prucha ed., *Documents of United States Indian Policy* (Lincoln: University of Nebraska Press, 2000), 1–2.
3. John O'Sullivan, "Annexation," *United States Magazine and Democratic Review* 17 (1845), 5–10.
4. Heinrich Popitz, *Phenomena of Power: Authority, Domination, and Violence*, trans. Gianfranco Poggi, Andreas Göttlich, and Jochen Dreher (New York: Columbia University Press, 2017), 39.
5. Popitz, 25.

6. Ari Kelman, *A Misplaced Massacre: Struggling Over the Memory of Sand Creek* (Cambridge, MA: Harvard University Press, 2013), 8–15.

7. Philip Joseph Deloria, *Playing Indian* (New Haven, CT: Yale University Press, 1998), 2.

8. Shari M. Huhndorf, *Going Native: Indians in the American Cultural Imagination* (Ithaca, NY: Cornell University Press, 2001), 20.

9. Kerri J. Malloy, "Renewing the World: Disrupting Settler-colonial Destruction," in Sara E. Brown and Stephen D. Smith eds., *The Routledge Handbook of Religion, Mass Atrocity, and Genocide* (New York: Routledge, 2022), 71.

10. Benjamin P. Bowser, Carl Word, and Kate Shaw, "Ongoing Genocides and the Need for Healing: The Cases of Native and African Americans," *Genocide Studies and Prevention* 15 (2021), 85.

11. Ibid.

24

Anarchist Airbenders
On Anarchist Philosophy in *Avatar: The Last Airbender*

Savriël Dillingh

Anarchists get a bad rap. More often than not, TV shows, comic-books, videogames and sometimes even serious journalism portray anarchists as lazy work-shirkers or as cartoonish evil villains, hell-bent on causing chaos for chaos's sake. Unfortunately, the world of *Avatar: The Last Airbender* isn't immune to this habit. Book Three of *Avatar: The Legend of Korra* even features an antagonist, Zaheer, who is nominally an anarchist. His reputation as a bringer of chaos is nothing less than deserved, but here's the funny thing: Zaheer isn't an anarchist! Aang, however, might be. In fact, anarchism can be found all over *ATLA*. In what follows, we'll see where.

What Is Anarchism?

What is anarchism and where in the four nations can it be found?[1] This is easier asked than answered, because unlike standard political theories such as liberalism or Marxism, anarchism isn't a cohesive body of thought. It isn't institutionalized, nor does it have an officially authorized canon. Now, this might seem like a pretty big problem, but anarchists consider this to be one of its strengths. Of course, anarchists agree on several fundamental things – and it is these things that star so prominently in Aang's journey across the four nations – but while these things are essential, they are secondary to anarchism's focus on *action*.

According to the anthropologist and anarchist activist David Graeber (1961–2020), anarchism recognizes that you can probably never convince another person to see the world exactly as you see it. And so, instead of trying to get everyone to agree on everything, it aims first and foremost to land on a plan that everyone can live with through anarchist deliberation

Avatar: The Last Airbender and Philosophy: Wisdom from Aang to Zuko, First Edition.
Edited by Helen De Cruz and Johan De Smedt.
© 2023 John Wiley & Sons, Inc. Published 2023 by John Wiley & Sons, Inc.

methods (such as consensus processes, or egalitarian decision-making practices).[2] Anarchists wouldn't need to agree on what is ethically speaking wrong with the Fire Nation's imperialist project; it is much more important that they agree on the fact that they need a plan to take down the Fire Lord. For this reason, anarchism is both practical and utopian; equal parts serious and playful. It believes we can find solutions that are acceptable to everyone, but doesn't pretend we can all see eye-to-eye on everything. Its focus, therefore, lies not on creating a theoretically unassailable framework, but on making the world anarchists want to live in *right now*. This, necessarily, involves much play, experimentation, and bravery. After all, "[g]rim, joyless revolutionaries who sacrifice all pleasure to the cause can only produce grim joyless societies."[3] And although Aang is undeniably a revolutionary, no one could call him grim or joyless.

What Do Anarchists Believe?[4]

Anarchists are continuously debating the best organizational principle or the best course of action, but all agree on the following.[5] Anarchism embodies the deeply held belief that power more often than not doesn't fix problems, but makes them worse. In fact, many of the world's problems that need fixing are subtly *due to* the very power we consider necessary to fix them. For instance, anarchists wouldn't look at the Earth Kingdom's secret police – the Dai Li introduced in "City of Walls and Secrets" – and think that an effective solution to their abuses of power would be to empower a *counter-police force* to make sure they never overstep their bounds. To suggest such a thing would be to carelessly accept that the Dai Li is necessary in the first place. And is it? Does Ba Sing Se really need secret police? These are the questions anarchism wants you to ask. Instead of erecting a counter-police force, anarchists would call for the Dai Li to be abolished, recognizing that granting several earthbenders so much official power wasn't a terribly good idea to begin with. They'd argue that the citizens of Ba Sing Se are perfectly capable of policing themselves in a democratic, communal way that doesn't unduly hand out power to only a few. Similarly, it is power itself that anarchists consider our world's biggest challenge. The less power people have over other people, the more harmonious human life will become, they argue.[6] According to anarchists, having power over one another makes people *unfree*.[7] Now, do you see why anarchists think that having a diversity of theoretical perspectives is a strength?

"But don't we need *some* power to organize at all?" you might be thinking. "Much less than you think," would be the anarchist's answer. Historically, there have been many societies that managed to get their stuff in order just fine without emperors, kings, or governments.[8] There's no reason to think that Ba Sing Se's citizenry wouldn't be able to do the same. In Katara's words: "why do boys always think someone has to be the leader?" ("Jet"). Still, there's undeniably some merit to the question, if only because so many people ask it. That's why Noam Chomsky, one of the world's most famous living anarchists, speaks of *unjustified hierarchies* rather than power. Chomsky argues that all forms of hierarchy – and all authoritarian institutions – have to prove they are justified *first*.[9] That last word is important! It means that, if there is no decent reason for it, it is at first glance *always* bad for one person to hold power over another. However, power may be justified in some situations. For instance, imagine that Toph has burned her feet and is, in a state of confused shock, stumbling toward a cliffside. You pull her aside and physically restrain her from walking toward what would almost certainly be death. Now, that's clearly an extremely authoritarian situation! You literally *overpower* Toph and so this action requires justification. But you *can* give a justification in this case – quite easily, in fact. Namely, Toph would tumble off the cliff because she is blind and requires her feet to use her earthbending to see. Chomsky simply states that, once you start looking into hierarchies in society, most of them will actually be unable to provide an adequate justification for their existence.[10] The "Toph walking off a cliff" example is easily defensible, but if you look into power structures in society, so anarchists argue, most hierarchies quickly show themselves to be unjustifiable.

The Dai Li say they need to establish a tyrannical rule to keep the Fire Nation from taking over Ba Sing Se ("City of Walls and Secrets"). However, it is a coup staged by the Dai Li that ultimately delivers the city into the hands of the Fire Nation. Ironically, unjustified hierarchies often bring about the very things they are supposed to prevent.

There Are No Unjust Hierarchies in Ba Sing Se

This attitude toward unjustified hierarchies plays a major role in *ATLA*. Let's consider some specific examples. In "The Storm," Aang reveals to Katara that he had eavesdropped on a conversation between his mentor Gyatso and High Monk Pasang. Against Gyatso's wishes, Pasang had unilaterally decided that Aang would be taken from Gyatso's care and be sent to the Eastern Air Temple to continue his Avatar training. In response, Aang ran away from the Southern Air Temple and encased himself and Appa in ice for what turned out to be a hundred years, leaving his people to be slaughtered by the Fire Nation. High Monk Pasang could order Gyatso around without his consent and make an impactful decision about Aang, based on an arbitrary, unjustified power structure, his rank in the hierarchy of Air Monks. Even though Gyatso, as Aang's mentor, would surely have been more knowledgeable about the situation, Pasang chose to dismiss his opinion, insights, and expertise. What's worse, no one thought to ask Aang himself! Now, with the power of hindsight, we can see that Pasang made a very wrong choice. In any event, we can be sure that if the senior Air Monk had taken time to find common ground with Gyatso and Aang, and had considered their views to be as important as his own, things could have gone quite differently. Perhaps Aang wouldn't have run away. Perhaps he'd even have chosen to go to the Eastern Air Temple himself, if he'd had a say in the matter and had been offered some time to think about it. *ATLA* explores this theme time and again: when people (even well-intentioned ones) wield their power in unjustified and arbitrary ways, calamity often ensues.

Another example: in "The Blue Spirit," Commander Zhao fails to convince a colonel to let him use the Yuyan Archers – an elite group of archers – to try and capture the Avatar. When a letter arrives informing Zhao that he has been promoted to admiral, he tells the colonel (now suddenly of lower rank) that his friendly request is now a command. The Avatar is caught, but escapes, leaving Zhao's fortress in tatters and his reputation besmirched. Zhao's entire character is a lesson in the dangers of unjustified hierarchies. A gifted firebender himself, Zhao expresses his belief that fire is "the superior element." On the basis of this belief he argues it is right and just for the Fire Nation to dominate all other peoples, leading Zhao to force his will onto others, resulting in death, destruction, and eventually his own downfall.

Are there any justified hierarchies in *ATLA*, then? Yes, there are, and these hierarchies are surprisingly egalitarian. For example, Uncle Iroh, one of the most powerful firebenders during Aang's tenure as Avatar, mentors his nephew Zuko not through force or dominance, but through love and recognition. Zuko makes plenty of wrong, bullheaded, and downright senseless decisions during the show, but Iroh never uses his power to force Zuko's will to his own ends. And seeing Iroh's fearsome firebending skills, we can be sure he could do that if he wanted. Instead, in "Sozin's Comet, Part 2: The Old Masters," Iroh makes it clear that all he ever wanted for Zuko was for him to find his own path. This reveals something about when anarchists feel power is used in just ways. Specifically, power that is *self-effacing* is just. This means power that is used to *empower* others. After all, power used in this way *lessens* your own power over others as a result. Consider, for instance, that when Katara taught Aang waterbending, it made her a less powerful bender by comparison! She could have also withheld her teachings, of course, thereby forever remaining a more powerful waterbender than the Avatar. And, in fact, most anarchists would consider that an unjustified hierarchy.

This is why anarchism defends sharing information widely and freely: because it is, in a very real way, *sharing power*.[11] Anarchists would never jealously guard knowledge in a personal library, like the owl spirit Wan Shi Tong ("The Library"). They would distribute it across the four nations for all to know. That's why, in our own world, most anarchists' writings can easily be found in free online repositories. Even anarchists who hold positions at universities and publish in scholarly journals will generally make sure their work is easily accessible (for example, by making it available on their personal website). However, sharing knowledge and power comes with a lot of responsibility. Since no one can tell you how and what to believe, you will have to put in the work and make up your own mind. The Avatar state provides a useful analogy. In this state, the current Avatar has access to the accumulated knowledge of all the past Avatars. In "Sozin's Comet, Part 2: The Old Masters," Aang asks several of his previous iterations how to combine his Air Nomad values of respecting all life with killing Ozai, now the newly styled Phoenix King. To his great sadness, all of the previous Avatars tell him that killing Ozai is the only real choice he has. In the end, however, Aang follows his own path and takes away the Phoenix King's firebending powers instead of killing him. This is exactly what anarchism encourages; listen to others, take them seriously, learn from them, but always make up your own mind and think for yourself.

Human Nature and Mutual Aid

Anarchism involves a radical commitment to democracy – sharing power – and an opposition to unjust hierarchies. But there's more. Anarchism also involves a way of looking at human beings and human interaction. This perspective is encapsulated in the anarchist principle "mutual aid," which is often ascribed to the Russian biologist and philosopher Pyotr Kropotin (1842–1921). Like most anarchists, he generally considered mutual aid – as well as opposition to unjust hierarchies – as a tendency in human nature that has played a major role in our species' evolutionary trajectory.[12] The principle of mutual aid is straightforward: people have a responsibility to take care of each other and voluntarily share their community's resources. Anarchism thus acknowledges that we owe each other in a very real, tangible way. In fact, we are forever connected through our shared past, present, and future – you wouldn't be reading this if someone hadn't thought of the alphabet, or of books, or of the printing press, for instance. For that matter, you wouldn't be here at all without your ancestors, without the people producing your food, the people who built your house, the people who taught you. Most importantly, you wouldn't be here reading this book if someone didn't think of making *ATLA*! We're all inextricably connected, or, as the swampbender Huu explains, "We're all living together, even if most folks don't act like it. We all have the same roots and we are all branches of the same tree" ("The Swamp"). Anarchism takes these facts to their logical conclusion: because we are all inextricably dependent on each other, we owe each other mutual aid.

Practicing mutual aid might sound a little utopian. But this is only because, while the principle sounds rather straightforward, it incorporates a complex and very specific way of looking at humans and human interactions. And we're not used to thinking of ourselves in the way mutual aid encourages us to! Back in Kropotkin's time (and no less so today) people tended to think that human beings, deep down, are savages.[13] We would destroy each other, or at the very least be entirely unable to cooperate, without a ruler to keep us in check (hence the idea that power and hierarchy are necessary). Mutual aid is based on a very different idea of human nature. According to Kropotkin, human beings aren't fundamentally *bad* – instead, we're fundamentally *cooperative*. Nature bestows huge evolutionary boons on those species that are social and manage to work together rather than those that only compete. Human beings are so far on top of the food chain not because we're ruthless, but because we're so uniquely capable of cooperating![14] Note that Kropotkin doesn't argue that human beings are fundamentally *good*; anarchists certainly don't think humans have no imperfections. However, as Kropotkin showed, we certainly have the ability to work together in egalitarian ways without hierarchical structures keeping us in check through violent means. In this ability, anarchists see proof that a better world is possible. Mutual aid only seems utopian to most of us because our economic, political, and social paradigms are fundamentally geared toward an individualistic conception of human nature. But *even in this paradigm*, mutual aid is exactly what happens (almost automatically) in disaster situations. For instance, mutual aid groups sprang up in many places after Hurricane Katrina in 2015, and during the COVID-19 pandemic of the 2020s. Clearly, Kropotkin was onto something when he argued mutual aid is a very powerful human impulse.

By facilitating our cooperative nature and by keeping out authoritarian institutions and practices, anarchism proposes that human beings will be able to live together more harmoniously. Iroh tells Zuko as much in "The Avatar and the Fire Lord," when he explains to his nephew that "evil and good are always at war inside you, Zuko. It is your nature. Your legacy. But, there is a bright side . . . Born in you along with all the strife, is the power to restore balance to the world." Zuko's character arc illustrates this conflict between the authoritarian and the anarchist views of human nature. The prince is visibly torn between these two philosophies. Ever since he was a child, he's been taught that the Fire Nation was superior to the other elemental polities and their denizens. He, as its prince, was on top of the highest hierarchy. Think, for instance, of "The Headband." In this episode, Aang accidentally infiltrates a Fire Nation school, where he is forced to recite the Fire Nation oath which includes reference to a "March of Civilization" – the Fire Nation's self-appointed task of "civilizing" the other elemental communities. The genocide of the Air Nomads was apparently a part of this civilization process. Moreover, in several episodes, including "Sozin's Comet Part 4: Avatar Aang," we see Princess Azula refer to non-royalty as "filth." It's not so strange that Zuko, having grown up in such an environment, had started to believe that human nature needs to be suppressed by power. However, under the tutelage of his uncle, Zuko learns how to come to terms with his own darkness. Iroh fosters the part of Zuko that is loving and cooperative. Finally, Zuko rejects the imperialist politics of his family and joins the Aang Gaang. This time, however, instead of trying to force them to accept him (like a younger version of him certainly would have), Zuko realizes that they all have their separate qualms with him that all deserve to be addressed. For most of the second half of Book Three, Zuko has to work hard to convince each member of the Aang Gaang that he is worth trusting. Clearly, Zuko's outlook on human nature has somewhat changed from an authoritative one to a more egalitarian, anarchist view, and his own behavior has followed suit. In the final episode, the newly crowned Fire Lord Zuko vows to build a "new era of love and peace," but this time *together* with the Avatar. Unfortunately, Zuko's transformation isn't total: an anarchist would disagree with the existence of the institution of a Fire Lord altogether! But Zuko's progress is undeniable.

We've seen that the view of human nature underlying mutual aid can be found in *ATLA*, but mutual aid in the practical sense – the actual *practice* that involves helping, caring, and sharing with your community – also features prominently in the show. Think, for instance, about the guided tour of Ba Sing Se ("City of Walls and Secrets") in which Team Avatar see that the city segregates the rich and the poor, and that citizens are actively disinclined to help each other.[15] Contrast this with "Winter Solstice, Part 1: The Spirit World," in which the citizens of Senlin Village ask the Avatar to help them banish the angry spirit Hei Bai. After Aang has managed to do so – with some minor hiccups – Sokka asks the village elder for some supplies and money, to which he happily agrees. The small villages the Aang Gaang visit during their adventure are consistently portrayed as places where people know each other and take care of each other. But perhaps a more illustrative example of mutual aid (and how painful it can be when it is not forthcoming) appears in "The Chase." Toph, coming from a wealthy family with servants, has just joined the Aang Gaang and she has difficulty coming to grips with the sense of community that exists between Aang, Katara, and Sokka. Katara softly prompts "So, Toph, usually when setting up camp, we try to divide the work," to which Toph responds "I can carry my own weight." She repeats this phrase three times during the episode, not understanding that the entire team is *carrying each other's weight*. Later, an enraged Aang incisively points this out when he tells her: "You're always talking about how you carry your own weight, but you're not. *He* is! Appa's carrying your weight!" Hurt and offended, Toph runs off, but has the good fortune of running into Iroh. The wisdom he offers her points toward mutual aid: "You sound like my nephew, always thinking you need to do things on your own, without anyone's support. There is nothing wrong with letting people who love you help you." This leads Toph to realize that helping others also involves letting yourself be helped – the very essence of mutual aid and the holistic, cooperative view of human nature underlying it.

The Anarchist You Are

At the end of the day, anarchism is more something you *do* than what you *are*.[16] In this sense, there are many anarchists in the world of *ATLA* – they just don't call themselves that. Aang was an anarchist when he made time to have fun in a world under siege; Iroh was an anarchist when he loved his nephew without coercing him. And it's not so different in our own world. There are plenty of people who feed the homeless in their spare time, who create community networks, who resist unjust hierarchies – they do all this without the need for an authority. These are ostensibly anarchist actions, even if the people who perform them wouldn't call themselves so. Ultimately, anarchism carries hope, and the promise for a better future. The only way to really change the world is to be a joyful rebel who believes, perhaps against all odds, that true love will prevail. Indeed, Aang is the embodiment of this hope.

Notes

1. A well-known anarchist credo is "No Borders, No Nations." Yet *ATLA* stars the four nations that, undoubtedly, have borders on all sides. Still, this might rather be a point in favor of rather than against finding anarchism in *ATLA*! This is because the wisest characters in the show repeatedly emphasize that the separation between the four nations, like the separation between the elements, is only an illusion (see also Chapter 4: "The End of the World").
2. David Graeber, *Fragments of an Anarchist Anthropology* (Chicago: Prickly Paradigm Press, 2004), 7–9.
3. Andrej Grubacic and David Graeber, "Anarchism, or the Revolutionary Movement of the Twenty-first Century," *The Anarchist Library*, January 6, 2004, at https://theanarchistlibrary.org/library/andrej-grubacic-david-graeber-anarchism-or-the-revolutionary-movement-of-the-twenty-first-centu.
4. There are a great many online resources through which you can find out all the (differing) things anarchists believe. To start you out, I recommend the classic Errico Malatesta, *Anarchy*, available at http://theanarchistlibrary.org/library/errico-malatesta-anarchy, and Emma Goldman, *Anarchism and Other Essays*, at http://theanarchistlibrary.org/library/emma-goldman-anarchism-and-other-essays, but also the more modern Peter Gelderloos, "Anarchy Works," at https://theanarchistlibrary.org/library/peter-gelderloos-anarchy-works, as well as the very basic Peter Storm, *Anarchism: Basic Concepts and Ideas*, at http://theanarchistlibrary.org/library/peter-storm-anarchism-basic-concepts-and-ideas.
5. Some "schools" of anarchism even choose to name themselves after an organizational principle, such as anarcho-syndicalism, anarcho-communism, anarchist cooperativism, anarcho-capitalism, and market anarchism.
6. See, for perhaps the most thorough defense of this argument, David Graeber and David Wengrow, *The Dawn of Everything: A New History of Humanity* (New York: Farrar, Straus & Giroux, 2021).

7. Another anarchist credo: "No Gods, No Masters."

8. See, for both historical and contemporary examples, Harold Barclay, *People without Government: An Anthropology of Anarchy* (London: Kahn and Averill, 1990).

9. Noam Chomsky, *On Anarchism* (London: Penguin, 2014), 32–33.

10. Chomsky, 33.

11. After all, as the philosopher Francis Bacon (1561–1626) famously said: "knowledge is power."

12. Pyotr Kropotkin, *Mutual Aid*, at https://theanarchistlibrary.org/library/petr-kropotkin-mutual-aid-a-factor-of-evolution.

13. The classic example of this sentiment is Thomas Hobbes's *Leviathan*, at https://gutenberg.org/files/3207/3207-h/3207-h.htm.

14. Pyotr Kropotkin, *Ethics: Origin and Development*, chapter 4, at https://theanarchistlibrary.org/library/petr-kropotkin-ethics-origin-and-development.

15. See Chapter 16: "The Earth King, Ignorance, and Responsibility."

16. This is a slight paraphrase of a sentence David Graeber had in his Twitter bio for years.

25

A Buddhist Perspective on Energy Bending, Strength, and the Power of Aang's Spirit

Nicholaos Jones and Holly Jones

When Aang exits the Avatar State after besting Fire Lord Ozai (now the Phoenix King) in battle, Ozai hurls a critical accusation: "Even with all the power in the world, you are still weak!" Ozai's accusation frames power as a tool for domination, and strength as a willingness to dominate at any cost. From Ozai's perspective, Aang has all the power in the world because the Avatar State enables Aang to conquer any foe, but Aang is weak because, when exiting the Avatar State, he shows an unwillingness to defeat the Fire Nation by killing his enemy. Because he views Aang as weak, Ozai is confident that Aang cannot use his power to win. Ozai thus moves to attack once more.

Aang is unwilling to kill Ozai in order to secure peace. But this unwillingness allows Aang to find a winning strategy that does not reproduce Ozai's violence. Aang's alternative involves making his spirit vulnerable to Ozai's. Binding Ozai in place with earth, Aang places one hand on Ozai's forehead, another on his chest. When their spirits mingle, Ozai's energy begins to consume Aang's. Aang is very nearly corrupted by Ozai. But Aang prevails. Energy erupts from Aang's eyes and proceeds to engulf Ozai. Aang secures peace, not by killing his enemy, but by removing the firebending ability that made Ozai fearsome and powerful.

During Aang's intermingling with Fire Lord Ozai, the voice of a Lion Turtle hints at the reason why Aang prevails. "In the era before the Avatar, we bent not the elements but the energy within ourselves. To bend another's energy, your own spirit must be unbendable or you will be corrupted and destroyed." The Lion Turtle's remark indicates that Aang's alternative strategy involves bending Ozai's energy, and that Aang is victorious because his spirit is unbendable while Ozai's presumably is bendable. This raises several questions.

Avatar: The Last Airbender and Philosophy: Wisdom from Aang to Zuko, First Edition.
Edited by Helen De Cruz and Johan De Smedt.
© 2023 John Wiley & Sons, Inc. Published 2023 by John Wiley & Sons, Inc.

1. What is it for a spirit to be unbendable?
2. What is it to bend another's energy?
3. Does Aang's ability to bend Ozai's spirit refute Ozai's accusation that Aang is weak?
4. What does Aang's ability indicate about what it means to be powerful?

The Lion Turtle's remark directly motivates the first two questions. Aang's final confrontation with Ozai motivates the other two. As we shall see, none of the answers are obvious, but Buddhism can help us understand the answers and the story.

Powerful Vulnerability

Ozai's conception of power and strength offers one approach to answering these questions. On his conception, bending another's energy is a matter of dominating their spirit in order to manipulate their powers, and someone's spirit is unbendable whenever it is capable of resisting any such manipulation by others. So Aang defeats Ozai by dominating Ozai's spirit, and Aang's spirit is unbendable because the power of the Avatar allows Aang to resist Ozai's energy. Moreover, on this conception, Aang is clever but not weak. Aang is willing to do whatever it takes to dominate Ozai, but his cleverness allows him to find a non-lethal strategy for doing so. This cleverness, together with the superior power of the Avatar, allows Aang to bend Ozai's spirit. Power, so understood, coincides with strength, and Aang is powerful by virtue of having a stronger spirit than Ozai.

Tempting as these answers might be, they do not sit well with the narrative arc of Aang's journey. The preceding answers valorize resistance to opposition and domination over others. But Aang's journey involves letting go rather than dominating, learning acceptance rather than mastering resistance. Moreover, Aang is not willing to do whatever it takes to dominate Ozai. Aang exits the Avatar State during his battle with Ozai precisely because he is unwilling to win by killing. Moreover, Aang is not willing to dominate Ozai at all. The mingling of Aang's and Ozai's spirits indicates that Aang's alternative strategy involves opening himself to Ozai's corruption. This vulnerability precludes domination, because dominating another involves confronting them while defending against openings through which they might attack. (Consider, by analogy, strategies for domination in chess or boxing that involve giving opponents an opening to attack in order to induce them to unbalance or overextend themselves.)

Better answers to the preceding questions derive from teachings of Buddhism. On this alternative, Buddhist-inspired approach, bending another's energy is a matter of merging with their spirit in order to manipulate their powers, and someone's spirit is unbendable when it is thoroughly vulnerable to others, lacking all resistance to being manipulated by others. So Aang defeats Ozai, not through domination or resistance, but through making his spirit entirely vulnerable to Ozai. This vulnerability is the vehicle through which Aang merges his spirit with Ozai's, and this merging allows Aang to control Ozai's powers as if they are his own. Moreover, on this alternative approach, Aang's weakness is precisely the quality that secures victory over Ozai. Aang's vulnerability makes him weak (by Ozai's standard), but it also makes Aang's spirit unbendable and allows him to take away Ozai's capacity for firebending. Power, so understood, coincides with the capacity to realize one's own goals, and Aang is powerful by virtue of having the capacity to make himself more vulnerable than anyone else. Or so we shall argue.

Unbendable Spirit

When speaking with Aang, the Lion Turtle offers some cryptic wisdom about what it is for a spirit to be unbendable. "The true mind can weather all the lies and illusions without being lost. The true heart can tough the poison of hatred without being harmed" ("Sozin's Comet, Part 2: The Old Masters"). According to the Lion Turtle, having an unbendable spirit requires having a true mind and a true heart. But the Lion Turtle does not explain what it is for a mind or a heart to be true.

Buddhist teachings address both requirements. Briefly, according to these teachings, a true heart is one free from emotional hindrance, and a true mind is one free from delusion. Emotional hindrance and delusion foster what Buddhists refer to as *duḥkha*, a condition of suffering and dissatisfaction with the way things are. Freedom from emotional hindrance and delusion, by contrast, promotes encountering pain and failure – as well as pleasure and success – calmly and fearlessly. When Aang defeats Ozai, he embodies this fearless calm. His spirit is unbendable, not because his Avatar powers allow him to dominate Ozai, but because he lets go of his emotional muck and embraces his role as the Avatar.

Buddhist teachings identify five fundamental hindrances that foster *duḥkha*. Each hindrance is a kind of emotional muck that encourages domination of others and sustains resistance to the way things are. The *Discourse on Worthy Deeds*, the sixty-first discourse in the fourth book of the *Numerical Discourses* (*Aṅguttara Nikāya*), presents these hindrances as impediments to wisdom.[1]

> And what is accomplishment in wisdom? If one dwells with a heart overcome by longing and unrighteous greed, one does what should be avoided and neglects one's duties, so that one's fame and happiness are spoiled. If one dwells with a heart overcome by ill-will . . . by dullness and drowsiness . . . by restlessness and remorse . . . by doubt, one does what should be avoided and neglects one's duties, so that one's fame and happiness are spoiled.

When . . . a noble disciple has understood thus: "Longing and unrighteous greed are a defilement of the mind," he abandons them. When he has understood thus: "Ill will . . . dullness and drowsiness . . . restlessness and remorse . . . doubt [are defilements] of the mind," he abandons [them].

When . . . a noble disciple has understood thus . . . and abandoned [them], he is then called a noble disciple of great wisdom, of wide wisdom, one who sees the range, one accomplished in wisdom. This is called accomplishment in wisdom.[2]

Aang struggles with all five hindrances, but he ultimately overcomes them and has a true heart.

The first hindrance concerns sensory desire, longing for pleasure through the bodily senses. Aang struggles with this hindrance as a young child. He enjoys fruit pies, airball, and comradery with his friends, and he flees his responsibilities as the Avatar, in part, from a desire to retain these pleasures. He overcomes his grief at the loss of these pleasures when clearing his fourth chakra with Guru Pathik, and he overcomes his resistance to being the Avatar when he clears his fifth chakra ("The Guru").

The second hindrance is ill will. Ill will involves aversion, wanting to reject what one has. It can manifest as anger, bitterness, hostility, or resentment. Aang's struggles with ill will center upon change and loss. He shows anger when he discovers the destruction of the Southern Air Temple ("The Southern Air Temple"). He is similarly hostile when he witnesses a mechanic destroy a statue at the Northern Air Temple in order to make room for a bathhouse. Aang's loss of Appa in the desert also prompts several bouts of anger, as when Aang yells at Toph for not preventing Appa's kidnapping. While traveling through the desert, he lashes out at Katara after extracting water from a desert cloud. When confronting sandbenders he suspects of stealing Appa, Aang destroys several of their sailers and, entering the Avatar State, generates a massive sandstorm. Insofar as Aang's anger arises from grieving about change and attachment to that which is lost, Aang overcomes ill will arising from change when clearing his fourth chakra with Guru Pathik, and he overcomes most of his ill will arising from attachment – everything except his attachment to Katara – when working on his seventh chakra ("Bitter Work").

The third hindrance is dullness and drowsiness. This manifests as depression or inertia. Aang struggles most with this hindrance when Appa goes missing. For example, when Aang, his friends, and some refugees reach the Serpent's Pass, they find a sign that says, "Abandon hope." Ying, one of the refugees, comments that hope is all they have. Aang's curt reply indicates a latent depression about Appa's absence: "The monks used to say that hope was just a distraction, so maybe we do need to abandon it . . . Hope is not going to get us into Ba Sing Se, and it's not going to help find Appa" ("The Serpent's Pass"). Aang responds to his hopelessness by focusing on the task at hand – getting the refugees across the Serpent's Pass. Success in this endeavor does not resolve his hopelessness, but it does allow for a circumstance that does. After crossing the pass, Ying gives birth to a daughter, whom she names Hope. When Aang meets the baby, Ying remarks, "I want our daughter's name to be unique. I want it to mean something." Ying's gesture of hopefulness reminds Aang that he should not flee from his feelings, that his love for Appa – and for his friends – is valuable even when circumstances are bleak. "I've been going through a really hard time lately. But you've made me . . . hopeful again. I thought I was trying to be strong. But really I was just running away from my feelings. Seeing this family together, so full of happiness and love, it's reminded me how I feel about Appa . . . and how I feel about you [Katara, Suki, Sokka, and Toph]." The love of his (found) family allows Aang to overcome his depression, and he departs with newfound resolve to find Appa.

The fourth hindrance is restlessness and remorse. Aang's struggles with this hindrance are most apparent when he is preparing for an inevitable confrontation with Fire Lord Ozai ("Nightmares and Daydreams"). Aang can't sleep. When he does sleep, he has absurd nightmares in which he is unprepared for the confrontation. He is also restless. He trains constantly in response to worries that he won't be able to stop the Fire Lord, and he criticizes his friends for not being diligent in their own preparations. Katara eventually calls Aang's behavior to his attention. "Aang! I know you're just trying to help, but you *really* need to get a grip. You're unraveling" ("Nightmares and Daydreams"). Aang's friends offer well-intentioned advice – yoga, talking, screaming into a pillow, massage. The distractions don't work. Aang's nightmares persist. He overcomes his worry only when his friends voice their confidence in him. Katara takes the lead. "Listen, you've been training for this since the day we met. I've seen your progress. You're smart, brave, and strong enough" ("Nightmares and Daydreams"). Sokka and Toph voice similar encouragements. When Aang falls asleep shortly thereafter, he dreams of Ozai once more – but this time it is Ozai, rather than Aang, who is unprepared.

The fifth and final hindrance is doubt. Doubt can manifest as indecision, uncertainty, lack of conviction, and lack of trust. Aang admits to Katara that his doubt is long-standing, and he suggests that doubt is what prompted him to flee from his home. "I was afraid and confused, I didn't know what to do" ("The Storm"). But Aang most often struggles with doubt and uncertainty when trying to master his ability to bend elements other than air. For example, when learning earthbending from Toph, Aang becomes frustrated and wants to give up: "I know, I know, I know, I know! I get it, all right? I need to ace it head on like a rock, but I just can't do it. I don't know why, but I can't" ("Bitter Work"). Despite these doubts, he eventually masters all four elements. For example, Aang overcomes doubts about earthbending while saving Sokka from an attack by a wild animal. Sokka is trapped in the ground, about to be attacked by a saber-tooth moose lion. When the moose-lion charges, Aang stands his ground in order to protect Sokka. Shortly thereafter, Toph reminds Aang of the courage he showed. Aang's conviction in his strength then dissolves his doubt and allows him to bend a rock into a nearby canyon wall.

By overcoming his emotional hindrances, Aang comes to have a true heart. He comes to have a true mind, as well, but this achievement is more intellectual than emotional. Aang's path to having a true mind involves overcoming delusions that foster resistance to his circumstances and obligations.

Buddhist teachings identify many delusions. Paradigmatic examples include erroneous views about the sources and remedies for *duḥkha* as well as misconceptions about cause–effect relations and the ephemerality of all things. The contemporary Vietnamese Buddhist teacher Thích Nhất Hạnh contrasts the deluded mind with true mind.

> The world of birth and death is brought about by deluded mind. Wrong impulses arise from this mind. Impulses, in turn, produce seeds that make up consciousness. The cycle of birth, old age, and death based on ignorance brings us much suffering.
>
> There is also a world conditioned by true mind. This world has sunlight, bird song, the wind in the pine trees - just as in the world we see around us - but it does not have being and nonbeing, coming and going, same and differ-ent, birth and death. The world that has true mind as its seed cause is the world of the Avatamsaka Sutra, where the one encompasses the all, where there can be no fear. True mind is the means for understanding birthlessness and deathlessness.[3]

Delusions ensnare us, making us experience the world as an aimless succession of pleasures and pains, successes and failures. The delusions also get us to experience this succession with attachment, so that our own consciousness alternates between moments of calm and moments of suffering or dissatisfaction. By contrast, the true mind frees us from the cycles of *duḥkha*, allowing us to live calmly and without fear of change or failure.

Perhaps the most fundamental delusion, according to Buddhist teaching, is that the self is separate from and independent of others. Buddhism con-ceptualizes the ideal person as one who is fully aware of how their existence and identity arise by virtue of their relations to others, and thereby concep-tualizes those who strive for self-sufficiency and independence as delu-sional. Aang overcomes this delusion when conversing with Huu in the swamp, learning that "Everything is connected" ("The Swamp"). Aang reiterates this insight when training with Guru Pathik ("The Guru"). His insight contrasts with Fire Lord Ozai's ambition to be a supreme ruler who controls others without those others, in turn, affecting his plans or identity.[4]

Aang comes to have a true mind by overcoming the delusion that he is separate from and independent of others. He comes to have a true heart by overcoming various emotional hindrances. Ultimately, his true mind allows Aang to discern a path to victory against Fire Lord Ozai that does not involve violence, and his true heart allows Aang to merge spirits with Fire Lord Ozai without being harmed by Ozai's rage and lust for power.

Strength and Vulnerability

In coming to have a true heart and a true mind, Aang abandons any intention to dominate or resist the way things are. His spirit becomes unbendable, not because he is strong by Fire Lord Ozai's standards, but because he is thoroughly vulnerable. Aang's vulnerability allows Ozai's spirit to penetrate his own – and, conversely, *his* spirit to penetrate Ozai's and thereby bend Ozai's energy. Buddhist teachings depict this kind of mutual penetration with the metaphor of Indra's net. Indra is one of the most powerful divinities in the Buddhist pantheon. He is also a paragon of generosity. His net, composed as a lattice of mirror-like jewels, represents the way in which everything is connected. Each jewel reflects every other within itself and, in turn, appears as a reflection in every other jewel.

The reflection of one jewel in another is a metaphor for the way in which one thing penetrates into another. The mutually penetrating reflections of the jewels allow each jewel to exist in all other jewels freely and without resistance. This aspect of the metaphor is meant to depict the way in which interconnection involves different things entering into and influencing each other without resistance or domination, each vulnerable to the others and thereby also made to be what it is by those others.

Aang's final encounter with Fire Lord Ozai depicts a similar relation. When Aang connects with Ozai, his spirit enters into Ozai's, just as Ozai's spirit enters into Aang's. A willingness to be vulnerable, and the absence of a will to dominate or remain separate from Ozai, allows Aang to bend Ozai's energy and to remove his firebending.

The metaphor of Indra's net is apt for understanding Aang's relation to Ozai, because Aang's victory over Ozai resembles Indra's victory over demons. In the Story of the Eagle's Nest (*Kulāvaka-jātaka*), from a collection of tales known as the *Jātakamālā*, Indra banishes the demons of darkness from Mount Sumeru into the ocean. The demons vow to reclaim their residence in the heavens, and Indra engages them in battle at the border where ocean meets land. Indra's army retreats against the onslaught. But Indra persists. On the brink of victory, he notices that his offensive efforts are destroying trees that shelter the hatchlings of eagles. Moved by compassion, and risking defeat by exposing himself to his enemies, Indra halts his assault, offering his life as a sacrifice to preserve the eagles. This disorients his enemy. Thinking Indra's halt signals the impending return of a strengthened army, the demons flee in terror.[5]

There are, of course, discrepancies between Indra's victory over the demons of darkness and Aang's victory over Fire Lord Ozai. For example, Indra confronts his enemy with an army; Aang confronts Ozai alone. Indra wins when his enemy flees; Aang, when Ozai loses his firebending ability. But the similarities are overwhelming. Both Indra and Aang refuse to win at the cost of violence to others. Both secure victory through compassionate protection rather than life-destroying conquest. Perhaps most importantly, both are fearless when risking their life for the sake of winning the right way or not at all.

Fearlessness and Power

Sylvia Boorstein, a co-founding teacher at Spirit Rock Meditation Center in Woodacre, California, and a senior teacher at the Insight Meditation Society in Barre, Massachusetts, tells a story from the Zen Buddhist tradition that helps to explain the source of Aang's fearlessness.

> A fierce and terrifying band of samurai was riding through the countryside, bringing fear and harm wherever they went. As they were approaching one particular town, all the monks in the town's monastery fled, except for the abbot. When the band of warriors entered the monastery, they found the abbot sitting at the front of the shrine room in perfect posture. The fierce leader took out his sword and said, "Don't you know who I am? Don't you know that I'm the sort of person who could run you through with my sword without batting an eye?" The Zen master responded, "And I, sir, am the sort of man who could be run through by a sword without batting an eye."[6]

Boorstein's commentary on this story explains why, from a Buddhist perspective, fearlessness is a natural corollary of compassion.

> Fearlessness . . . comes from benevolence and goodwill in the face of whatever oppresses you. You are afraid, but instead of fighting what faces you, you embrace it and accept it – you develop loving-kindness as a direct antidote to fear.[7]

By virtue of overcoming emotional hindrance and delusion, Aang becomes a person who embraces obstacles and strives to overcome them through compassion rather than control.

Aang is not always fearless, of course. Much of his journey involves struggling with fear. This is apparent to Guru Pathik. "You've been through so much recently. Hurt and betrayed. So twisted up inside. You're still full of love. Ah. But fear has moved in where trust should be" ("Appa's Lost

Days"). Aang's central fear, perhaps, concerns his inevitable confrontation with Fire Lord Ozai. When Guru Pathik asks Aang what he is most afraid of, Ozai is one of many images Aang sees. Pathik advises Aang to surrender his fears and let them "flow down the creek" ("The Guru"). But the fear of Ozai lingers, and Aang articulates to Sokka the reason why. "He's the baddest man on the planet! I'm supposed to defeat him and save the world!" ("Nightmares and Daydreams") Nonetheless, Aang is fearless in his final confrontation with Fire Lord Ozai. This is not because he is certain that the power of the Avatar will allow him to kill Ozai, but because, following Guru Pathik's advice, Aang is willing to embrace the consequences of fighting Ozai with compassion rather than violence.

By virtue of being unwilling to do whatever it takes to dominate others for the sake of peace, Aang renders himself thoroughly vulnerable to his enemies. If, as Ozai would have it, power is a tool for domination, and if strength is a willingness to dominate at any cost, Aang is powerless to achieve his goals and thereby maximally weak. But ATLA shows an alternative conception of power whereby Aang is more powerful than Ozai precisely because he is weak by Ozai's standards. Uncle Iroh intimates this alternative when teaching Prince Zuko about fire. "Fire is the element of power. The people of the Fire Nation have desire and will, and the energy to drive and achieve what they want" ("Bitter Work"). According to Iroh, one has power by virtue of having a desire to achieve one's goals and the energy to pursue those desires. By extension, one has more power than another by virtue of realizing one's goals better than the other. Aang's goals involve helping others, alleviating their pain, and fostering peace. His fearlessness sustains these desires, and his vulnerability gives him the energy to realize those desires. So Fire Lord Ozai's accusation against Aang, that he remains weak despite having all the power in the world, is more correct than Ozai likely intended. Aang is weak, by Ozai's standards, because his compassion subverts any desire to dominate others and win at any cost. But this weakness is precisely what gives Aang the power to defeat Ozai and secure peace.

Notes

1. The *Numerical Discourses* are one of several collections of canonical scriptures in the Buddhist tradition, composed as early as the first century BCE but preserved through oral tradition for several centuries prior.
2. *The Numerical Discourses of the Buddha*, trans. Bhikku Bodhi (Boston: Wisdom Publications, 2012), 450.
3. Thích Nhât Hạnh, *Understanding Our Mind* (New Delhi: HarperCollins, 2008), 190.
4. See also Chapter 27: "The Avatar Meets the Karmapa."

5. See Viggo Fausböll, *The Jātakamālā, Volume 1*, trans. T.W. Rhys Davis (London: Trubner & Co., 1890), 284–287.
6. Sylvia Boorstein, "The Gesture of Fearlessness and the Armor of Loving-kindness," *Lion's Roar*, May 25, 2017, at https://www.lionsroar.com/fear-and-fearlessness-what-the-buddhists-teach.
7. Ibid.

26

Ahimsa and Aang's Dilemma
"Everyone . . . [has] to be treated like they're worth giving a chance"

James William Lincoln

As *Avatar: The Last Airbender* concludes, Aang faces an ethical challenge. He is an Air Nomad and is devout in his belief that all life is sacred. Yet, he is also the Avatar and is tasked with "bringing balance to the world" by stopping Fire Lord Ozai's war for world domination. Unfortunately, this latter task seemingly requires Aang to kill Ozai. As a result, Aang is trapped in an *ethical dilemma*. He must choose between killing Ozai as the Avatar or sparing Ozai as an Air Nomad.

Aang's ethical dilemma, henceforth referred to as "Aang's Dilemma," asks us to consider several important philosophical questions: What makes a situation a dilemma in the first place? Are ethical dilemmas resolvable? Does the scope of one's ethical considerations influence which obligations override others? How does one intervene in non-harmful ways against people doing harmful things? As we'll see, Ahimsic practice and the Buddhist virtues known as *the Four Sublime States* can empower us to reshape the conditions upon which an ethical dilemma is grounded, thereby helping us discover ways to resolve dilemmas. This is the lesson of Aang's Dilemma.

Ethical Dilemmas

Philosopher Terrance McConnell notes that many people think of ethical dilemmas as occurring when a person "regards herself as having moral reasons to do each of two actions, but doing both actions is not possible."[1] To illustrate, consider the moral rule that you should always tell the truth. Now, imagine your friend Sam asks you to hide them from a murderer and, moments after hiding your friend, the murderer arrives at your home only to ask you to reveal Sam's location. You seemingly have two choices in this situation: (i) lie to the murderer or (ii) reveal Sam's location. Notably, you have ethical reasons to do (i), out of benevolence to your friend Sam, and

Avatar: The Last Airbender and Philosophy: Wisdom from Aang to Zuko, First Edition.
Edited by Helen De Cruz and Johan De Smedt.
© 2023 John Wiley & Sons, Inc. Published 2023 by John Wiley & Sons, Inc.

(ii), because you think lying is wrong. However, you cannot do both: (i) and (ii) are contrary actions and you seemingly face an ethical dilemma. Yet, is this dilemma genuine?

The answer to this question depends on whether you believe that it is ethically more important to protect Sam than to tell the truth, or vice versa. You might be saying to yourself: "Of course I should lie; I must protect my friend and the murderer wants to do immoral things." If so, then you believe that your ethical obligations, your duties to your friend, can override your duty to tell the truth in certain situations. Notably, philosopher W.D. Ross (1877–1971) thought that there were many obvious cases where the details of a situation could influence what is ethically required of us.[2] Ross famously argued that the specifics of a situation help determine which obligations have a higher ethical priority than others. So, does protecting your friend from the murderer override your ethical obligation to tell the truth?

This question reveals something interesting about ethical dilemmas in general: if a person must choose between two incompatible actions (both of which are supported by good moral reasons), but they also have a good moral reason to pursue one action over another, then there is no genuine dilemma in the first place. In the murderer case, if you have a pressing moral reason to choose lying over truth telling, say because Sam deserves not to be harmed and the murderer has ill-intent toward them, then your ethical conflict dissolves. If one ethical duty can be overridden by another, then we don't really have a dilemma on our hands at all.[3]

Philosopher Lisa Tessman refers to obligations that can be overridden as negotiable ethical duties and ones that cannot as non-negotiable ethical duties, ones which would result in "a cost that no one should have to bear" should they go unmet.[4] If a person faces a genuine dilemma, then all their choices must be non-negotiable. An ethical dilemma is genuine when no obligation can be overridden by another, and no other alternatives are currently possible. This is true in cases where you face two non-negotiable choices, as in the murder case, or where you face three or more non-negotiable options. Regardless of the number of choices you face, the conflict is friction-like. Conflicts between two or more non-negotiable duties result in ethical friction because the opposing duties rub each other the wrong way. This contrasts with cases where a person merely lacks the knowledge needed to sort out their choices. These conflicts are about one's misunderstanding – they are not really dilemmas. With this in mind: is Aang's Dilemma real? Is it genuinely friction-like?

Air Nomad Philosophy

Fire is the element of power. The people of the Fire Nation have desire and will and the energy and drive to achieve what they want . . . Earth is the element of substance. The people of the Earth Kingdom are diverse and strong. They are persistent and enduring . . . Air is the element of freedom. The Air Nomads detached themselves from worldly concerns and found peace and freedom . . . Water is the element of change. The people of the Water Tribes are capable of adapting to many things . . . Understanding others, the other elements, and the other nations, will help you become whole.

(Iroh to Zuko, "Bitter Work")

In the show's final episodes, specifically "Sozin's Comet, Part 2: The Old Masters," Aang communes with his past lives and receives four pieces of advice about his future confrontation with the Fire Lord: "You must be decisive," from Avatar Roku of the Fire Nation. "Only justice will bring peace," from Avatar Kyoshi of the Earth Kingdom. "You must actively shape your own destiny and the destiny of the world," from Avatar Kuruk of the Water Tribes. "Selfless duty calls you to sacrifice your own spiritual needs and do whatever it takes to protect the world," from Avatar Yangchen of the Air Nomads. From all this, Aang concludes that, in his role as the Avatar, he is obligated to confront and kill Ozai to save the world. Aang comes to believe that bringing balance to the world, even if it requires one to kill another human being, is a non-negotiable duty for the Avatar. Yet, during his exchange with Yangchen, Aang remarks that "all life is sacred . . . I'm even a vegetarian. I've always tried to solve my problems by being quick or clever, and I've only had to use violence for necessary defense, and I've certainly never used it to take a life." From this we can see that Aang also believes that protecting the sanctity of life is a non-negotiable duty for Air Nomads. Unsurprisingly, these two realizations cause Aang to feel fated to fail morally in some way, either as the Avatar or as the last Air Nomad. To unpack this, let's look briefly at Air Nomad philosophy and Avataric philosophy.

Air Nomads live a quasi-monastic life of non-attachment, peace, and freedom. Aang, as an Air Nomad, is generally portrayed as deeply compassionate, even as he struggles with having to grow up in wartime. For example, during "Winter Solstice, Part 1: The Spirit World," he confronts a rampaging spirit who is abducting villagers because of the destruction of its forest home. Seeing that violence does not work, Aang turns to empathy. Building on his compassion for the spirit, he soothes its trauma and, thereby, resolves the conflict, returns the villagers to their home, and alleviates suffering for all involved, the spirit included. Aang displays many Buddhist virtues during this interaction and throughout the series. His behavior is emblematic of the Buddhist virtues called the Sublime States: loving kindness (*metta*), compassion (*karuna*), sympathetic joy (*mudita*), and equanimity (*upekkha*). Additionally, Aang's respect for life is emblematic of Ahimsa: a willingness to respect the innate worth of all living beings by forsaking paths that lead to harm in our thoughts, words, or deeds. Taken together, the Sublime States and Ahimsic practice make up the core of Air Nomadic philosophy.

The central claim of all Buddhist traditions is that suffering is a pervasive feature of our reality. As a result, who we become depends on our
ability to notice and respond to this issue. When the Buddha achieved
enlightenment while meditating under the Bodhi tree, he saw through the
illusion of separation to realize our fundamental *dependent origination*
and, through it, came to understand that one person's suffering is always
connected to others. As the Dalai Lama puts it, this dependent origination
operates on three levels:

> At the first level, the principle of cause and effect, whereby all things and
> events arise in dependence on a complex web of interrelated causes and con-
> ditions is invoked. This suggests that no thinking or event can be construed
> as capable of coming into, or remaining in, existence by itself . . . On the
> second level, [dependent origination] can be understood in terms of the
> mutual dependence which exists between parts and wholes. Without parts,
> there can be no whole; without a whole, the concepts of parts make no
> sense . . . On the third level, all phenomena can be understood to be depen-
> dently originated because, when we analyze them, we find that, ultimately,
> they lack independent identity.[5]

These insights are similar to Huu's, the plantbender from "The Swamp."
If you recall, he found enlightenment under the banyan-grove tree, a tree
which grows outward to such an extent that the entire swamp itself is
really one huge, interconnected, organism. The Buddha–Bodhi tree symbolism in this episode reflects the nature of reality in the Buddhist worldview of dependent origination. That is, one of the Buddha's most profound
realizations is that since all life, all reality, is interconnected then all
suffering must be interconnected as well.

Grounded in the understanding that everything is interconnected, the
Sublime States cannot be understated in their capacity to empower individuals to proactively and positively shape their world to alleviate
suffering in pursuit of Ahimsa. What Aang represents, as an Air Nomad
pursuing these states/virtues, is the capacity and commitment of the
human spirit to heal a world plagued by suffering. These virtues may take
a lifetime to cultivate but the story of Avatar Aang suggests that there is a
power to alleviate suffering in the world within each of us – that we are
each capable of healing the world's wounds and we ought to be treated
like we are worth giving a chance to do so. As summarized by Zen
Buddhist Master Thích Nhất Hạnh, the Sublime States can be understood
in the following way: (i) *loving-kindness* – "extending unlimited, universal
love and good-will, to all living beings without any kind of discrimination";
(ii) *compassion* – that which is found in the heart that shudders for "all
living beings who are suffering"; (iii) *sympathetic joy* – that which is
expressed as a "serene response to others' success, welfare, and happiness"; and (iv) *equanimity* – the capacity to see through the illusion of
separateness without prejudice.[6]

Considering Aang's philosophical commitments as an Air Nomad, it is no surprise that the show's creators were inspired by Buddhist philosophies and Ahimsic principles when they created the show. Ahimsa is a cornerstone for Buddhist Philosophy, and, in different ways, it is also essential to Hinduism and Jainism.[7] Ahimsa always seems to be on Aang's mind. During the episode "The Avatar and the Fire Lord," Aang learns that the origin of the conflict he is tasked with ending began with a falling out between Roku, the Avatar before Aang, and Sozin, the Fire Lord before Ozai. Together with Aang we learn that the deep friendship between Roku and Sozin was torn apart by Sozin's betrayal of Roku and the beginning of the Great War. Yet, in classic Air Nomad style, Aang sees this story as proving that "anyone's capable of great good and great evil. Everyone, even the Fire Lord and the Fire Nation, have to be treated like they're worth giving a chance." Such is the nature of, what we can call, *Sublime Ahimsic Practice*.

Sublime Ahimsic Practice, in its *positive* form, means to exercise a deep love for other living things in thought, word, and deed through loving-kindness, compassion, sympathetic joy, and equanimity out of the recognition that all living things are worth giving the chance to realize who they are, who they could be, and to pursue a life of peace. In its *negative* form, it means to practice non-harm and non-violence in thought, word, and deed by renouncing ill-will, antipathy, and jealousy toward other living beings out of the recognition that all living things are worthy of being free from suffering – to be given a chance for peace. This is what Air Nomad Aang means when he says that we must treat people like "they are worth giving a chance": we are all interconnected beings in possession of an essential dignity which makes our worthiness to be loved non-negotiable. "To be treated like you are worth giving a chance" is to be treated in ways that affirm your equal value as a living being among others. One cannot adopt Air Nomadic values and wish to live with the consequences of rejecting the duties associated with Sublime Ahimsic Practice. Thus, treating people like they are worth giving a chance is a non-negotiable Air Nomadic duty. As such, Aang cannot kill Ozai.

Avataric Philosophy

In contrast to Sublime Ahimsic Practice, Avataric philosophy pulls its inspiration from a different source. At its core, it is concerned with unity through harmonious balance. It parallels Daoist attitudes about the relationship between yin and yang in addition to its predilection for finding wisdom in the forces of nature.[8] The Avatar is tasked with preserving the spiritual balance between the four elements (earth, air, water, and fire) by modeling what personal, internal, balance looks like. This entails a balance between each of the virtues *ATLA* associates with these elements: fire's passion and drive, earth's steadfastness and endurance, air's creativity and freedom, and water's resiliency and adaptability. The Avatar is also responsible for taking up a position at the center of the four elementally aligned nations to maintain a harmonious, inclusive, political landscape among them.

Given their role in *ATLA,* the consecutive incarnations of the Avatar fulfill their obligations to the world when they counteract the human propensity for disruption because the human creature too often desires power over the world – a distinctly anti-Daoist approach to life.[9] Where humans are prone to propagate disharmony, the Avatar helps to maintain a state of the world that unifies each element and nation as a mutually supported and interdependent part of the whole. In their Daoist guardianship of the world, an Avatar's task is threefold: to synthesize the four elemental philosophies into a unified spiritual worldview in order to share that wisdom, to promote peace between the elemental nations, and to guard against human disruption of the world's harmony.

What is more, to be the Avatar is to tacitly accept one's duty to promote harmony and spiritual balance. Being the Avatar means adopting certain obligations in the same way that we might say a child has certain obligations to their parents. I didn't ask to be born and I didn't ask to have the parents that I do. However, in the absence of abuse or mistreatment, it is reasonable to expect that I have certain obligations to my parents. In the case of the Avatar, those obligations are to the world even if one didn't ask for that burden. Avataric philosophy should be understood as making nonnegotiable demands upon the Avatar because of the unique place and power they wield in *ATLA* and, thus, they must act whenever they find themselves confronted with political or spiritual disharmony in the world. If the Avatar's duty, motivated by Daoist values, is to pursue balance in the world and they choose not to do so, or to pursue imbalance, then we would expect the fabric of the natural order within *ATLA* to fray and tear itself apart, as is clear in the show: Aang initially fled his duty and responsibilities as Avatar, and this brought about the disharmony between the elements and the Great War. Given that such an event would promote extensive suffering and war, as the show illustrates, we should take Avatar Aang's responsibility to restore balance to the world, even if it means killing Ozai, to be a non-negotiable duty.

Overcoming Dilemmas

Aang's dilemma seems to be genuine: his Avataric duties and Air Nomadic beliefs prescribe non-negotiable obligations that pull in different directions. This would, on its own, offer a compelling narrative to the show's conclusion – that the hero's journey often requires him to deal with tragic forms of moral failure. However, this is not the lesson the writers chose to convey. Instead, they use Aang's Sublime Ahimsic Practice to illustrate how it can empower us. Sublime Ahimsic Practice empowers us to reshape the conditions upon which an ethical dilemma is grounded. *ATLA* illustrates how this can happen and why this practice can be valuable to our ethical lives. In a primary sense, it inoculates Aang against believing that killing Ozai is the right thing to do. In a secondary sense, it keeps Aang connected to people and resources by maintaining his openness to the world. This allows him to make contact with the last Lion Turtle and to learn energybending ("Sozin's Comet, Part 2: The Old Masters"), and it helps him to preserve Phoenix King Ozai's life, while stripping him of his firebending and political power ("Sozin's Comet, Part 4: Avatar Aang"). Without this power, Aang was doomed to fail morally but thanks to it, his dilemma is overcome. In doing so, he ends the war while preserving core Air Nomadic ethical beliefs.

ATLA doesn't suggest that it's possible to overcome all ethical dilemmas through Sublime Ahimsic Practice. Rather, it illustrates the same lessons that Martin Luther King Jr., Mahatma Gandhi, and more contemporary liberation movements like the Women's March and Black Lives Matter have been teaching – that a liberated and compassionate world is possible and can be achieved by walking a path that allows us to alter the fundamental conditions of this world by becoming different people. Yet, in a world ravaged by suffering and populated by systems which perpetuate it or, in some cases, reward people for causing suffering to others, we are not treated like we are worth giving a chance. Sublime Ahimsic Practice aims to remind us that we are all worthy of being treated like we are worth giving a chance. Ultimately, *ATLA* shows its viewers that they are worthy of such consideration and capable of showing others the same kindness.

Notes

1. Terrance McConnell, "Moral Dilemmas," in *The Stanford Encyclopedia of Philosophy*, at https://plato. stanford. edu/entries/moral-dilemmas.
2. W.D. Ross, *The Right and the Good* (Oxford: Clarendon Press, 1930).
3. Walter Sinnott-Armstrong, *Moral Dilemmas* (Oxford: Blackwell, 1988).
4. Lisa Tessman, *Moral Failure: On the Impossible Demands of Morality* (New York: Oxford University Press, 2016), 44.
5. Dalai Lama, *Ethics for the New Millennium* (New York: Riverhead Books, 1999), 36–37.
6. Thích Nhất Hạnh, *The Heart of the Buddha's Teaching: Transforming Suffering into Peace, Joy, and Liberation: The Four Noble Truths, the Noble Eightfold Path, and Other Basic Buddhist Teachings* (New York: Harmony Books, 1988), 169–175.
7. Raghavan Iyer, *The Moral and Political Thought of Mahatma Gandhi* (Delhi: Oxford University Press, 1973).
8. Laozi, *Tao Te Ching*, trans. Ursula K. Le Guin (Boston: Shambhala Publications, 1997), 4, 8.
9. Zhuangzi, *The Complete Works of Zhuangzi*, trans. Burton Watson (New York: Columbia University Press, 2013), 53–67, 134–143.

27

The Avatar Meets the Karmapa
Interconnections, Friendship, and Moral Training

Brett Patterson

Each episode of *ATLA* begins with an introduction that sets the stage and tone for the series. Once we've seen it a few times, we dismiss it, wanting to get along with the story. We may view it superficially, thinking that the Avatar, the only one who can master the four elements, the only one who can defeat the "ruthless firebenders," is the sole person who will "save the world." However, if we pause and consider who is speaking and what she says, we realize that the Avatar is not a lone superhero, a radical individual like a Wild West gunslinger. Let's focus on that moment when Katara says Aang "has a lot to learn before he can save anyone." The series as a whole portrays Aang's journey from being a scared boy, who ran from his training, to becoming Avatar Aang, who is able to face Fire Lord Ozai. That journey in one sense does belong to Aang, but in another crucial sense, also belongs to each person who travels with him along the way. As the series progresses, we see others investing in that ongoing project, others who join Katara in professing that the playful, exuberant boy can become the one who saves their world.

The series beautifully illustrates the relational quality of human life that contemporary Tibetan Buddhist leader the Karmapa Ogyen Trinley Dorje describes in his book *Interconnected: Embracing Life in Our Global Society*. Counter to much emphasis in our global, consumer culture, which fosters division and competition, human beings exist fundamentally in "webs of interdependence."[1] Although the Karmapa consistently draws from Buddhist teachings, he argues that interdependence is an essential reality of human life; we only succumb to illusions if we declare that we are discrete individuals who depend on nothing other than ourselves. We should embrace this social reality with gratitude and foster practices that

Avatar: The Last Airbender and Philosophy: Wisdom from Aang to Zuko, First Edition.
Edited by Helen De Cruz and Johan De Smedt.
© 2023 John Wiley & Sons, Inc. Published 2023 by John Wiley & Sons, Inc.

help us value these connections and extend compassion to those who share the journey with us.[2] Dorje proposes that we should see ourselves as "interdependent" or "interconnected" individuals, people who live and grow in a network of relationships with other human beings, with animals, and with the world around us.[3] He insists, playfully, that even an "exalted" person such as himself must depend on friendships and connections. *ATLA* similarly emphasizes such connections in its portrait of Aang's quest, for his journey toward maturity draws on the work and play he shares with many others before the series comes to its conclusion.

Can the Avatar or the Karmapa Have Friends?

From the first episode ("The Boy in the Iceberg") we learn that Aang faces a significant obstacle. He is running from the responsibilities that come from his role. When Katara first asks Aang if he knows anything about the Avatar, he guiltily dodges the question; it is not until Zuko confronts him that Aang admits he is the Avatar. Katara later ("The Avatar Returns") asks why he didn't tell her who he really was, and Aang says he never wanted the title. The third episode ("The Southern Air Temple") gives us a brief glimpse into that backstory, showing Aang's relationship with his teacher Gyatso a hundred years before. Aang proposes that the monks misidentified him, but Gyatso affirms the calling, saying that their mistake was that they didn't wait until he was 16 to tell him.

Those of us who are curious about Aang's background have to wait until Episode 12 ("The Storm") before we learn that the leadership of the Air Nomads identified him as the Avatar from the toys he chose to play with, since these were relics connected to previous Avatars. The identification immediately sets Aang at odds with his friends; boys who previously played games with him now will not allow him to play since it wouldn't be fair for a team to have the Avatar. Gyatso tries to protect Aang's childhood, allowing him to continue to play games with him, but the other monks, feeling desperation over an imminent war, push to increase Aang's training and plot to remove Aang from Gyatso's care. When Aang overhears that they plan to move him to the Eastern Air Temple, he runs away, only to meet a storm at sea and to fall into the water, where an iceberg preserves him and Appa, dormant for 100 years.

Ogyen Trinley Dorje expresses a similar awareness of the weight of an exalted title in his experience as the Karmapa. At the age of seven he had to face the expectations of a Buddhist community who identified him as the seventeenth incarnation of the Karmapa, the head of the Karmu Kagyu lineage of Tibetan Buddhism. Buddhist leaders took Dorje from his family and introduced him to a serious course of training that led to his installment at Tsurphu Monastery at the age of eight. Throughout *Interconnected* Dorje openly shares how challenging that separation from his family was.

(He could only see them once or twice a year.) In a candid section entitled "Introducing His Loneliness," Dorje explains that even though people surround him every day, when they treat him as the "reincarnation of a 900-year-old historical figure," their expectations create a divide that makes friendship difficult: "For so holy and exalted a personage, it is a little complicated to go about finding friends."[4] He later comments that we all must face conditions in life that we didn't choose, as he relates having to leave his family at the age of seven. Even though others might expect him to be perfect, he has had to learn to see the positive in the relationships that arise from his position. When people come to him with their problems, he has learned to celebrate moments when his training and teaching have been useful to them; such encounters give meaning to his life.[5] He understands such relationships are essential; even he cannot stand alone.

Only with time does Aang begin to learn this lesson as well, and some crisis points develop later in his quest when he forgets the lesson ("Nightmares and Daydreams"). In Book One, Aang despairs that he has no teacher to show him what it means to be the Avatar ("Winter Solstice, Part 1: The Spirit World"). He finds that the Fire Nation has killed Gyatso, along with his monastic community and the rest of the Air Nation. At this crucial point, Katara and Sokka declare that they, along with Appa and Momo, are Aang's new family ("The Southern Air Temple"). Aang draws strength from this declaration and continues to draw from their encouragement in succeeding episodes. That family, of course, comes under stress as Aang faces both adulation and derision from the different peoples they meet in their travels. If Aang lets the adoration of the crowds go to his head, Katara is there to frown and pull him back on course ("The Warriors of Kyoshi") or Toph is there to call him "Twinkle Toes" ("The Blind Bandit"). The title Avatar often separates Aang from the others, but just as often, Katara and Sokka, and later Toph and others, relate to him also as Aang.

Moral Training: A Shared Journey

ATLA excels in portraying the richness of these friends who surround and support Aang – the Warriors of Kyoshi, the deviously unpredictable King Bumi, the various villagers who put their trust in Aang to save their towns from tormented spirits or Fire Nation occupation, and the Robin-Hood-like Jet and his gang. The list grows with each episode (obviously also with some antagonists along the way), and the writers enjoy bringing characters introduced in earlier chapters back in later adventures, notably in Book Three as the series reaches its final confrontations. The characters connect with Aang and his mission as he also celebrates and benefits from his relationships with them.

Aang's journey moves away from the stereotypical hero's quest that portrays an individual who pushes out beyond the community, crossing various thresholds, into a new world, defeats a villain or monster, and returns with the elixir to save the world.[6] Raised on images of democratic, capitalistic liberalism, Americans often portray heroes as rugged individuals who find strength in their autonomy. *ATLA*, on the other hand, presents a more communal model of the hero. As the Karmapa warns, pushing away from our inherent connections to others often is an "egocentric pursuit of self-interest"; we should instead embrace our relationships with others.[7] So, Aang's quest is not primarily about celebrating his gifts and showing how different he is from everyone else, but about finding self-control. The Karmapa emphasizes that the Tibetan concept of freedom derives from self-control – moving away from jealousy, anger, attachment, greed, resentment, and prejudice.[8] Thus, a Buddhist "hero" would avoid indulging in personal whims and instead patiently wait for discernment to find the option that would both satisfy self and others. Such a character would not stand alone.[9] In such a story, as we see in Aang's journey, there is much more emphasis on the community.

Because of this emphasis on a shared journey, training becomes a crucial concept for the series: when Aang (and others) train, they draw on the wisdom of many masters. As the story unfolds, many people contribute to Aang's training. In the episodes that highlight someone training Aang, we see such an affirmation of interconnections, as well as an exploration of the responsibilities and opportunities that arise from these relationships. Even though Aang early on is excited about the possibility of learning water-bending together with Katara, the encounter with Roku, reminding him of Sozin's comet and the need to master all four elements by then, adds pressure and makes Aang panic. When Katara offers to teach him, a competitive situation quickly develops as Katara realizes that Aang learns faster than she does. When Aang pushes the boundaries of his knowledge, a wave hits Sokka for comic relief, but then also washes their supplies down the river. At the end of the chapter, Katara recognizes her mistake and apologizes for fostering competition that led to envy ("The Waterbending Scroll").

Several chapters pass before Aang finds a firebending master in Jeong Jeong, who consistently warns him that he is not ready for training in this element. Jeong Jeong only agrees when a vision of Roku convinces him to try. Aang initially shows respect for his teacher, but later grows impatient. Ignoring Jeong Jeong's cautions, Aang pushes ahead, loses control of his flames, and burns Katara in the process ("The Deserter"). Feeling shame at hurting her, Aang shows reticence in his further training, particularly avoiding firebending. It may contribute to his initially boycotting the next master, the waterbending master Pakku, who refuses to train Katara. Only when Katara pushes him forward does Aang continue his training. When he decides to share what he has learned with her, Pakku angrily confronts him for disrespecting the social practices of the Northern Water Tribe. Then, after a duel between Katara and Pakku which reveals Katara's talent and leads to the revelation that she is the granddaughter of the woman Pakku loved but did not marry, the old master finally agrees to teach her alongside Aang ("The Waterbending Master").

Even though he is the reincarnated Avatar, Aang has to go through the painstaking process all over again, and in these encounters we see his weaknesses. Whenever he tries to short-cut his training, he ends up making a mistake, taking a step back, or hurting someone. We continue to see this pattern while he works with Toph ("Bitter Work"). Toph's style of training also leads to a debate between her and Katara over the best method of teaching, the harsher style of Toph, which involves yelling criticism, or the "gentle nudge" Katara suggests, which centers on encouraging praise. By the end of the episode, both teachers play the role of *sifu* to Aang.

Katara, Sokka, and Toph make overt contributions to the quest; past Avatars share insights; masters of diverse elements take Aang under their wing. Even Appa and Momo give their best (affirming a connection to animals) to help him in his mission. Fundamentally, training is more than just learning the movements of bending; it is about making connections, learning self-control, and embracing one's gifts and responsibilities.

Aang grows in the community, illustrating the Karmapa's words about the importance of relying on others. Dorje emphasizes that we often learn about connections and community through our families.[10] We never see Aang's biological family, but we see Team Avatar providing those familial moments for Aang, supporting each other when someone is suffering and when their moral vision needs reinforcement. Family cares for us in vulnerable moments (as Uncle Iroh tries to tell the raging Zuko in "The Avatar State" and a repentant Zuko in "Sozin's Comet Part 2: The Old Masters").[11] In community we build courage and do not lose heart.[12] In community we learn that individual actions affect the collective and that people with diverse gifts can contribute to the group's flourishing.[13] Communities train us in interdependence – helping us to develop awareness and to engage in action.[14] We all have the potential for virtue, but we need support.[15] We anchor ourselves in shared aspirations.[16] As we connect with friends with "shared virtues," we gather courage to face the challenges that previously seemed impossible.[17] Aspirations flourish when shared.[18]

As we progress morally, Dorje argues, we widen our sense of family. After we build confidence on a local, intimate level, we graduate to a larger social environment.[19] The Karmapa was taken from his family at age seven and could only see his parents once or twice a year, but his circumstances pushed him to learn the lesson of being part of a larger family more quickly. Aang's situation is similar.[20] As we see ourselves as part of a family, we understand community brings meaning to our lives, and, as Buddhism teaches, the local community should always lead us out to the expansive human community.[21] As we move ever outward to a universal community, we wrestle with both aversion and attachment: we learn to see former enemies as people who suffer from insecurity, fear, or misguided strategies;

and we see turns in our relationships that show that we do not listen to others (attachment is about me, but love is about the other).[22] We reorient our relationships to establish harmony.[23]

We see these last lessons in that difficult moment in Aang's training with Guru Pathik, a close friend of monk Gyatso, at the Eastern Air Temple ("The Guru"). Pathik leads Aang through opening the seven chakras of the body to control the Avatar State. Aang carefully addresses the first six – earth (survival), water (pleasure), fire (willpower), air (love), sound (truth), light (insight) – by facing each corresponding block – fear, guilt, shame, grief, lies, and illusion. In this process Aang works through his weaknesses and moves outward to embracing the unity of the four elements and the four nations. However, the last chakra – cosmic energy – proves a serious challenge, for the block is earthly attachment. Aang objects that he cannot leave those he loves behind, particularly Katara; he says it doesn't make any sense when the opening of the fourth chakra was an affirmation of love, which he must now seemingly abandon to take on his role as Avatar. Although he tries to open this chakra, a mental image of Katara suffering interrupts the training and Aang abandons the process, counter to Pathik's wishes. Viewers sympathize with Aang, but those aware of Buddhist teachings see here an illustration of the Karmapa's point that attachments on the local level can become obstacles on the path to universal compassion.[24] Aang's choice does allow him to rescue Katara, but it also contributes to the block (along with an injury incurred from Azula's attack from behind in "The Crossroads of Destiny") that sets up significant challenges in Book Three.

Alienation, Betrayal, and Repentance: Zuko's Path to Team Avatar

Of all the relationships that shape Aang's quest, Zuko's takes the most dramatic turn. From the very first episode and often throughout the series, episodes portray Zuko's story in counterpoint to Aang's – crucially in "The Storm" and "Bitter Work." Zuko wrestles with banishment and with his own isolation, even as Uncle Iroh consistently watches over him. In exile Zuko confronts suffering and becomes obsessed in his search for the Avatar, his key to returning home and restoring his place in the Fire Nation. Aang learns from these encounters about the seriousness of the threat that the Fire Nation poses, and viewers see Zuko's alienation juxtaposed against Aang's growing in community.

When we learn Zuko's backstory, we see that his father has fostered an environment that sidelined his uncle Iroh (Ozai's brother and the true heir to the throne), led to the mysterious disappearance of Zuko's mother, and fed the destructive, competitive spirit of his sister Azula. Zuko's family illustrates problems that the Karmapa believes are in our society today that work against our drawing strength from our connections. Dorje highlights the

Buddhist teaching that competition creates the illusion that life is a zero-sum game and that it undermines our happiness.[25] Certain social environments promote jealousy, greed, and anger, which impair our inherent empathy toward other life.[26] Zuko's mother offers the one significant consenting voice in her love and encouragement, but Ozai removes her and creates a crisis that haunts Zuko and pushes him into despair, loneliness, and rage.

Ironically, Zuko's exile originated because he spoke up at a war council ("The Storm"), defending troops a commander was going to sacrifice for the sake of a military maneuver. Zuko was expressing compassion, and his father chose to emphasize a military order over supporting his son. Thus, hurt and scorned, Zuko goes out into the world, seeking to "restore his honor" by capturing the Avatar. Uncle Iroh is the steady voice of compassion for Zuko in exile. Zuko's is a long journey from an obsession with capturing the Avatar, until Aang extends compassion to him by not leaving him in the cold Northern tundra ("The Siege of the North, Part 2") – to wandering through the Earth Kingdom, searching for himself, until he betrays Iroh, Katara, and Aang to get a ticket back to the Fire Nation ("The Crossroads of Destiny") – to finally coming to his senses that he is not beholden to his father's quest to conquer the world ("The Day of the Black Sun, Part 2: The Eclipse").

Aang's eventual positive response to Zuko's desire to join Team Avatar is crucial for the development of Aang's moral character. The Avatar can help turn an enemy into a friend. As Dorje reminds us, compassion allows us to see that those who appear as enemies are enslaved to their own "disturbing emotions."[27] When we move beyond the problem and focus on the person, we recognize opportunities to grow.[28] Egocentrism is a prison of our own making (as we see in Azula's turn toward madness at the end of the series).[29] Team Avatar's forgiveness sets up Zuko as Aang's final bending teacher. Zuko pushes Aang in ways that are reminiscent of the monks who wanted to take Aang away from Gyatso – and reminiscent of Toph, who pushed Aang through rigor and criticism ("Sozin's Comet, Part 1: The Phoenix King"). Few viewers of the first chapters of the series would have predicted the partnership between Aang and Zuko in the rebuilding of their world after the defeat of Ozai, Azula, and the Fire Nation armies. Zuko's path is a rough one, filled with angst and suffering, but he moves eventually from competition through failure and betrayal to humility and eventually confidence. Dorje carefully describes this movement from pride and competition to confidence and humility.[30] He argues that embracing interdependence (learning one's place in the vast net of life) brings contentment – something we see in Zuko's smile in the last scenes of the series.[31]

Journey's End and a Vision of a New Community

After all the training, within a year marked by notable connections and several setbacks, Aang rises to the occasion and faces Ozai, but only with the help of Katara, Sokka, Toph, Zuko, the Order of the White Lotus, and numerous other friends. As we watch the thrilling confrontations of the last episodes, it is important to note that Aang's confrontation with Ozai also occurs while Zuko and Katara fight with Azula; while Sokka, Suki, Appa, and Toph destroy the fleet of fire ships; and while the Order of the White Lotus, under Iroh's guidance, liberates the city of Ba Sing Se ("Sozin's Comet, Part 3: Into the Inferno" and "Sozin's Comet, Part 4: Avatar Aang").

As the Karmapa emphasizes, interconnectedness does not negate individuality. Aang still has to make his own stand.[32] He is still the Avatar and must play his role.[33] Dorje clarifies that not everyone is always "in a good position to act virtuously" – some play specific roles, but others can "encourage good people to be more active in manifesting their goodness."[34] But what happens if you face conflicting advice?

This struggle appears in the last major challenge Aang must face. He must reconcile the pacifism he learned from the Air Nomads with the advice given by several previous Avatars, Zuko, and seemingly everyone else – namely, that killing Phoenix King Ozai is the only way to stop him. The conflict even drives Aang away from Team Avatar to a retreat where he has to weigh matters on his own – but Momo goes with him, and the retreat ends with an encounter with the ancient Lion Turtle, who gives him a vision that is crucial for his final move against Ozai ("Sozin's Comet, Part 2: The Old Masters"). Aang's story here illustrates Dorje's point that embracing our connectedness allows us to grow beyond our current capacities and draw on the power of our imagination to find a solution to our problems.[35]

As Aang resists Ozai, his friends also make their own stands that contribute to stopping Ozai's conquest. Aang completes his journey as an "interdependent individual"[36] and leads the deliverance of their world from Fire Nation conquest. The defeat of the destructive forces of the Fire Nation is an affirmation of the "connectedness" of all life in their world. Team Avatar have embraced their responsibilities. The Karmapa reminds us that "responsibility is the opportunity to experience our connections in interdependence as love."[37] As Zuko joins Aang in shaping a new era of peace, we see a new spirit of cooperation and generosity, aspirations which Dorje states are essential to sustain the "lifelong process" of fulfilling our responsibilities.[38] When we join our life-affirming aspirations together, as Team Avatar has, our efforts have greater effect and move us closer to changing the world.[39]

Notes

1. The Karmapa, Ogyen Trinley Dorje, *Interconnected: Embracing Life in Our Global Society* (Somerville, MA: Wisdom Publications, 2018), Loc. 189 (ebook).
2. Dorje, Loc. 318–355.
3. Dorje, Loc. 446–483.
4. Dorje, Loc. 626–635.

5. Dorje, Loc. 1026–1044, 2019.
6. Here I refer to the idea made popular by Joseph Campbell's work, especially *The Hero with a Thousand Faces* (Novato, CA: Joseph Campbell Foundation, [1949] 2020), with the boost given by George Lucas in his descriptions of how he wrote *Star Wars*. Many writers, including those working for prominent production companies, have consulted the paradigm of the hero's quest ever since, as Christopher Vogler describes in *The Writer's Journey* (Studio City, CA: Michael Wiese Productions, 2020).
7. Dorje, Loc. 1848.
8. Dorje, Loc. 1875–1884.
9. Dorje, Loc. 1939–1957.
10. Dorje, Loc. 2592.
11. Dorje, Loc. 2815.
12. Dorje, Loc. 3065.
13. Dorje, Loc. 2545, 2573, 2582.
14. Dorje, Loc. 2609.
15. Dorje, Loc. 3192.
16. Dorje, Loc. 3200.
17. Dorje, Loc. 3210.
18. Dorje, Loc. 3219.
19. Dorje, Loc. 2618.
20. Dorje, Loc. 2727.
21. Dorje, Loc. 2493, 2519.
22. Dorje, Loc. 2926–2959.
23. Dorje, Loc. 3029.
24. Dorje, Loc. 2926–2959.
25. Dorje, Loc. 2222, 2247.
26. Dorje, Loc. 1432, 1440, 1530.
27. Dorje, Loc. 1557.
28. Dorje, Loc. 1753.
29. Dorje, Loc. 925.
30. Dorje, Loc. 943–970.
31. Dorje, Loc. 980.
32. Dorje, Loc. 887, 926.
33. I feel the Karmapa would nod here in understanding. He states in *Interconnected* that he has his "grand title," but he does not view it as a sign of his superiority, but as a means for helping others (Loc. 2200). He acknowledges his debt to his own teachers (Loc. 2191).
34. Dorje, Loc. 3227.
35. Dorje, Loc. 3128, 3155.
36. Dorje, Loc. 821.
37. Dorje, Loc. 2019.
38. Dorje, Loc. 2073.
39. Dorje, Loc. 2101, 3227.

Index

Avatar: The Last Airbender and Philosophy: Wisdom from Aang to Zuko, First Edition.
Edited by Helen De Cruz and Johan De Smedt.
© 2023 John Wiley & Sons, Inc. Published 2023 by John Wiley & Sons, Inc.